Foreign Trade and Economic Growth in Italy

Published in cooperation with
the University of Michigan Graduate
Research Seminar in International Economics

PRAEGER SPECIAL STUDIES IN INTERNATIONAL ECONOMICS AND DEVELOPMENT

Foreign Trade and Economic Growth in Italy

Robert M. Stern

FREDERICK A. PRAEGER, Publishers
New York · Washington · London

The purpose of the Praeger Special Studies is to make specialized research monographs in U.S. and international economics and politics
available to the academic, business, and government communities. For
further information, write to the Special Projects Division, Frederick
A. Praeger, Publishers, 111 Fourth Avenue, New York, N.Y. 10003.

FREDERICK A. PRAEGER, PUBLISHERS
111 Fourth Avenue, New York, N.Y. 10003, U.S.A.
77-79 Charlotte Street, London W.1, England

Published in the United States of America in 1967
by Frederick A. Praeger, Inc., Publishers

© 1967 by Robert M. Stern

Library of Congress Catalog Card Number: 66-17366

Printed in the United States of America

TO LUCETTA

PREFACE

The purpose of this study is to examine the role which the export sector in particular has played in Italy's postwar economic growth. Both in relation to its own past experience and in comparison to that of other Western nations in the postwar period, at least until 1963, Italian growth has been remarkable. Indeed, Italy's average annual rate of growth in real gross national product (GNP) of 6.3 per cent between 1953 and 1963 was exceeded only by one other major industrial nation, Japan (9.4 per cent), and matched the rate achieved in West Germany. The average annual rates of increase in GNP in the United States and Great Britain during this period were in contrast 2.8 and 3.0 per cent, respectively.[1] The factors explaining Italy's unusual growth would thus appear to be of great interest both to economists and to those responsible for economic policy in industrial and underdeveloped countries alike.

The Italian experience is interesting, furthermore, because the rate of growth diminished considerably in 1964 and 1965 to about 3 per cent annually. This raises the question as to whether there were special factors accounting for Italy's rapid growth until 1963 and, if so, whether the events of 1964 and 1965 were indicative of certain structural changes occurring in the economy. We shall unfortunately not have much to say about these recent events mainly because data for 1964 and 1965 were not yet available in comprehensive form at the time of writing. It is hoped that a useful purpose can nevertheless be served by our attempting to enhance the understanding of the period of rapid growth which ended in 1963, even if in fact important structural changes in the Italian economy have taken place since that time.

The reason for focusing upon the role of exports in the growth process is because exports are of considerable importance relative to GNP in many industrial countries and apparently have been a source of strength especially in the postwar expansion which has taken place in Italy, the other Common Market countries, and Japan.[2]

The plan of the study is as follows. We begin in Chapter 1 with a brief presentation and interpretation of the major outlines in the growth of the Italian economy from 1950-64. Chapter 2 contains a recapitulation of the important postwar developments which have occurred in Italy's merchandise export and import trade. The remaining substantive Chapters 3-5 consider the question of whether exports can be assigned a special role in the Italian growth experience. We close in Chapter 6 with a discussion of the main findings of the study and an examination of the implications which these findings may have for Italy's economic growth in the future.

The research underlying the present study was carried out during the 1964-65 academic year in residence at the Banca d'Italia in Rome under the auspices of a Ford Foundation Faculty Research Fellowship. I would like to express my appreciation to Governor Guido Carli and General Manager Paolo Baffi for extending the facilities of the Banca d'Italia to me. I owe a special debt of gratitude to Francesco Masera, head of the Servizio Studi of the Banca d'Italia, for looking after my day-to-day needs and for providing me with excellent working conditions and counsel on matters of research and data. I wish above all to thank Antonio Fazio and Guido Rey of the Ufficio Ricerche of the Banca d'Italia for giving so freely of their time in making arrangements for computer facilities, discussing technical questions of research, and in offering comments upon earlier drafts of the manuscript, especially Chapters 2-5.

In December, 1964, and January, 1965, I had the privilege of delivering an earlier version of Chapter 3 of this work to a special seminar at the Banca d'Italia, to an informal group convened in Rome by Luigi Spaventa and Antonio Pedone, and to a group of students and staff members of the Faculty of Economics in Namur, Belgium. W. Beckerman also read and commented on this earlier version of Chapter 3. Somewhat altered versions of Chapters 3 and 4 were prepared for delivery in March, 1965, to a group organized by Augusto Graziani at the Center for Advanced Training and Research in Agricultural Economics of the University of Naples at Portici. A similar presentation was made in April, 1965, to Luigi Spaventa's course on the Italian economy at the Johns Hopkins University Bologna Center.

The second and fourth parts of Chapter 2 were published in a slightly altered form in an article in the March, 1965, issue of the Quarterly Review of the Banca Nazionale del Lavoro. Luigi Ceriani, editor of the Review, was kind enough to give me permission to include the bulk of this article in the present study.

Most of the data utilized were drawn from official sources. I would, however, like to give special thanks to Mario Amendola who made available to me his work sheets on the industrial composition of

Italy's foreign trade in the postwar period. My research was also facilitated by obtaining access in the Banca d'Italia and in the Istituto Centrale di Statistica to certain data estimates and details which were not directly ascertainable from published sources.

Drafts of Chapters 1-5 were presented to my Graduate Seminar in International Economics at the University of Michigan at different times during the 1965-66 academic year. I am very grateful to the members of this Seminar for their unflinching criticisms and helpful suggestions concerning details of the individual chapters. I want to thank my colleagues, W. H. Locke Anderson and Harold T. Shapiro, for their careful reading of the main chapters and for their aid in clarifying a number of important points of theory and statistical procedure. A. Lamfalussy and Augusto Graziani are also to be thanked for reading and commenting on Chapters 3-5. Alan L. Ginsburg and Giuseppe Ruggeri provided me with computational assistance in the later phases of the research.

The bulk of the typing was done by Colleen Eccleston, who managed to maintain an unfailingly good humor in the face of what may have seemed like a countless number of drafts of the individual chapters of the manuscript. Patricia Dapprich and members of the departmental secretarial pool also furnished an important helping hand.

I wish finally to express my thanks to my wife for her continuous encouragement in the undertaking and completion of the study and for her empathy especially during the final stages of labor.

Robert M. Stern
Ann Arbor, Michigan

CONTENTS

xi

LIST OF TABLES

xiv

LIST OF FIGURES

Figures in the Appendix

ABBREVIATIONS

EEC	European Economic Community
EFTA	European Free Trade Area
GDP	Gross domestic product
GNP	Gross national product
ISCO	Istituto Nazionale per lo Studio della Congiuntura
ISTAT	Istituto Centrale di Statistica
OECD	Organization for Economic Cooperation and Development
OEEC	Organization for European Economic Cooperation
SITC	Standard International Trade Classification
SVIMEZ	Associazione per lo Sviluppo dell'Industria nel Mezzogiorno
U. N.	United Nations

Foreign Trade and Economic Growth in Italy

CHAPTER 1 AN OVERVIEW OF POSTWAR ITALIAN ECONOMIC GROWTH

The purpose of this chapter is to analyze briefly and to interpret the major outlines in the growth of the Italian economy in the postwar period. We shall focus on the behavior of the most important economic aggregates during the years 1950-64, and in doing so we shall make reference to some of the economic forces and general policy measures which were important during the period. Since the intention here is to offer a selective rather than an exhaustive treatment of the events of these years, the reader interested in greater detail on matters of chronology, institutional background, and specific policies will of necessity have to consult other sources. [1]

The year 1950 was chosen as the starting point in examining the record of postwar growth in order to minimize the effects on the data of the early postwar reconstruction and Marshall Plan years. To exclude these years is not to imply, however, that they were unimportant. Rather, the opposite is the case for it was during this time that the authorities made important strides in the attainment of the objectives of monetary stabilization and the rebuilding of official foreign-exchange reserves. [2] The expansion of the economy subsequent to 1950 would surely have been less impressive, therefore, if the necessary groundwork had not been so successfully laid in the immediately preceding years.

As will be evident from the discussion which follows, the pursuit of monetary stabilization and of a strong balance-of-payments position was continued by the authorities with an apparently high degree of success throughout the 1950's and into the beginning of the 1960's. However, with the appearance of inflationary forces in 1962 and especially in 1963, the joint realization of domestic stabilization and external-payments goals has presented grave difficulties.

NATIONAL PRODUCT AND EXPENDITURE

The basic data for gross national product (GNP) and expenditure at current prices and at 1954 prices are set forth in Tables 1 and 2 of Appendix I for the period 1950-64. The GNP data by expenditure sector at 1954 prices have been plotted in Figure 1. It is evident that GNP somewhat more than doubled during this 15-year period. Real private consumption about doubled, while public consumption increased about 2.5 times. In contrast to consumption, there was about a threefold rise during the period in gross-fixed-capital formation and fivefold rise in the exports of goods and services. The increase in imports of goods and services was also between four and five times.

The data for real gross domestic product (GDP) at factor cost have been plotted in Figure 2. They show that the output of the agriculture, forestry, and fishing sector rose by about one-third between 1950 and 1963. The output of the mining and quarrying sector (not shown in the figure) increased in contrast four times, the manufacturing sector three times, and the construction sector nearly 4.5 times during the period. Product originating in the public utilities sector rose 2.4 times and in all other sectors somewhat more than 1.5 times.

These differences in increases over the period as a whole were reflected in changes in the relative importance of the individual expenditure and production sectors. As is evident from Appendix Table 3, private consumption as a percentage of GNP fell from slightly over 70 at the beginning of the period to between 62 and 65 per cent at the end of the period. Public consumption remained more of less the same in relation to GNP during the period. Gross-fixed-capital formation increased, however, from just over 17 per cent to well over 20 per cent, while exports of goods and services as a percentage of GNP more than doubled from slightly over 10 to more than 20 per cent. Imports of goods and services as a percentage of GNP also roughly doubled during the period.

As far as the sectors of GDP were concerned, the percentage originating in agriculture, forestry, and fishing fell steadily throughout the period from somewhat more than 25 per cent in the early 1950's to just over 17 per cent by 1963. Output in manufacturing increased in contrast from a little under 30 per cent at the beginning to more than 40 per cent of the total by the end of the period. The percentage accounted for by construction doubled during the period from 3.3 to 6.8 per cent. Product originating in public utilities increased slightly to about 10 per cent of the total, while the percentage accounted for by all the other sectors fell from about 30 to somewhat less than 25 per cent of the total.

Figure 1

Italy: Gross National Product at 1954 Prices, 1950-64
(Billions of Lire)

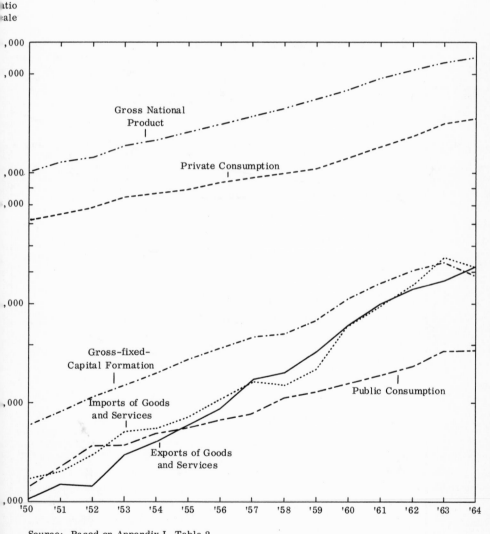

Source: Based on Appendix I, Table 2.

Figure 2

Italy: Gross Domestic Product at 1954 Prices, 1951-63
(Billions of Lire)

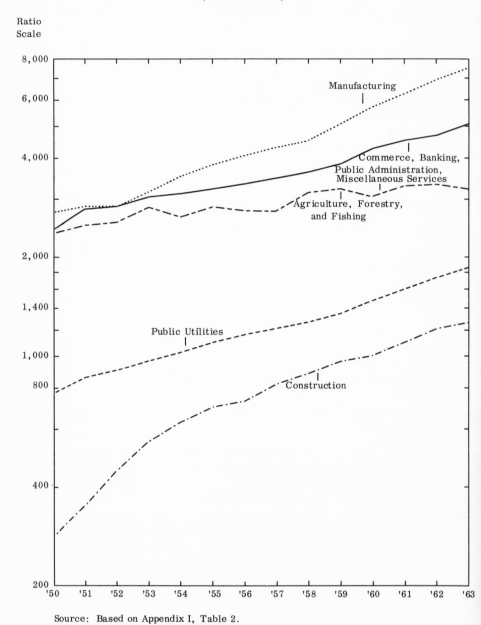

Source: Based on Appendix I, Table 2.

Some indication of the dynamic forces in the Italian economy is given by the annual rates of change in real national product and expenditure which can be inferred from Figures 1 and 2 and which are shown in detail in Appendix Table 4. The annual rates of increase in GNP during the period were truly remarkable on the whole, at least until 1964. Rates in excess of 7 per cent were achieved in 1951, 1953, 1959, and 1960. The maximum rate of increase recorded was 8.4 per cent for 1961. This rate fell considerably, however, in 1962 and again in 1963 when the occurrence of inflation together with a sizable deficit in the balance of payments led the monetary authorities to introduce measures to restrict home demand. The rate of growth in GNP declined still further to 3.0 per cent in 1964 as the effects of the restrictive policies were still being felt.[3] Preliminary information for 1965 indicated that the economy was relatively slow in responding to easier policies as the rate of growth remained about at the 1964 level.[4]

Looking at the components of GNP, there was a substantial rise in the rate of increase in private consumption in 1953. The rise in 1954 was comparatively small, however, and the increases were fairly modest in the next three years. There was again only a relatively small increase in 1958. But the rate of increase jumped markedly from 1959 and reached a postwar high of 9.3 per cent in 1963. The increase of only 2.4 per cent in 1964 reflected the contractionary domestic policy influences mentioned above.

The rate of increase in public consumption evidently fluctuated a good deal. There was some indication of countercyclical effects in 1952-53 and again in 1957-59. But the 11.6 per cent increase in 1963 seems clearly to have reinforced rather than offset the sharp rise in private consumption. The comparatively minor increase in 1964 of 1.1 per cent certainly imparted only a negligible stimulus to growth in that year.

The rates of increase in gross-fixed-capital formation show that investment provided a substantial impetus to growth during 1951-57, and that the impact in 1958 was minor. The most pronounced rates of increase in investment clearly occurred during 1959-61. There was a tapering off in 1962-63, and for the first time in the postwar period a significant absolute decline in 1964. The annual rates of change in the accumulation or decumulation of inventories were apparently sizable. As is evident from Appendix Table 4, the substantial reduction in stocks may have contributed significantly to the 1952 slowdown, while the build-up was expansionary during 1953-55. Changes in stocks seem to have behaved countercyclically during 1956-58 and then to have had an expan-

sionary effect in 1959-60. It is interesting that there were net decumu-
lations beginning in 1961 and that these became substantial in 1963-64.

Except for 1952 and 1958, the annual rates of increase in exports
of goods and services were substantial during the 1950's. As was the
case with investment, exports also jumped considerably during 1959-
61, although they tapered off noticeably in 1962-63. This tapering off
was reversed in 1964 when the rise in exports accounted evidently for
a substantial proportion of the relatively small rate of increase in GNP.
A significant rise in exports apparently also occurred in 1965. The annual rates of increase in imports were sizable during the 1950's, except for 1954 and for 1958 when imports actually fell in absolute terms.
Imports picked up in 1959, however, and jumped remarkably by 36.9
per cent in 1960. Substantial rates of increase were recorded also in
1961-62. As was mentioned above, the next jump, in 1963, brought in
its wake a sizable balance-of-payments deficit. The consequent introduction of restrictive domestic policies evidently restrained home demand sufficiently in 1964 so as to result in an absolute decline in imports. Imports in 1965 were slightly below the level of the previous
year.

When we look at the annual rates of increase in output by sectors,
it is evident that there was a good deal of variation from year to year
in the agriculture, forestry, and fishing sector. It is interesting that
this sector is still important enough in the Italian economy that bounti-
ful harvests and shortfalls can be seen to have had a perceptible impact
on the annual rates of increase in domestic product. This was evident
in 1962 and especially in 1963 when agricultural output fell, unfortunately
at a time when consumption pressures were mounting. This accounted
in considerable part for the significant increase in 1963 of imported
foodstuffs in particular.

The rates of increase in the output of the mining and quarrying sector noted in Appendix Table 4 were substantial during 1951-57 and relatively low in 1958. There was some pickup in 1959-61, little change in
1962, and an absolute decline in 1963. The manufacturing sector also
grew rapidly during the 1950's, except for 1952 and 1958. The increases
in 1959-60 were especially large--as one would have expected from the
way we have noted that investment and foreign trade behaved in these
years. Beginning in 1961 and continuing thereafter, however, the
growth of the manufacturing sector tapered off.

Construction grew rapidly in the early 1950's, then slowed down
somewhat in 1956, and subsequently followed a path of alternating in-
tensity. The growth in public utilities was on the whole fairly steady
during the period, although there were sizable spurts of activity, es-

pecially in 1951 and 1960. The growth of all the other sectors was somewhat variable around a relatively low rate of annual increase for most years.

A further indication of the dynamic factors in Italian development is provided by Appendix Table 5 which enables one to determine the contribution made by individual sectors to the rate of increase in GNP for individual years from 1951-64. The 1959-61 boom years are especially interesting in showing the contributions which gross investment and exports made to global demand as reflected in the total use of resources and in GNP. The tapering off of investment and exports in 1962-63 and the concomitant rise in consumption and imports can also be seen clearly. Finally, the importance of the increase in exports and reduction in imports is evident in 1964.

Appendix Tables 6 and 7 contain data on gross investment by sector and total saving at current prices and at 1954 prices for the period 1950-64. The last three rows of these tables show total fixed investment, fixed "productive" investment (i.e., dwellings are deducted from the total), and saving as a percentage of GNP. These latter percentages, together with the absolute amounts of saving, fixed productive investment and investment in dwellings at 1954 prices, have been plotted in Figure 3.

It is interesting that total fixed investment as a percentage of GNP increased during the period from 17.2 per cent to the remarkably high level of 24.5 per cent in 1963. The increase during 1959-63 was especially noteworthy. However, the reduction of investment in 1964 lowered the percentage to about the level of 1959. When dwellings are excluded from total fixed investment, it can be seen that the increase in fixed "productive" investment as a percentage of GNP was comparatively much less rapid during the 1950's. It rose from slightly over 14 in 1950 to somewhat more than 15 per cent in 1959. It jumped sharply, however, in the following years, reaching 18.4 per cent in both 1963 and 1964. But the contraction in 1964 reduced it to the 1959 level.

Total saving, which is equal to total gross investment plus the foreign balance, fluctuated around 17.5 per cent of GNP from 1950-54. It then rose four percentage points from 1955-58, two more from 1958-60, and increased still further to over 25 per cent of GNP in 1961 and 1962. The very substantial deterioration of the foreign balance in 1963 reduced the ratio to 21.8 per cent in 1963. It increased slightly in 1964 due chiefly to the improvement in the foreign balance, but was nevertheless a little below the level of 1957-58.

Figure 3

Italy: Saving, Fixed Productive Investment,
and Investment in Dwellings in Total and as a Percentage of GNP at 1954 Prices, 1950-64
(Billions of Lire)

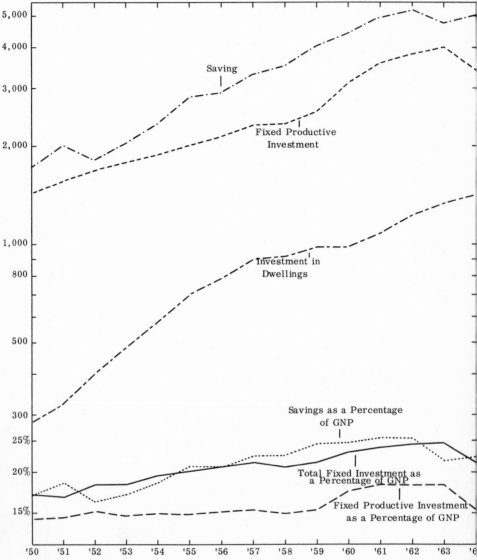

Source: Based on Appendix I, Table 7.

8

The picture which emerges from the foregoing discussion is thus one of a remarkably high and more or less continuous rate of over-all expansion in the Italian economy in the postwar period until 1963. The data for 1964 show that the policies introduced by the monetary authorities beginning in 1963 to curtail the increases in home demand and prices were successful as the rise in consumption was relatively small and imports were reduced in absolute terms. With favorable foreign demand conditions, there was fortunately a significant rise in exports which, as we shall see, helped greatly in generating a sizable surplus in the balance of payments. Less fortunate, however, was that gross investment fell in absolute terms. The net outcome was a rate of growth in real GNP in 1964 of 3.0 per cent, which was the lowest rate experienced by Italy since 1952. Conditions in 1965 seem to have paralleled on the whole those in 1964.

INDUSTRIAL AND PRIMARY PRODUCTION

We have already discussed the important changes which occurred during the postwar period in gross domestic product by sector. It may be of interest, however, to look at changes in production in somewhat greater detail. Thus, in Appendix Table 8 there are listed the indexes of industrial production applicable to the extractive industries, manufacturing and its major component industries, and electricity and gas. Also shown are the indexes covering the production of crops, animal products, and forest products. The data for these major groupings of industrial production and primary production have been plotted in Figure 4.

The production index for the extractive industries increased substantially until 1957, slackened in 1958, and then rose again though at a much reduced rate compared to that of pre-1958. The index dipped in 1963, but more than recovered its earlier level in 1964. The index of electricity and gas production increased steadily until 1958 and accelerated from 1959 onward.

The rate of increase in manufacturing production was substantial until 1957, slackened in 1958, and then jumped considerably during 1959-61. The increases in 1962-63 were also sizable though less than in the three preceding years. During 1963-64 the index was practically stationary, reflecting the slowdown in economic activity mentioned earlier, while in 1965 it apparently rose to some extent.

The production indexes for the individual manufacturing industries in Appendix Table 8 are noteworthy because they provide an indication of comparative growth patterns. It is evident that foodstuffs and bev-

Figure 4

Italy: Industrial Production and Primary Production, 1951–64 (1953=100)

A. Industrial Production

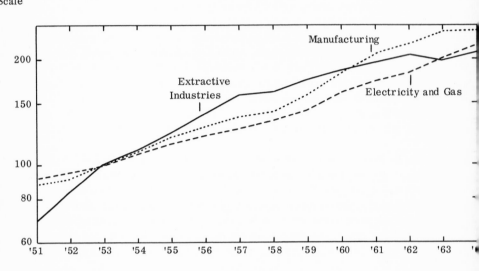

B. Primary Production

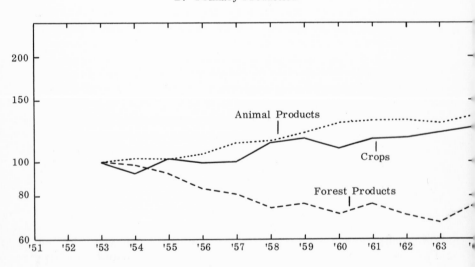

Source: Based on Appendix I, Table 8.

erages, tobacco, textiles, leather, shoes, wood, machinery, rubber, and paper grew significantly less than the over-all industry average. The individual industries registering the greatest increases were thus metallurgy, precision instruments, vehicles, stone, clay, and glass products, chemicals, petroleum and coal products, and synthetic fibers. These latter industries were in large measure the "newer" industries subject to dynamic change. As we shall see later, they figured importantly in the development of Italy's foreign trade in the postwar period.

Turning now to primary production, it can be seen from Figure 4 that the index of crop production was more or less stationary during 1953-57, rose substantially in the next two years, dropped in 1960, and then more than recovered its earlier levels. The production of animal products moved sharply upward during 1955-57 and then again in 1959-60. But it was practically stationary for the next three years which, as will be recalled, were the ones in which consumption pressures were building up. Increased imports, especially of foodstuffs, were thus unavoidable at this time as domestic production was insufficiently expanded. The production index for forest products can be seen, finally, to have declined markedly during the period since low cost domestic sources apparently became increasingly unavailable.

It is clear from the foregoing discussion that over-all industrial and primary production grew at widely disparate rates, and that there were also significant differences in the growth rates of the component sectors. The development of some of the newer lines of manufacturing activity was especially impressive, while the lagging output of crops and livestock products created some difficulties, particularly in 1962-63.

WHOLESALE PRICES, CONSUMER PRICES, AND THE COST OF LIVING

Turning now to an examination of the behavior of prices in the postwar period, Appendix Tables 9 to 11 contain indexes of the implicit price deflators for national product and expenditure, wholesale prices, consumer prices, and the cost of living. The annual rates of change in these indexes are shown for the implicit deflators in Appendix Table 12 and for the other series in Appendix Table 13. The implicit deflators and the summary indexes for the other price measures have been plotted in Figures 5 to 7.

Taking 1954=100, it is evident from Figure 5 that the GNP deflator increased by 10 per cent between this year and 1958. In the boom years following, it can be seen to have fallen slightly in 1959 and risen only moderately in 1960 and 1961. Inflationary pressures were

Figure 5

Italy: Implicit Price Deflators for Gross National Product, 1950-64 (1954=100)

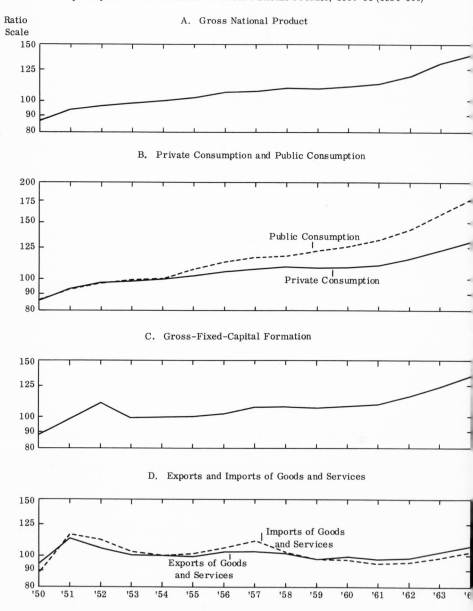

A. Gross National Product

B. Private Consumption and Public Consumption

Public Consumption

Private Consumption

C. Gross-Fixed-Capital Formation

D. Exports and Imports of Goods and Services

Imports of Goods
and Services

Exports of Goods
and Services

Ratio
Scale

Source: Based on Appendix I, Table 9.

12

evident in 1962 when the index rose by 5.7 per cent and again in 1963 when the increase was 8.8 per cent. The rise of 6.1 per cent in 1964 indicated that the inflationary pressures were reduced somewhat, but they were nevertheless still relatively substantial.

The increase in the deflator for private consumption was not materially different than the GNP deflator during the 1950's. The same general pattern of increase was also observed during 1960-64, but the level and rate of increase in the private consumption deflator were less than for GNP. The deflator for public consumption evidently increased substantially after 1954. It rose nearly 18 per cent from 1954-58, another 21 per cent from 1958-62, and an additional 24 per cent in the next two years.

The gross-fixed-capital-formation deflator was more or less unchanged during 1953-55, increased by 5.8 per cent in the next two years, and then remained relatively stable until 1961. It rose by 5.4 per cent in 1962, however, and then accelerated to 7.2 and 8.4 per cent in 1963 and 1964. It can be seen, finally, that the deflator for exports of goods and services fluctuated around 100 during 1954-58, moved downward until 1962, and rose in 1963-64. The deflator for imports of goods and services rose substantially in 1956-57 during the period of the Suez crisis and thereafter moved steadily downward until 1962. It then increased in 1963-64.

The gross-domestic-product deflator plotted in Figure 6 apparently followed the same general pattern of increase as the GNP deflator. The deflator for agriculture, forestry, and fishing seems to have followed alternating patterns above and below the base level until 1961, after which it increased substantially. The mining and quarrying deflator exhibited an almost continuous decline during the period until 1963, when it turned upward. The deflator for manufacturing fell considerably during 1952-54, remained nearly unchanged during 1954-62, and then increased by 5.4 per cent in 1963. The construction deflator rose significantly between 1952 and 1957, tapered off through 1960, and then jumped, especially in 1962-63. The deflator for public utilities rose more or less steadily throughout the period, but showed a marked increase in 1962-63. The deflator for the "other" sector which includes commerce, banking, public administration, and miscellaneous services rose very substantially until 1958. The rate of increase diminished considerably during 1959-61, but then jumped to 13.2 per cent in 1962 and 11.2 per cent in 1963.

Turning now to the other price indexes, it is evident that the general-wholesale-price index fluctuated only slightly around its 1953

Figure 6

Italy: Implicit Price Deflators for Gross Domestic Product, 1950-64 (1954=100)

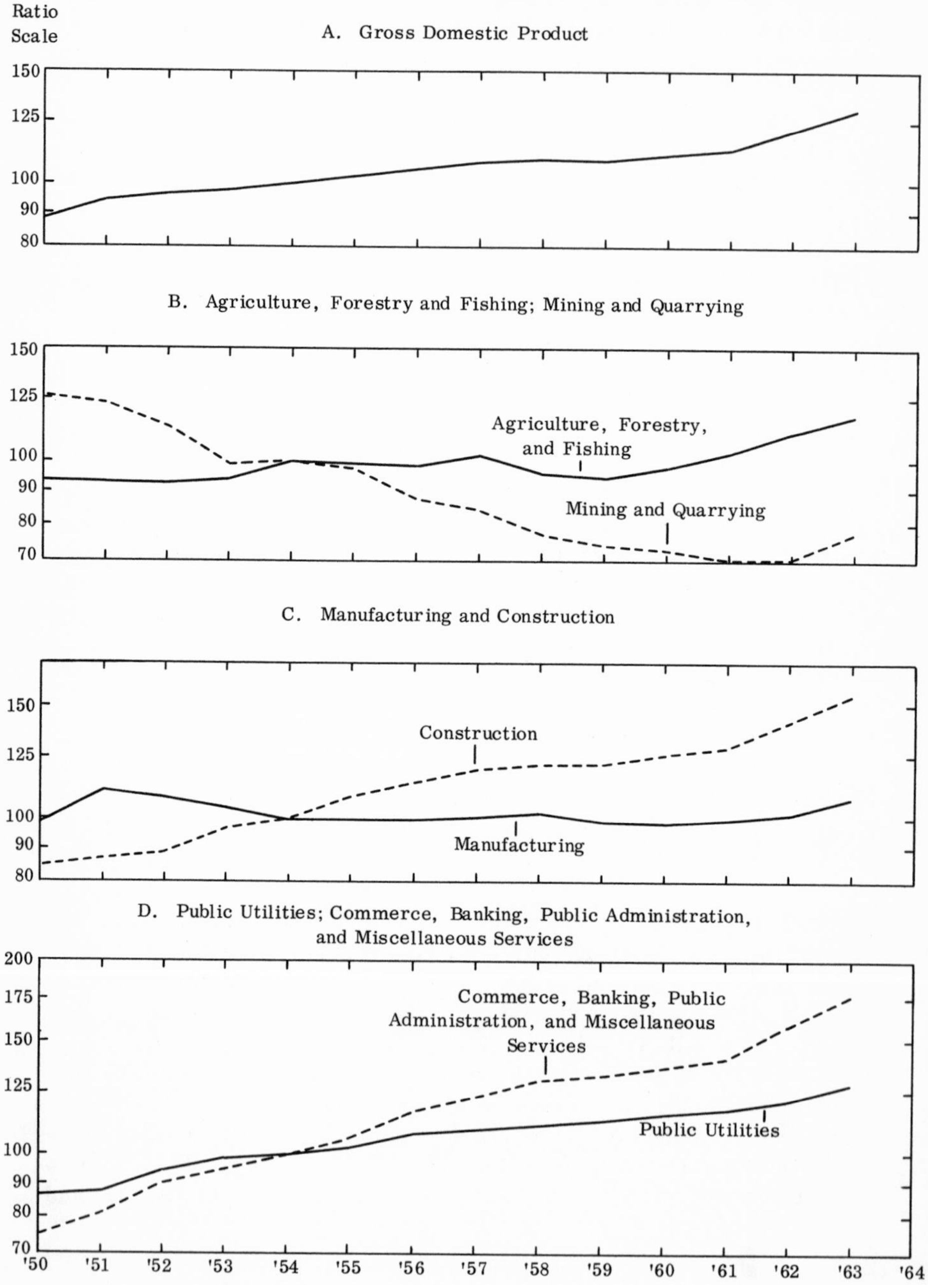
Ratio Scale
A. Gross Domestic Product
150
125
100
90
80
B. Agriculture, Forestry and Fishing; Mining and Quarrying
150
125
100
90
80
70
Agriculture, Forestry, and Fishing
Mining and Quarrying
C. Manufacturing and Construction
150
125
100
90
80
Construction
Manufacturing
D. Public Utilities; Commerce, Banking, Public Administration, and Miscellaneous Services
200
175
150
125
100
90
80
70
Commerce, Banking, Public Administration, and Miscellaneous Services
Public Utilities
'50
'51
'52
'53
'54
'55
'56
'57
'58
'59
'60
'61
'62
'63
'64

Source: Based on Appendix I, Table 9.

Figure 7

Italy: Wholesale Price, Consumer Price, and Cost-of-Living Indexes, 1951-64 (1951=100)

Ratio
Scale

A. Wholesale Prices: General Index

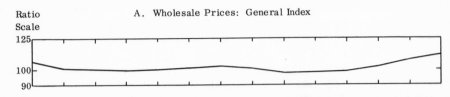

B. Wholesale Price Indexes of Agricultural and Nonagricultural Products

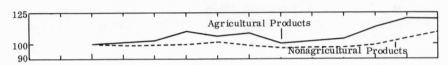

C. Wholesale Price Indexes of Consumer Goods, Investment Goods,
and Auxiliary Materials

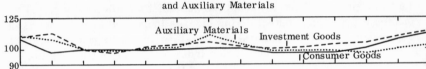

D. Consumer Price Index

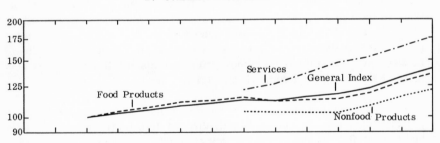

E. Cost-of-Living Indexes

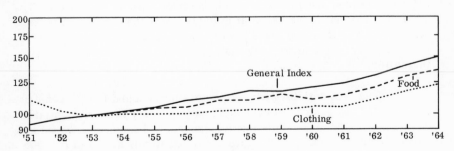

Source: Based on Appendix I, Tables 10 and 11.

15

base level during 1952-62, and that it increased subsequently by 5.2 per
cent in 1963 and by 3.4 per cent in 1964. It continued to rise slightly
in 1965. The wholesale price index for agricultural products was al-
ternately relatively low during 1953-55, high in 1956-58, and low from
1959-61. It then increased by 8.7 per cent in 1962 and by 6.1 per cent
in 1963. It was roughly the same in 1964 as in 1963. The index for nonagricultural products was comparatively stable throughout the period
until 1963-64. The same general pattern of comparative stability for
most of the period until 1962 was evident also for the wholesale price
indexes for consumer goods, investment goods, and auxiliary materials. Further data on wholesale price indexes by industry groups are
contained in Appendix Table 10. These will be discussed in detail in
Chapter 5 below.

The indexes for consumer prices and the cost of living apparently
increased considerably more during the period than was the case for
wholesale prices. That is, from the base of 1953=100, the general
consumer price and cost-of-living indexes increased to 140.3 and 149.1,
respectively, while the general-wholesale-price index rose to 110.9.
The increase in the consumer price index was fairly steady during
1953-58, showed a decline in 1959, and then a rapid rise especially
after 1961. This same pattern was evident for the food and the non-
food products indexes, while the index for services rose rapidly in contrast in the years shown, reaching a level of 177.3 in 1964. The levels
of the cost-of-living indexes were generally higher than the consumer
price indexes although the movements were basically similar. It is
noteworthy that both the consumer price and cost-of-living indexes continued to move upward somewhat in 1965.

This brief review of the behavior of prices in the Italian economy
has disclosed a more or less steady upward drift until 1961 in the GNP
and GDP deflators and in the indexes of general consumer prices and
the cost of living. These indexes as well as the index of wholesale
prices increased sharply in 1962-63, however, and again in 1964-65,
but at a somewhat lower rate. It is evident that the component indexes
did not always follow the same pattern as the general indexes prior to
1961, although most of the component indexes increased significantly
thereafter.

Thus, the deflators for public consumption and for the construction and "other" sectors of gross domestic product rose substantially
during the period. The deflators for exports and imports of goods and
services and for manufacturing were comparatively stable in relation to
the base year level, while the deflator for the mining and quarrying sector fell considerably. The wholesale price index for agricultural products

Figure 8

Italy: Labor Force, Employment, and Unemployment, 1951-64 (000's)

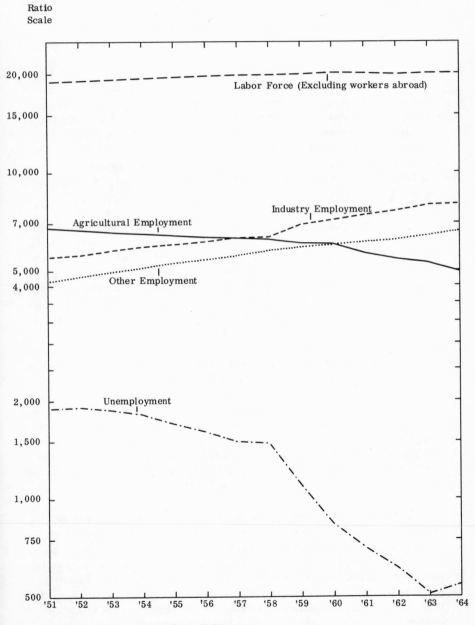

Source: Based on Appendix I, Table 14.

fluctuated more than the general index which was remarkably stable until 1961, and it then increased more than the general index in 1962-63. The consumer price index of services also increased significantly more than the general index in the period covered. It would appear important therefore in evaluating and projecting the general trends in prices to keep in mind the aforementioned differences in components.[5]

EMPLOYMENT, WAGES, AND PRODUCTIVITY

Appendix Table 14 contains estimates of the labor force, employ- ment by major sectors, unemployment, net emigration, and workers employed temporarily abroad for the period 1951-64. The labor force, employment, and unemployment data have been plotted in Figure 8. While caution is necessary in interpreting these series because of the manner in which part-time employment and workers abroad, especially, are treated, the trends seem nevertheless clearly enough established for analytical purposes.

The increase in the labor force present in Italy (i.e., excluding workers temporarily employed abroad) was evidently relatively small, from 18.9 million in 1951 to 20.1 million in 1964. Were it not for emi- gration, the total labor force increase would have been significantly larger.[6] This is clear from the fact that net emigration was well over 100,000 annually until 1963 and that at the end of the period nearly 500,000 workers were temporarily employed abroad in other parts of Western Europe.[7]

As far as employment was concerned, the major increases took place in industry, from 5.5 million in 1951 to 8.0 million in 1964, and in the "other" (tertiary) sector, from 4.7 million in 1951 to 6.6 million in 1964. Employment in agriculture fell from 6.8 million in 1951 to 5.0 million in 1964.[8] In relative terms, the percentage of total employment in agriculture dropped from 40.0 per cent at the beginning of the period to 25.4 per cent at the end. Employment in industry rose in contrast from 32.4 to 40.8 per cent of the total, while employment in the "other" sector increased from 27.6 to 33.8 per cent.

The data show that the increase in employment of 2.6 million workers during the period was drawn from an increase in the labor force of about 1.2 million and from a reduction of 1.4 million in the number unemployed. Employment apparently increased steadily in in- dustry and in the "other" sector during 1951-57 absorbing .8 million from an increase in and redistribution of the labor force and .4 million from reduced unemployment. After 1958, however, employment in industry jumped remarkably and by 1964 the industrial sector had ab-

sorbed more than 1.6 million additional workers. Employment in the
"other" sector rose during those years by nearly .9 million. Since
the total labor force increased only slightly, it appears that 1.3 million of the increase in employment came from a drop in agricultural
employment and nearly an additional million from the reduction in the
level of unemployment.

Unemployment as a percentage of the labor force thus dropped
from 10.1 per cent in 1951 to 7.5 per cent in 1958, and by 1963 it
amounted only to 2.5 per cent. With the 1964 slowdown, it increased
to 2.7 per cent and apparently exceeded 3 per cent in 1965.[9] The improvement in domestic employment opportunities by the end of the
period was also reflected in the considerable decline in net emigration
in 1962-63, and by the small reductions in these years of the total
number of workers employed temporarily abroad.

We have already seen the impact which the 1959-63 expansion
had on national product and expenditure and upon prices, particularly
in 1962-63 when consumption rose considerably. The employment data
just examined throw additional light upon this episode, for Italy had
apparently reached in effect a full-employment economy by 1963. Appendix Table 15 and Figure 9 which contain some estimates of wage and
productivity changes in the Italian economy for 1951-64 bring out clearly the developments which occurred in the labor market.

The first set of series plotted in Figure 9 refers to Organization
for Economic Cooperation and Development (OECD) estimates of hourly
earnings and output per man-hour in manufacturing. It is evident that
the gap between productivity and wages increased steadily until 1958
and then widened considerably.[10] But with hourly earnings spurting
greatly in 1962 and again in 1963, the increase in earnings exceeded
the growth in productivity in this latter year. The rise in earnings
abated slightly in 1964 but still exceeded the rise in productivity.[11]

The second set of series on hourly earnings and productivity was
based on estimates by the Banca d'Italia. These estimates were on the
whole similar to those of the OECD since both organizations used data
published in Ministry of Labor surveys. The Banca d'Italia estimates
of hourly earnings were generally just a little lower than the OECD estimates, but their estimates of output per man-hour were consistently higher
than those of the OECD. Thus, while the Banca d'Italia data showed the
dramatic narrowing of the gap between earnings and productivity that
began in 1961, the increase in productivity remained in excess of that of
earnings in 1963-64.

Figure 9

Italy: Wages and Productivity, 1951-64 (1953=100)

A. Manufacturing - OECD Data

Ratio
Scale

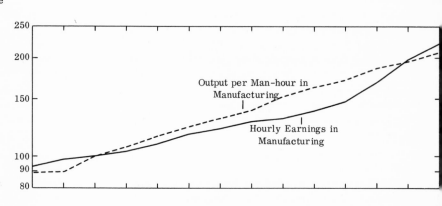

B. Manufacturing: Banca d'Italia Data

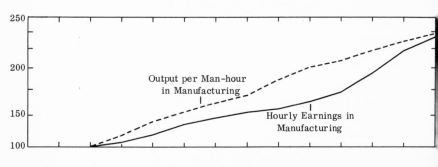

C. Industry: Banca d'Italia Data

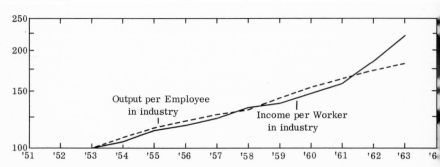

Source: Based on Appendix I, Table 15.

The final series plotted in Figure 9 cover income per worker and output per employee in industry. These series are not altogether comparable because the income and productivity of nonproduction workers may differ from that of production workers and because other industries besides manufacturing are included. In any event, even though the differential between productivity and earnings was much smaller than for manufacturing alone, the results were generally similar especially insofar as income per worker rose substantially in excess of output per employee in 1962-63.

The data on employment thus add a further dimension to our discussion of postwar developments in the Italian economy. The very considerable expansion of aggregate income and production during the period and especially after 1958 plus the opportunities available through emigration enabled large numbers of workers to be released from agriculture and from the ranks of the unemployed and underemployed in order to take advantage of newly created jobs. This was accomplished, for the most part, in a noninflationary manner during the 1950's. However, following the spurt in economic activity that began in 1959, Italy soon found itself in a position faced with inflationary price and wage conditions and a substantial balance-of-payments deficit. The day of full employment reckoning had arrived in effect.

FOREIGN TRADE AND THE BALANCE OF PAYMENTS

Reference has been made already to the substantial postwar expansion of Italy's exports and imports of goods and services. This can be seen also in Appendix Tables 16 and 17 which contain data on the value, quantum, and unit value of total world and total Italian exports, world and Italian exports of manufactures, and Italian imports in the postwar period. The quantum and unit value series have been plotted in Figure 10 and 11.

It is evident that total Italian exports increased much more rapidly than total world exports. That is, taking 1953 = 100, the quantum of total Italian exports rose to 180 in 1957 and to 453 in 1964. The corresponding increases in total world exports were to 130 in 1957 and to 205 in 1964. This was true also for the quantum of Italian exports of manufactures which doubled during 1953-57 and then tripled during 1957-64. The corresponding increases in the quantum of world exports of manufactures from 1953 were to 30 per cent in 1957 and another 56 per cent during 1957-64. As can be inferred from the unit value indexes plotted in Figure 10, a substantial proportion of the increase in Italian exports relative to world exports was apparently attributable to improvements in Italy's export price competitiveness. [12]

Figure 10

Total World and Total Italian Exports at 1953 Prices, World and
Italian Exports of Manufactures at 1958 Prices, and Unit Values, 1950-64

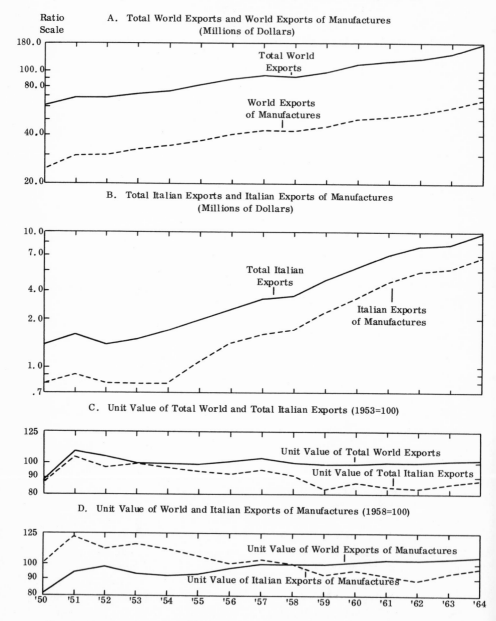

Source: Based on Appendix I, Table 16.

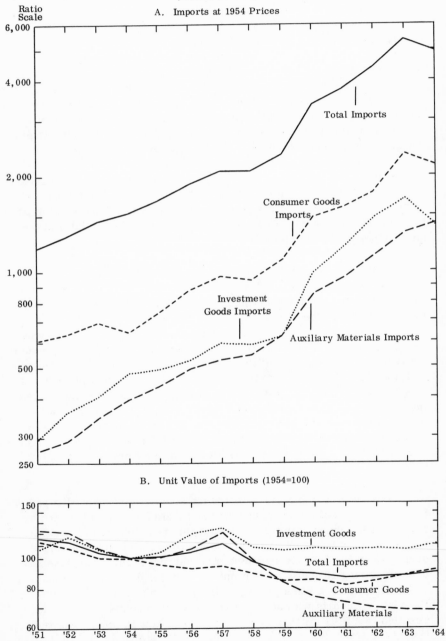

Figure 11
Italy: Imports at 1954 Prices and Unit Values, 1951-64 (1954=100)
(Billions of Lire)

A. Imports at 1954 Prices

Ratio Scale

Total Imports

Consumer Goods Imports

Investment Goods Imports

Auxiliary Materials Imports

B. Unit Value of Imports (1954=100)

Investment Goods

Total Imports

Consumer Goods

Auxiliary Materials

Source: Based on Appendix I, Table 17.

23

The pattern of Italy's import expansion which is plotted in Figure 11 showed a fairly steady increase until 1957, a slight decline in 1958, and then a substantial jump during 1959-63. There was an absolute decline in imports in 1964 as has already been noted. The same general pattern of increase was evident with minor exceptions in the three subgroups of imports in the period until 1958. After this year, investment goods imports increased relatively more than the other two groups, particularly during 1959-62. The unit value indexes also plotted in Figure 11 all showed a substantial decline after the Suez crisis period of 1957. This decline was most marked in the case of auxiliary materials imports, whereas the indexes for consumer and investment goods imports remained more or less unchanged until 1962-63.

Developments in the commodity composition and market distribution of Italy's foreign trade as well as the impact of foreign trade on domestic production also revealed some interesting changes in the postwar period. These will be examined in some detail especially in the next chapter and in Chapter 5.

Italy's balance of payments for the period 1950-64 is shown in summary form in Appendix Table 18. Its end-of-year official international reserves are listed in Appendix Table 19 for the period 1950-65. Figure 12 depicts the annual balance-of-trade deficit, surplus on invisibles, the consequent current account surplus or deficit, and the annual change in official reserves. It is evident that the balance-of-trade deficit averaged around $700 million during 1952-57, dropped significantly in 1958-59, increased to earlier levels by 1962, and then jumped to a record postwar high in 1963 of nearly $1.9 billion in the wake of greatly increased imports. A $400 million decline in imports coupled with a $900 million rise in exports in 1964 resulted in a substantial narrowing of the trade deficit. Preliminary data for 1965 revealed that imports were $79 million below their 1964 level, while exports rose by $1.2 billion.

The surplus on services increased steadily throughout the period from a level of $321 million in 1953 to just slightly over $1 billion by 1964. This coupled with the annual surplus realized on unilateral transfers resulted in substantial reductions in the current account deficit during 1952-56, followed by substantial current account surpluses especially during 1958-61. A current account surplus was sustained in 1962, although at a reduced level. But the combination of the substantial rise in imports with nearly stationary net receipts on invisibles resulted in a $701 million current account deficit in 1963. The reduction of the trade deficit in 1964, together with a sizable pickup in receipts from services, produced a current account surplus nearly equal

Figure 12

Italy: Balance of Payments, 1950–64
(Millions of Dollars)

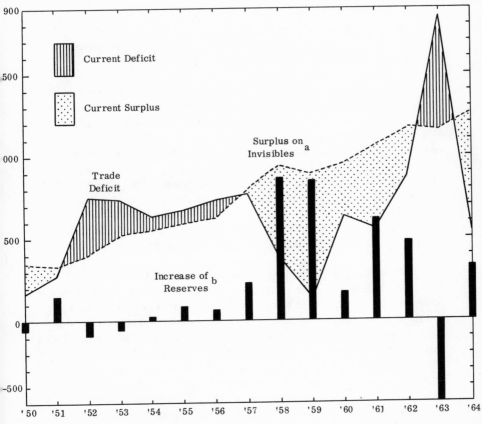

a Services and unilateral transfers.   b Official reserves and net IMF position.
Source: Based on Appendix I, Table 18.

in size to the deficit of the preceding year.

Capital movements plus errors and omissions yielded net receipts during 1951-61, thus offsetting the trade deficits during 1952-
56 and adding significantly to the trade surpluses in the years up to
1961. Net outflows were evident in 1962 and also in 1963 when they apparently aggravated the already sizable current account deficit. The
flows turned positive again in 1964, adding slightly to the surplus
realized on current accounts.

The financing of the annual over-all balances is indicated by
the net monetary movements shown in Appendix Table 18 and the
growth of official reserves in Appendix Table 19. Annual changes in
official reserves are shown by the bars drawn in Figure 12. [13] These
reserves were accumulated in substantial amounts from a total of
$768 million in 1953 to more than $3.8 billion by 1962. Reserves were
drawn down to some extent in 1963 to help finance the large over-all
deficit noted. But with the balance-of-payments surplus realized in
1964, reserves were built up again to roughly their 1962 level. And
with the realization of another surplus in 1965, reserves were accumulated even further to a total well in excess of $4 billion.

The foregoing discussion disclosed that Italy experienced a negative trade balance in each postwar year. This was offset increasingly,
however, by a surplus on services and unilateral transfers with the
result that the current account deficit was steadily reduced during
1952-56 and a surplus recorded thereafter through 1962. Since there
were net inflows of capital during 1951-61, the effect was to reduce the
over-all balance-of-payments deficits and to increase the over-all surpluses recorded in individual years. The balance of payments deterio-
rated markedly in 1963 with a recorded deficit of nearly $1.3 billion as
the consequence of the combined effects of a huge jump in imports
which produced a trade deficit of nearly $1.9 billion, stagnant invisible
net receipts, and a capital outflow of $551 million. The situation was
corrected in 1964, as we have seen, by the implementation of restrictive domestic monetary measures designed to curtail home demand and
inflationary pressures. The combination of reduced imports, an expansion of exports made possible by the lowered rate of increase in
domestic absorption and favorable foreign demand conditions, a pickup
in net receipts from invisibles, and a small net inflow of capital resulted in a balance-of-payments surplus of $774 million. Preliminary
indications for 1965 were for another sizable surplus of about $1.5
billion.

CONCLUSION

Let us now attempt to look back over the discussion of the preceding sections and see what conclusions can be drawn concerning the
characteristics of economic growth in postwar Italy. Suppose we begin
by concentrating on the favorable aspects of Italy's growth experience.
What are the factors which may explain this success? As Baffi has
pointed out in his perceptive analysis of postwar Italian development, [14]
we may note first that with the end of World War II substantial amounts
of productive resources were freed for use domestically. The government was no longer burdened with sizable expenditures for military
purposes, the maintenance of colonies, and service of the national
debt. This was beneficial not only to the domestic economy but also
to the balance of payments. It meant that nonessential imports could
be reduced and that the wartime excess capacity that had been generated in the engineering and textile industries, in particular, could be
diverted to domestic needs and also to markets for export.

With successful recovery both at home and abroad in the industrial countries, a second important development which occurred was
the progressive dismantling of trade restrictions. This had a two-
fold effect on Italy. Trade liberalization and the growth of foreign incomes served to encourage export expansion, while Italy's own liberalization of imports had the effect of exposing her domestic economy to
competition on a broad scale in many lines of manufacturing. The
authorities were able to take this risk of liberalizing imports in the
early 1950's since, as we have noted, they had been able as a prior
condition to build up the level of official foreign-exchange reserves.

The third point to be stressed is that the rapid postwar growth
was predicated on a relatively elastic supply of labor. It was shown
above that the expansion of employment in the industrial and tertiary
sectors absorbed a substantial number of new entrants into the labor
force, workers from the agricultural sector, and individuals from the
ranks of the unemployed. This was not taking into account the sizable
annual net emigration of workers to other parts of Western Europe and
elsewhere. Wage increases during the period were thus comparatively
restrained for the most part.

The fourth point to be emphasized is the pervasive influence of
technological progress. The conversion to a peacetime economy gave
existing industries an opportunity to introduce more up-to-date methods
of production. It was also possible to undertake completely new lines
of productive activity. The importance of manufacturing in the economy

thus increased and, as the indexes of manufacturing production showed, there were rapid advances in production especially in the newer industries that were subject to more dynamic changes. The data presented on productivity bear further witness to these changes.

Italy's postwar development might thus be characterized as stemming from favorable demand conditions at home and abroad combined with an elastic labor supply and a large reservoir of unexploited technological opportunities. This development took place, moreover, in the policy context of joint and largely successful striving for monetary stability and the building up of official foreign-exchange reserves. To achieve such rapid growth required the generation of an unusually large amount of saving and the successful completion of highly productive investment projects. It also required an expansion of bank credit consistent with stabilization objectives.

The dynamic expansion of saving and investment in the postwar period was stimulated significantly by a substantial increase in public sector investment in excess of public saving. At the same time, with the continued expansion of Italian exports and net receipts from invisibles and capital inflows, the monetary authorities were thus able to build up their official reserves and, concomitantly, to manage a stable domestic monetary expansion. This building up of official reserves provided, moreover, a significant base from which credit expansion by the commercial banks could proceed. A major part of this credit expansion was directed to the private sector without serious interruption and it was reinforced by the sizable amounts of profits that this sector ploughed back into new investment. There was some indication, finally, that the rapid expansion of liquidity at the end of the 1950's, when the balance of payments was in substantial surplus, had the effect of reducing interest rates to some extent. The Italian economy was able therefore to generate substantial amounts of saving and investment and grow rapidly until the beginning of the 1960's without any major disturbances to the general level of prices and the balance of payments.

The data presented in the preceding sections give testimony to the fact that certain basic changes were taking place in the Italian economy in 1962 as the consequence of the boom that had started three years previously. The very rapid expansion of the industrial and tertiary sectors resulted in a substantial redistribution of the labor force from agriculture as well as absorption on a large scale of the unemployed. Italy was thus moving up quickly toward a full-employment ceiling. It was not surprising that with the continuation of relatively easy credit policies, wages and prices increased significantly in 1962-63. The resulting changes in the distribution of income led to sizable increases in consumption and imports, and balance-of-payments difficulties followed.

With the application of restrictive domestic policies in late 1963, as we have noted, the effect in 1964 was to arrest the rate of increase in consumption, slow down inflation, and reduce imports. Since exports increased considerably, the balance of payments improved in 1964. The price for the aforementioned changes, however, was a significant reduction in capital formation and some rise in unemployment. Incomplete evidence for 1965 available at the time of writing suggests that conditions were not improved materially as compared to 1964. That is, the rate of increase in GNP in 1965 was about 3 per cent, inflationary forces were still present to an important degree, and the level of unemployment was slightly higher. On the favorable side, exports increased $1. 2 billion in 1965 while imports were slightly lower. Official reserves increased as a consequence by around $600 million. [15]

What is clear from our discussion is that the Italian economy apparently reached a turning point in its postwar development in 1963. The experiences of 1964 and 1965 may, of course, prove to be transitory. But given the relatively low level of unemployment attained in recent years, it is doubtful whether the unusually high pre-1963 growth rates could be sustained repeatedly in the near future unless sizable increases in investment and gains in factor productivities were realized.

Having thus completed our general survey of economic growth in postwar Italy, we shall confine our attention in the next four chapters to developments in Italy's foreign trade. The major focus will be on exports and the special role that they have played in Italy's postwar growth. We shall then return in the final chapter to some of the more general considerations set forth in the present chapter, hoping thereby to provide perspective for our concentration on the export sector.

CHAPTER **2** POSTWAR DEVELOPMENTS IN
ITALY'S FOREIGN TRADE

What is proposed in the present chapter is a recapitulation of
the important developments which have been reflected in the remarkable expansion of Italy's foreign trade in the postwar period. We
shall begin by presenting some regression measurements of the elasticities of demand for Italian exports in the postwar period. We will
then attempt to determine the extent to which the observed changes in
exports may be attributable to changes in the commodity composition,
market distribution, and competitiveness of these exports. The third
part of the chapter contains some regression measurements of Italy's
elasticities of demand for imports. Imports are then examined further with reference particularly to changes in their commodity composition and regions of origin.[1] The chapter closes with some con-
cluding remarks.

ELASTICITIES OF DEMAND FOR ITALIAN EXPORTS

Estimation of the demand elasticities for Italy's exports may
help to afford some understanding of the role that these demand factors have played in the expansion of exports in the postwar period.
The problems of estimating and interpreting elasticities in international trade are, of course, well known. They relate principally to the
difficulties of applying ordinary least squares regression methods to
time series data when shifts in the relevant demand and supply sched-
ules cannot be identified independently. There is also the fact that
these data may be seriously inadequate due to the difficulties which
arise in the formulation and construction of aggregative index numbers
with reference especially to manufactured goods.[2] Subject to these
caveats, elasticity measurements are, nevertheless, of considerable
interest.

Three sets of estimates were constructed for present purposes.
The first set noted below refers to total exports on an annual basis for
1950-64 and total exports on a quarterly basis from 1953 to the first
quarter of 1965, which was the latest available at the time of writing.
The theory underlying these equations is that total Italian exports in

constant dollars depend positively on world income and negatively upon the average price of Italy's exports relative to the average price of total world exports. Since data on world income are unfortunately not available, it is necessary in fitting these equations to find some alternative measure. One which is commonly used and which we employ here is a measure in constant dollars of the value of total world exports excluding those from Italy. What equations (1) and (2) amount to saying, therefore, is that Italian exports, X_{It}, are taken to be some particular marginal fraction of X_{Wt}, the exports of the rest of the world, and are modified due to the influence of changes in $\frac{P_{XIt}}{P_{XWt}}$, Italy's export prices relative to those of the rest of the world.[3]

The data used in these regressions and in others to be discussed presently are listed in Tables 16 and 17 of Appendix I. All the regressions were fitted in linear logarithmic form.[4] The regression coefficients can thus be interpreted in terms of elasticities which have been constrained to be constant. The results for equations (1) and (2) are shown below. The standard errors are noted in parentheses beneath the regression coefficients. The coefficient of determination corrected for degrees of freedom ($\bar{R}^2$) and the Durbin-Watson statistic measuring the presence or absence of serial correlation are indicated to the right of each equation.

Equation (1) - Total exports, 1950-64 (annual data)

$$\log X_{It} = -.64 + 1.69 \quad \log X_{Wt} - 2.20 \log \frac{P_{XIt}}{P_{XWt}} \quad \bar{R}^2 = .98 \ D.W. = 1.71$$
$$\phantom{\log X_{It} = -.64 +} (.16) \phantom{\quad \log X_{Wt}} (.66)$$

Equation (2) - Total exports, 1953- 1 Q., 1965 (quarterly data)

$$\log X_{It} = -1.91 + 1.91 \log X_{Wt} - 1.84 \log \frac{P_{XIt}}{P_{XWt}} \quad \bar{R}^2 = .97 \ D.W. = 1.78$$
$$\phantom{\log X_{It} = -1.91 +} (.11) \phantom{\log X_{Wt} - 1.84 \log} (.37)$$

The results of equations (1) and (2) provide a clear indication that both world exports and relative prices were important determinants of total Italian exports in the postwar period.[5] The elasticity of demand with respect to total world exports implied in the results was 1.69 for the annual data and 1.91 for the quarterly data, while the comparable price elasticities were -2.20 and -1.84.

The second set of elasticity estimates refers to manufactured goods alone on an annual basis in equation (3) for 1950-64 and on a

quarterly basis for 1960-64. Quarterly data prior to 1960 were not
readily available. The relationships estimated were of the same form
as equations (1) and (2). That is X_{Im}, Italian exports of manufactured
goods in constant dollars, were taken to depend positively on X_{Wm},
world exports of manufactured goods excluding those from Italy, and
negatively on $\dfrac{P_{XIm}}{P_{XWm}}$, the price of Italy's exports relative to the rest
of the world.[6] The results were as follows:

Equation (3) - Manufactured goods exports, 1950-64 (annual data)

$$\log X_{Im} = 1.14 + \underset{(.39)}{1.54} \log X_{Wm} - \underset{(.80)}{1.68} \log \frac{P_{XIm}}{P_{XWm}} \quad \bar{R}^2 = .93 \ \ D.W. = .71$$

Equation (4) - Manufactured goods exports, 1960-64 (quarterly data)

$$\log X_{Im} = 1.70 + \underset{(.13)}{1.57} \log X_{Wm} - \underset{(.43)}{1.81} \log \frac{P_{XIm}}{P_{XWm}} \quad \bar{R}^2 = .88 \ \ D.W. = 2.25$$

The results of equations (3) and (4) do not differ greatly from
those just noted for total exports, although the coefficient of the relative price variable in equation (3) was not statistically significant at
the .05 level. Also, there was evidence of serial correlation in the
residuals of equation (3) so that the true standard errors may be larger
than those shown. In any event, the elasticity of demand with respect
to world exports of manufactures implied in the results was 1.54 for
the annual data and 1.57 for the quarterly data, while the comparable
price elasticities were -1.68 and -1.81.[7]

The third and final elasticity estimates were more or less
identical in principle and time period with those in equation (5) for
manufactured goods. The chief difference was that $\dfrac{C_{Im}}{C_{Wm}}$, relative
unit labor costs in manufacturing, was used in the equation in order
to test whether it was a good proxy for relative price, as is often implied. The assumption here is that the ratio of wages to labor productivity (i.e., unit labor costs) in each country's domestic manufacturing
industry should be an accurate indication of its export prices. Thus,
the relative unit labor cost ratio is hypothesized to have a negative
sign. It should also be noted that because data on unit labor costs were
not available for all the industrial countries, the variable X^*_{Wm} des-
ignated in equation (5) does not correspond exactly to the comparable

one in equation (3). The results were:

Equation (5) - Manufactured goods exports, 1950-64 (annual data)

$$\log X_{Im} = -4.14 + 2.40 \log X^*_{Wm} + .27 \log \frac{C_{Im}}{C_{Wm}} \quad \bar{R}^2 = .91 \quad D.W. = .69$$
$$\phantom{\log X_{Im} = -4.14 + } (.33) \phantom{\log X^*_{Wm} } (.66)$$

It is evident that the relative unit labor cost variable was not statistically significant and that it had a positive rather than the expected negative sign. One possible explanation of this result is that the data used were not particularly reliable. It may be, however, that changes in relative unit labor costs were not really decisive in promoting the growth of exports from the statistical point of view, especially once allowance was made in the estimate for the influence of the world manufactures export variable.

Considering the foregoing results as a whole, it seems reasonable to conclude that the rapid postwar development of Italy's exports has been promoted both by favorable world demand conditions and by Italy's achievement of a favorable competitive position in terms of its relative export prices.

CHANGES IN THE COMMODITY COMPOSITION, MARKET DISTRIBUTION, AND COMPETITIVENESS OF ITALIAN EXPORTS

We shall now adopt a somewhat different approach to the analysis of Italian exports by estimating the portions of the changes in these exports that can be attributed to factors operating on both the demand and supply sides. [8] That is, from some given base period we can attribute changes in the demand for Italy's exports to such factors as: (1) changes in world demand as measured by the total value of world trade; (2) changes in the commodity composition of import demand in a given foreign market due to changes in the level and distribution of real income, tastes, technology, commercial policy, or the competitiveness of import-competing industries in the given market; and (3) changes due to the reasons just mentioned in the market distribution pattern of the different national and regional markets which comprise the total world market for imports from various countries.

Changes on the supply side serving to increase the relative competitiveness and thus the volume of Italy's exports can be attributed to such factors as: (1) differential rates of increase in productivity and the levels of prices; (2) differential rates of improvement in the quality of goods exported and in the development of new exports;

(3) differential rates of improvement in the efficiency of marketing or in the terms of financing the sale of export goods; and (4) differential changes in the ability for prompt fulfillment of export orders. [9]

While a precise accounting of all the foregoing factors cannot be made, those on the demand side, at least, are susceptible to quantitative measurement. Thus, in what follows, estimates have been made of the changes in Italy's exports to the extent that they were reflected on the demand side in changes in the total value, commodity composition, and market distribution of world trade. Given the difficulty of measuring individually the supply factors mentioned above, the portion of the increase in exports remaining after the demand factors have been accounted for is thus considered attributable to the role which the supply factors jointly have played in increasing the general competitiveness of Italian exports.

The procedure adopted for purposes of analysis is outlined in algebraic form in Appendix II. [10] It consisted of three steps. The amount by which Italy's exports would have increased from an initial year if they had grown at the same rate as the total value of world demand was first calculated. World demand was measured here by the total value of world exports to all importing areas excluding Italy.

The second step was to estimate the increases which Italy would have realized if its exports of each major commodity group had risen at the same rate as world exports of the particular commodity group, and then to subtract from these amounts the amounts by which each group would have increased if it had risen at the same rate as total world exports. Thus, if world demand expanded more than proportionately for those commodities in which Italy specialized in the initial year, the effect would be positive. Otherwise, it would be negative.

The third step was to estimate the increase in Italy's exports of each commodity group if Italy had only maintained its share in each major market for that group, and to subtract from these amounts the amounts by which each commodity group would have increased if it had risen at the same rate as world exports of that particular group. Accordingly, if world demand grew more than proportionately in those markets in which Italy was concentrated in the beginning year, the effect would be positive. Otherwise, it would be negative.

Finally, the sum of the amounts calculated in the manner just described was deducted from the total increase in Italy's exports in order to arrive at the remainder, which can be considered the result of the increased competitiveness of these exports. It bears repeating that this remainder is an indication of general competitiveness in the sense that it reflects not only price competitiveness, but, as well, the influence of quality variations, the introduction of new exports, promotional expenditures, possible changes in marketing arrangements, and the ability to service export orders promptly. [11] It would, of course, be of great interest to attempt to disaggregate this residual of general competitiveness in order to assess the relative importance of the price and nonprice factors. This will not be undertaken in the present study, however, due to the lack of information on these latter factors and the relatively few data points which could be computed for purposes of analysis. [12]

The calculations were based upon seven Standard International Trade Classifications (SITC) commodity groups and upon ten importing areas, as specified in Appendix II. The classification of manufactured goods in particular into only three groups is far from satisfactory because of the heterogeneity of the goods included especially in SITC groups 6 and 8. Time and resources unfortunately precluded both the utilization of data for the few available subgroup components of the major manufactured goods groups and the expansion of the calculations to cover a significantly larger number of importing areas. [13]

The results of the detailed calculations are shown in Table 1. The first five columns indicate the absolute changes in total exports for particular years and for the entire decade of 1955-64. [14] The attributions of these changes to the various demand factors are listed in the first, second, and third rows, while the fourth row constitutes the attribution of the residual remaining to increased competitiveness. The relative importance of the individual attributions can be assessed from the last five columns of the table.

It is evident that the increases in the value of world trade explained about 40 per cent of the increase in Italy's exports from 1955-59, about 25 per cent from 1959-62, around 60 per cent from 1962-63, and over 40 per cent again from 1963-64. The percentage explained for the period as a whole was 36.8. The changes due to the commodity composition and the market distribution of the expansion in world trade were comparatively small. Only 5 per cent or less of the increase in Italy's exports from 1955-62 could be attributed to the commodity composition. This factor was actually slightly unfavorable from 1962-63. The over-all market distribution was somewhat unfavorable from 1955-59 and somewhat favorable after that time.

Table 1

Analysis of Changes in Italy's Exports, 1955-64
(Millions of dollars)

	1955-59	1959-62	1962-63	1963-64	1955-64
Change in total exports	$ 1,058	$ 1,784	$ 376	$ 889	$ 4,107
1. Due to increase in value of world trade	443	476	228	366	1,513
2. Due to commodity composition of increase in world trade	53	64	- 8	a	109
3. Due to market distribution of increase in world trade	- 55	53	12	18	28
4. Due to increased competitiveness of Italy's exports	617	1,191	144	505	2,457
Percentage distribution of change in total exports	100.0%	100.0%	100.0%	100.0%	100.0%
1. Due to increase in value of world trade	41.9	26.7	60.6	41.2	36.8
2. Due to commodity composition of increase in world trade	5.0	3.6	- 2.1	a	2.7
3. Due to market distribution of increase in world trade	- 5.2	3.0	3.2	2.0	.7
4. Due to increased competitiveness of Italy's exports	58.3	66.7	38.3	56.8	59.8

[a] Included in change due to increased competitiveness.
Source: Based upon Table 2.

The residual portion which measures the increase in Italy's exports due to increased competitiveness can thus be seen to have been substantial. It represented nearly 60 per cent of the increase from 1955-59, about 66.6 from 1959-62, nearly 40 per cent from 1962-63, and well over 50 per cent from 1963-64. The percentage for the entire period was 59.8.

The summary data in Table 1 are broken down in Table 2 according to the regions of destination of Italy's exports. It can be seen that the major increases in Italy's exports from 1955-59 were to the industrial countries of North America, the European Economic Community (EEC), and the European Free Trade Area (EFTA), and that a substantial proportion of these increases was attributable to increased competitiveness. This was also the case from 1959-62, in particular as far as exports to the EEC were concerned. That is, $839 million of the $1,784 million increase in exports during these years went to the EEC, and close to $600 million was attributable to increased competitiveness. The proportion of the increase due to the market distribution was relatively minor by contrast, even given the very rapid growth in income which the EEC countries experienced. It would of course be interesting to determine what part, if any, of the increase in Italy's competitiveness between 1959 and 1962 was due to the differential impact of EEC commercial policies which favored Italy. However, since this would require detailed information on changes in tariffs within the EEC, it was considered to be beyond the scope of the present study. [15] In any case, there can be no doubt of the pervasiveness of the increase in Italy's competitiveness which was evidenced strongly, as well, in all of the other importing regions.

Italy's exports from 1962-63 increased to all regions with the exception of EFTA. While the proportion of the increase due to competitiveness declined somewhat in comparison to the earlier years noted, it was nevertheless still relatively substantial. [16] More than half of the remarkable increase in Italy's exports from 1963-64 was accounted for by the EEC, and close to 30 per cent went to EFTA and other Western European countries combined. Nearly three-fourths of the EEC and other Western European countries increases were attributable to increased competitiveness, while the comparable percentage for EFTA was around 30.

Table 3 contains an analysis of Italy's exports for the period from 1955-63 according to the major SITC commodity classes. The greatest part by far of the increases in exports from 1955-59 was in machinery and transportation equipment and other manufactured goods, and, as would be surmised, a substantial proportion of these increases was attributable to increased competitiveness. It is also clear that the increases from 1959-62 and 1962-63 were similarly concentrated in

Table 2

Analysis of Changes in Italy's Exports by Region of Distribution, 1955-64

(Millions of dollars)

	North America	Latin America	EEC	EFTA	Other W. Europe	Austr., New Zealand, and U. of S. Africa	Japan	Other Asia and Africa (a)	Eastern Europe	All Other	TOTAL
Exports in 1955 to:	176	190	434	432	181	46	12	288	59	38	1,856
Exports in 1959 to:	380	257	797	648	192	55	11	400	120	54	2,914
Exports in 1962 to:	490	319	1,636	963	310	87	25	529	242	97	4,698
Exports in 1963 to:	527	321	1,802	961	342	99	42	609	271	100	5,074
Exports in 1964 to:	567	333	2,268	1,088	469	131	40	678	276	113	5,963
A. Change in exports, 1955-59	204	67	363	216	11	9	-1	112	61	16	1,058
1. Due to increase in value of world trade	42	45	104	103	43	11	3	69	14	9	443
2. Due to commodity composition	2	11	36	12	4	-2	-5	-7	5	-3	53
3. Due to market distribution	16	-27	21	-39	-26	-12	2	-5	21	-6	-55
4. Due to increased competitiveness	144	38	202	140	-10	12	-1	55	21	16	617
B. Change in exports, 1959-62	110	62	839	315	118	32	14	129	122	43	1,784
1. Due to increase in value of world trade	45	49	111	111	47	12	3	74	15	9	476
2. Due to commodity composition	3	8	40	17	-3	-	-	-3	5	-3	64
3. Due to market distribution	-36	-35	95	3	47	-7	5	-30	13	-2	53
4. Due to increased competitiveness	98	40	593	184	27	27	6	88	89	39	1,191

C. Change in exports, 1962–63	37	2	166	– 2	32	12	17	80	29	3	376
1. Due to increase in value of world trade	22	23	53	53	22	6	1	35	8	5	228
2. Due to commodity composition	3	– 5	6	3	– 6	– 4	–	– 7	–	2	– 8
3. Due to market distribution	– 9	– 27	31	– 6	20	2	5	2	1	– 7	12
4. Due to increased competitiveness	21	11	76	– 52	– 4	8	11	50	20	3	144
D. Change in exports, 1963–64	40	12	466	127	127	32	– 2	69	5	13	889
1. Due to increase in value of world trade	34	38	80	85	36	8	3	57	11	8	366
2. Due to market distribution	– 8	– 7	55	3	– 2	3	2	– 25	1	– 4	18
3. Due to combined influence of commodity composition and increased competitiveness[b]	14	– 19	325	39	93	21	– 7	37	– 7	9	505

[a] Includes exports to Mainland China   [b] These influences are shown jointly because of unavailability at the time of writing of world commodity exports by region of destination for 1964.

Sources and notes: Italy's exports by region of destination were taken from U.N., Yearbook of International Trade Statistics 1958, Volume II and from the OEEC-OECD sources cited in Table 3. Exports to the Union of South Africa for 1959–63 were taken from OECD, Foreign Trade, Series C, Trade by Commodities, and were deducted from the total of Italy's exports to Africa indicated in the OECD Series B source. Data on world exports for 1955–63 by commodity classes and regions of destination were taken from the U.N., Monthly Bulletin of Statistics, March, 1961 and 1965; the data for 1964 were based upon the total values of world exports by provenance and destination given in the Monthly Bulletin of Statistics, June, 1965. The adjustment made for exports to Italy was as noted in Table 3.

Table 3

Analysis of Changes in Italy's Exports by Commodity Classes, 1955–63
(Millions of dollars)

	Food, Beverages, and Tobacco	Crude Materials, Oils, and Fats	Mineral Fuels and Related Materials	Chemicals	Machinery and Transport Equipment	Other Manufactured Goods	TOTAL
Exports in 1955:	412	130	166	127	371	650	1,856
Exports in 1959:	536	140	214	208	758	1,058	2,914
Exports in 1962:	717	182	263	360	1,432	1,723	4,699
Exports in 1963:	692	196	280	387	1,579	1,910	5,074
A. Change in exports, 1955–59	124	10	48	81	387	408	1,058
1. Due to increase in value of world trade	98	31	40	30	89	155	443
2. Due to commodity composition	-29	-19	-11	21	69	16	47
3. Due to market distribution	6	-9	-11	-	-2	-33	-49
4. Due to increased competitiveness	49	7	30	30	231	270	617
B. Change in exports, 1959–62	181	42	49	152	674	665	1,785[a]
1. Due to increase in value of world trade	106	33	42	33	95	167	476
2. Due to commodity composition	-39	-25	-3	14	81	29	57
3. Due to market distribution	-2	-	-6	1	42	25	60
4. Due to increased competitiveness	116	34	16	104	456	444	1,192[a]

C. Change in exports, 1962–63	-25	14	17	27	147	187	375[a]
1. Due to increase in value of world trade	51	16	21	15	45	80	228
2. Due to commodity composition	2	-6	-2	7	14	-10	5
3. Due to market distribution	-15	-1	-	2	-3	16	-1
4. Due to increased competitiveness	-63	5	-2	3	91	101	143[a]

[a] Total includes $22 million for 1959–62 and $8 million for 1962–63 of transactions and commodities not elsewhere specified (SITC 9).

Sources and notes: Italy's exports in 1955 were taken from OEEC, Statistical Bulletins, Foreign Trade, Series IV, Italy, Foreign Trade by Commodity and Area of Origin and Destination, January/June 1958; the 1959, 1962, and 1963 exports were taken from OECD, Foreign Trade, Series B, Italy, Analytical Abstracts, January–December, 1961 and 1963. Data on world exports by commodity classes and regions of destination were taken from U.N., Monthly Bulletin of Statistics, March, 1961 and 1965. These data were adjusted to exclude exports to Italy on the basis of the c.i.f. import values shown for Italy in the OEEC and OECD sources just noted. This procedure was necessitated because exports to Italy were not specified separately in the U.N. source.

41

manufactured goods and that the relative importance and absolute magnitudes represented by increased competitiveness were impressive indeed. Although the analysis by commodity classes could not be extended beyond 1963 because data were not yet available at the time of writing, the 1963-64 results given in Table 2 according to region of destination would suggest that increased competitiveness in manufactured goods exports was of considerable importance also in 1964.

In interpreting the statistical results presented in the foregoing tables, one must be cognizant of course of the limitations inherent in the method of calculation, the data and the level of aggregation, and the inability to specify more exactly the components of competitiveness. Thus, it has been assumed in the method of calculation that the various factors specified are independent and additive, and that they can be fully and unambiguously isolated.[17] Moreover, the data classifications and levels of aggregation employed cannot be broken down readily to analyze the changes which may have occurred for particular commodities or importing nations within the major commodity and regional groups. Since the data on individual manufacturing industries to be presented in Chapter 5 below suggest that new and improved lines of manufactured goods may have bulked large in the increase in Italy's exports in the period under study, a more disaggregated system of data classification might possibly yield, therefore, results that would give more weight especially to changes in the commodity composition of exports. But in any case, the picture which emerges from the present results establishes without doubt the predominant role of increased competitiveness in the remarkable increase in Italy's exports in the past decade.

ELASTICITIES OF DEMAND FOR ITALIAN IMPORTS

Turning now to imports, we shall begin with the discussion and presentation of some estimates of Italy's elasticity of demand for imports.[18] Four different estimates were constructed. These involved total imports, imports of consumption goods, investment goods, and auxiliary materials. Imports in constant lire were taken in each equation to depend positively on some measure of income, negatively upon the average price of imports, and positively on the average price of related domestic goods. The price variables were treated individually in order to distinguish more clearly if imports were sensitive to the prices of domestically produced goods.

The dependent variables for imports in 1954 lire in equations

(6), (7), (8), and (9) below were as follows: M_T, total imports; M_C, consumer goods imports; M_I, investment goods imports; and M_{AM}, auxiliary materials imports. The income variables in 1954 lire in equations (6), (7), and (8) were: GNP, gross national product; C, consumption expenditures; and I, investment expenditures. These measures were used in the absence of a measure of disposable income. MP, the index of manufacturing production, was used in equation (9) for auxiliary materials imports. The import prices used in the individual equations were: P_{M_T}, for total imports; P_{M_C}, for consumer goods imports; P_{M_I}, for investment goods imports; and $P_{M_{AM}}$, for imports of auxiliary materials. The prices of domestic goods used were: P_{GNP}, the implicit GNP deflator; P_C, the implicit deflator for consumption expenditures; P_I, the implicit deflator for investment expenditures; and P_{AM}, the wholesale price index for auxiliary materials.

The equations were estimated using annual data as shown in Tables 2 and 17 of Appendix I for the period 1951-64. All the regressions were fitted in logarithms so that the coefficients can be interpreted as elasticities. The results were as follows:

Equation (6) - Total imports, 1951-64

$$\log M_T = -5.32 + 1.95 \log GNP + .32 \log P_{M_T} - .11 \log P_{GNP}$$
$$\quad\quad\quad\quad (.31) \quad\quad\quad\quad\quad (.42) \quad\quad\quad (.61)$$
$$\bar{R}^2 = .98 \quad D.W. = 1.25$$

Equation (7) - Imports of consumer goods, 1951-64

$$\log M_C = -8.71 + 3.58 \log C + 1.25 \log P_{M_C} - 2.64 \log P_C$$
$$\quad\quad\quad\quad (.44) \quad\quad\quad (.41) \quad\quad\quad (.84)$$
$$\bar{R}^2 = .98 \quad D.W. = 2.19$$

Equation (8) - Imports of investment goods, 1951-64

$$\log M_I = -3.00 + 1.31 \log I - .74 \log P_{M_I} + 1.33 \log P_I$$
$$\quad\quad\quad\quad (.12) \quad\quad\quad (.51) \quad\quad\quad (.49)$$
$$\bar{R}^2 = .98 \quad D.W. = 1.42$$

Equation (9) - Imports of auxiliary materials, 1951-64

$$\log M_{AM} = -.19 + 1.41 \log MP - .21 \log P_{M_{AM}} + .18 \log P_{AM}$$
$$\quad\quad\quad\quad (.12) \quad\quad\quad (.26) \quad\quad\quad (.48)$$
$$\bar{R}^2 = .99 \quad D.W. = 1.85$$

It is evident from equation (6) that the elasticity of demand for total imports with respect to GNP was close to 2. Neither the price of imports nor the GNP implicit price deflator was significant. The elasticity of consumer goods imports with respect to consumption expenditures in equation (7) was 3.58. The coefficients for both the price of consumer goods imports and the price deflator for consumption goods expenditures were statistically significant, but they had signs opposite to those that were hypothesized. What these results mean from the economic point of view is not clear, although they may possibly be due to changes in the composition of expenditures favoring higher-priced imports and lower-priced domestic goods.

The elasticity of investment goods imports with respect to investment expenditures in equation (8) was 1.31. The coefficients for the price variables had the expected signs, but they were not statistically significant. The elasticity of auxiliary materials imports with respect to manufacturing production in equation (9) was 1.41. While the coefficients for the price variables had the hypothesized signs, in effect they did not differ significantly from zero.

The foregoing results thus imply that imports were relatively sensitive to income but not to prices. How plausible is this conclusion? This would seem to depend upon a number of factors. First, one cannot be certain about the accuracy and representativeness of the data, especially with reference to the price series used. There may also be certain statistical drawbacks in the results due to the predominance of the income variables.[20] Finally, the existence of multicollinearity may have complicated matters.[21] Now there may well be grounds for arguing that Italian importers were price insensitive and that domestic supplies of goods were inadequate or qualitatively different from imports. But before this conclusion is accepted, it would be worthwhile to investigate the aforementioned factors more thoroughly, especially with regard to individual commodities.[22]

CHANGES IN THE COMMODITY COMPOSITION AND REGIONS OF ORIGIN OF ITALIAN IMPORTS

Taking now a broader view of imports, it is evident that changes in Italy's import demand in total and according to major commodity groups will be determined by changes in a number of the factors discussed earlier in connection with exports. These factors included changes in the level and distribution of income, tastes, technology, commercial policy, or the competitiveness of Italy's import-competing industries. Similarly, on the supply side, the share of particular regions of origin in Italy's imports will depend upon changes in their relative price competitiveness, quality variations and the introduction of new exports, promotional expenditures and changes in marketing arrangements, and the ability to service export orders promptly.

Since a detailed examination of the foregoing factors was considered to be beyond the scope of the present undertaking, an attempt was made instead to adapt the procedure used above in the analysis of exports to an examination of the changes which have occurred in Italy's imports between 1955 and 1964. This adaptation is set forth in algebraic form in Appendix II.

The amounts by which Italy's imports, according to each major commodity group and region of origin, would have increased from an initial year if these imports had increased at the same rate as total imports were first calculated. The sum of these amounts will be equal by definition to the actual increase in total imports between the initial year and some given year.

The next step was to calculate for each commodity group and region of origin the increase in imports that would have been realized if the share in total imports of each commodity group and region of origin had remained the same as in the initial year, and to subtract from these amounts the amounts by which imports of each commodity group or region of origin would have increased if they had risen at the same rate as total imports. Thus, if Italy's demand for imports increased more than proportionately for those commodity groups which were less important in the beginning year, the effect would be positive. Otherwise, it would be negative. The combined effects should sum to zero since they refer to components of the change in total imports.

Finally, the calculated increase in imports that would have been realized by each region of origin if its share in Italy's total imports of each commodity group had remained unchanged was subtracted from the total amount of imports in a given year in order to arrive at a remainder, which can be taken as indicative of the change in competitiveness of individual regions of origin. Consequently, if Italy's demand for imports expanded proportionately more with respect to regions or origin that were less important in the initial year, the effect would be positive. Otherwise, it would be negative. Here again the combined effects should sum to zero since they refer to the components of the change in total imports. Note further that for the individual regions the change in competitiveness must be interpreted broadly, as in the analysis of exports, to comprehend both price and nonprice factors.

The calculations were based upon the same commodity groups and regions as utilized in the analysis of exports. The same drawbacks that were mentioned earlier with respect particularly to the heterogeneity of the components for manufactured goods are thus applicable here as well. The results of the detailed calculations made for 1955-64 are presented in Table 4 according to commodity class and in Table 5 according to region of origin. The small positive or negative figures indicated in the Total column in each table are the consequence of rounding.

The results in Table 4 indicate that from 1955-59 the commodity composition, which reflects the changes in Italy's demand for imports brought about by changes in the level and structure of income and output, was roughly neutral for foodstuffs, negative for crude materials and mineral fuels, and positive for chemicals and manufactured goods. With a near doubling of total imports in the subsequent period from 1959-62, the commodity composition revealed that imports of foodstuffs, crude materials, and mineral fuels dropped substantially in relative importance compared to the very sizable increases in the imports of the two categories of manufactured goods.

The commodity composition of the $1.5 billion increase in imports from 1962-63 was concentrated particularly upon foodstuffs and manufactured goods as compared to crude materials, mineral fuels, and chemicals. It can be seen, finally, that the $350 million decline in imports from 1963-64 as a consequence of restrictive domestic policies had its impact chiefly on imports of crude materials and manufactured goods.

The results in Table 5 provide an indication of the factors which have influenced the shares in Italy's imports of the individual regions of origin. Thus, the total increase shown in Italy's imports from each region is broken down into the portion due to the increase in the value of imports from all regions, the portion due to changes in the commodity composition of imports by region, and a residual portion due to changes in competitiveness.

From 1955-59, Italy's imports increased from all regions except North America and Australia, New Zealand, and the Union of South Africa, which exhibited negative influences for commodity composition and competitiveness. The EFTA countries had a small negative influence due to reduced competitiveness, while the commodity composition was unfavorable for the less-developed countries of Asia and Africa. The substantial increase in imports from 1959-62 was concentrated in large part on the industrial countries. The commodity composition can be seen to have been unfavorable to all of the nonindustrial regions, especially other Asian and African countries. As far as competitiveness was concerned, the chief increases noted were for North

America, the other EEC countries, other Western European countries, and Eastern Europe, while there were substantial decreases evident for EFTA and other Asian and African countries.

From 1962-63, imports from North America were subject, as from 1955-59, to the negative influences of commodity composition and competitiveness, while imports from the other countries of the EEC continued to reflect strong positive influences in these respects. Interestingly enough, the EFTA countries exhibited a further decline in competitiveness, as did Australia, New Zealand, and the Union of South Africa and other Asian and African countries. Imports from these latter regions were also subject to a pronounced negative influence due to commodity composition.

The decline in imports from 1963-64 was concentrated particularly upon the EEC and EFTA countries and to a lesser extent upon North America, other Western European countries, Japan, and Eastern Europe. The decline due to commodity composition was reflected especially in imports from the EEC, EFTA, and North America, Australia, New Zealand, and the Union of South Africa, while this influence was positive for Latin America, and particularly for other Asian and African countries. As far as competitiveness was concerned, a decline was again evident for EFTA and also for other Western European countries, Japan, and Eastern Europe, while there were increases for all of the other regions.[23]

When we consider Tables 4 and 5 together, it is thus clear that changes in the commodity composition of Italy's imports from 1955-63 were concentrated in favor of manufactured goods in comparison to crude materials and mineral fuels. This was not the case for 1963-64, mainly due to the reduced demand for imports of manufactured goods owing to the contraction of the domestic economy. The pattern of change was also against foodstuffs from 1959-62, but was reversed sharply in 1963 when imports of foodstuffs rose significantly. The reversal continued in 1964, although on a much smaller scale.

The chief beneficiaries of the increase in Italy's imports from 1955-63 were the industrial countries, particularly the other members of the EEC that benefited both from the commodity pattern of the increase and from their increased competitiveness. The EFTA countries especially and, to some extent, North America were adversely affected by reduced competitiveness. The primary producing regions, in particular the less-developed nations of Asia and Africa, fared relatively poorly in the increase in Italy's imports due to an unfavorable commodity composition and also to some reduction in their competitiveness.

Table 4

Analysis of Changes in Italy's Imports (C.I.F.) by Commodity Classes, 1955-64
(Millions of dollars)

	Food, Beverages, and Tobacco	Crude Materials, Oils, and Fats	Mineral Fuels and Related Materials	Chemicals	Machinery and Transport Equipment	Other Manufactured Goods	TOTAL[a]
Imports in 1955:	451	841	532	141	299	441	2,706
Imports in 1959:	561	1,007	586	232	379	582	3,351
Imports in 1962:	846	1,535	814	393	1,207	1,292	6,101
Imports in 1963:	1,331	1,680	928	435	1,572	1,596	7,581
Imports in 1964:	1,355	1,558	1,018	461	1,442	1,354	7,231
A. Change in imports, 1955-59	110	166	54	91	80	141	645
1. Due to increase in value of total imports	107	199	126	33	71	105	641
2. Due to commodity com-position	3	- 33	- 72	58	9	36	4
B. Change in imports, 1959-62	285	528	228	161	828	710	2,750
1. Due to increase in value of total imports	459	856	541	144	304	448	2,753
2. Due to commodity com-position	- 174	- 328	- 313	17	524	262	- 3
C. Change in imports, 1962-63	485	145	114	42	365	304	1,480
1. Due to increase in value of total imports	247	460	292	77	164	242	1,483
2. Due to commodity com-position	238	- 315	- 178	-35	201	62	- 3

48

D. Change in imports, 1963–64	24	– 122	90	26	– 130	– 242	– 350
1. Due to increase in value of total imports	– 59	– 109	– 69	–18	– 39	– 58	– 352
2. Due to commodity composition	83	– 13	159	44	– 91	– 184	2

[a]Includes transactions and commodities not elsewhere specified (SITC 9).

Sources: OEEC, Statistical Bulletins, Foreign Trade, Series IV, Italy Foreign Trade by Commodity and Area of Origin and Destination, January/June, 1958;

OECD, Statistical Bulletins, Foreign Trade, Series B, Italy, Analytical Abstracts, January-December, 1961 and 1963; and UN, Commodity Trade Statistics, 1964, Vol. XIV.

Table 5

Analysis of Changes in Italy's Imports (C.I.F.) by Region of Origin, 1955-64
(Millions of dollars)

	North America	Latin America	EEC	EFTA	Other W. Europe	Austr., New Zealand, and U. of S. Africa	Japan	Other Asia and Africa (a)	Eastern Europe	All Other	TOTAL
Imports in 1955 from:	434	180	648	471	117	143	6	627	68	12	2,706
Imports in 1959 from:	405	232	895	598	141	139	15	765	155	6	3,351
Imports in 1962 from:	960	355	1,899	901	346	229	49	1,019	333	10	6,101
Imports in 1963 from:	1,108	498	2,489	1,174	369	235	90	1,173	426	19	7,581
Imports in 1964 from:	1,047	539	2,365	1,034	316	240	68	1,233	370	19	7,231
A. Change in imports, 1955-59	- 29	52	247	127	24	- 4	9	138	87	- 6	645
1. Due to increase in value of total imports	103	43	154	112	28	34	1	149	16	3	643
2. Due to commodity composition	- 4	5	31	22	- 4	- 6	1	- 50	- 1	1	- 5
3. Due to increased competitiveness	- 128	4	62	- 7	-	- 32	7	39	72	- 10	7
B. Change in imports, 1959-62	555	123	1,004	303	205	90	34	254	178	4	2,750
1. Due to increase in value of total imports	441	183	659	479	119	145	7	637	69	12	2,751
2. Due to commodity composition	30	- 56	233	131	- 16	- 39	-	- 279	- 9	11	6
3. Due to increased competitiveness	84	- 4	112	- 307	102	- 16	27	- 104	118	- 19	- 7

C. Change in imports, 1962-63	148	143	590	273	23	6	41	154	93	9	1,480
1. Due to increase in value of total imports	238	98	355	258	64	79	3	344	38	7	1,484
2. Due to commodity composition	- 40	48	85	57	- 3	-43	-1	- 131	-	24	- 4
3. Due to increased competitiveness	- 50	- 3	150	- 42	-38	-30	39	- 59	55	- 22	-
D. Change in imports, 1963-64	- 61	41	- 124	- 140	-53	5	-22	60	-56	-	- 350
1. Due to increase in value of total imports	- 56	-23	- 85	- 61	-15	-19	-1	- 82	- 9	- 2	- 353
2. Due to commodity composition	- 21	14	- 62	- 47	- 2	11	1	112	5	2	13
3. Due to increased competitiveness	16	50	23	- 32	-36	13	-22	30	-52	-	- 10

Sources and notes: Same sources as Table 4, with adjustments to make the regions comparable with the United Nations classification shown in Table 2.

51

The changes from 1963-64 were, on the whole, unfavorable to the industrial countries as compared to the primary producing regions. But this seems due mainly to the effects of the domestic recession upon imports of manufactured goods in particular. It is thus likely that a revival of expansionary forces in the Italian economy would tend to restore the pattern observed prior to 1964.

CONCLUSION

We have attempted in this chapter to analyze the chief forces lying behind and reflected in the remarkable increases in Italy's merchandise exports and imports in the postwar period. It was clear both from the regression analysis and the more detailed consideration of changes in the commodity composition and market distribution of exports that a substantial improvement in Italy's international competitiveness in terms of price as well as nonprice factors was responsible in large measure for the expansion of its exports.

The regression analysis of import demand disclosed that imports were relatively sensitive to income but not to prices. There were, however, some possible drawbacks in the data and in the statistical procedures which require further investigation before this conclusion can be more firmly established. Examination of the commodity composition of the changes in imports showed that manufactured goods imports were especially important. It was shown that the increases in imports came chiefly from the industrial countries. Imports from the EEC were of particular significance and a relatively large proportion of these imports was apparently attributable to the increased competitiveness of the EEC as compared to other regions.

Thus having completed our review of the major postwar developments in Italy's foreign trade, we can now turn to our main object. This is to determine how these developments, particularly in exports, were related to Italy's economic growth in the postwar period. We begin accordingly in the next chapter by reviewing certain of the so-called export-led models of economic growth that have appeared in the literature in recent years. We then proceed in Chapter 4 to subject two of these models to empirical test in the light of Italian postwar export and growth experience. The analysis is then carried further in Chapter 5 where a number of different aspects of foreign trade are investigated on the individual industry level.

CHAPTER 3

"EXPORT-LED" MODELS OF ECONOMIC GROWTH

In addressing attention to the role of exports in the Italian growth experience, we are fortunate that there have appeared in the literature since 1960 some "export-led" models of economic growth which may provide a useful framework for analysis. Since, however, these models differ in their points of emphasis, the degree to which they have been articulated, and their amenability to empirical verification, it seems appropriate before turning directly to Italy's experience to examine the assumptions, key relationships, and workings of the various models. The present chapter will thus be devoted to the exposition and evaluation of the most noteworthy recent contributions to the subject of export-led growth made by C. P. Kindleberger, A. Lamfalussy, and W. Beckerman and B. Balassa.

THE KINDLEBERGER MODEL

Our consideration of export-led growth models can well begin with Kindleberger's writings dealing with the impact of trade on growth, for his writings are rich both in their historical perspective and current relevancy.[1] Kindleberger's work is also a valuable reminder of the essentially partial and imprecise nature of our existing theories of economic growth and, hence, of our lack of any general theory of growth.[2] Moreover, because his analyses demonstrate that foreign trade may stimulate growth under some conditions and retard it under others, it becomes important to specify the particular circumstances which affect the choice of the relationships to be formulated and applied in an individual case.[3]

While Kindleberger distinguishes three possible models in which exports may lead, balance, or lag behind growth, our interest here will be only in the first of these.[4] The basic characteristic of his export-led model is thus that an increase in foreign demand for a country's exports will in turn stimulate its domestic growth. He then goes on to distinguish a number of different factors or submodels which specify the possible connections between exports and growth:[5]

53

1. With full employment, an increase in foreign demand or a cost-reducing innovation at home will expand exports and therefore income. Income will be further expanded through greater savings and investment along Harrod-Domar lines.

2. With unemployment or underemployment, expanded exports will allow resources to be drawn into the more highly productive sector. Alternatively, the expansion of exports may call the attention of entrepreneurs to investment opportunities either in the export industry or in ancillary industries.

3. Expanded exports may permit firms to take advantage of decreasing costs through internal economies of larger-scale production.

4. By putting pressure on domestic resources, expanded exports may induce entrepreneurs to devise cost-reducing processes.

In contrast to the foregoing possibilities, Kindleberger has stated that increased exports may conceivably retard growth because of a nation's inability to adapt or transform its domestic resources:[6]

1. Depending upon the factor endowment and social structure of the economy, increased exports may increase the demand for non-labor factors (e.g., land) and alter the distribution of income in favor of groups (e.g., landowners) whose consumption and savings pattern do not contribute significantly to growth.

2. The expansion of exports may make only limited technical demands upon producers and workers, with resultant specialization at relatively low and/or comparatively fixed levels of productivity.

In evaluating Kindleberger's model, the following points seem relevant:

1. It is not clear in Kindleberger's first submodel how an increase in foreign demand will stimulate growth under conditions of full employment, for there would surely be some limitation on productive capacity. The connection between the increase in demand and the expansion of output would thus appear to be roundabout rather than direct. It is conceivable, for example, that export prices would be bid up initially so that an increase in real income would stem from improved terms of trade. Forced saving might consequently occur under such excess demand conditions, and it is possible that investment might be expanded to increase capacity. This is more like Hicksian ("trade cycle") growth rather than Harrod-Domar growth, however, since

Harrod-Domar growth is limited by ex ante saving and makes no allowance for forced saving.

The balance-of-payments implications of the foregoing case are by no means favorable. There will be induced imports both from the initial increase in real income and from the further increase which follows when investment is expanded. A continued rise in real income might be seriously hampered, moreover, to the extent that prices rise as the expanding industries bid for resources. The initial balance-of-payments improvement might therefore be erased and possibly turned into a deficit by the induced effects of these income and price changes. If, in contrast, the expansion of exports was due to a cost-reducing innovation at home rather than an increase in foreign demand, the expansion of output would be somewhat easier because of the increase in effective factors supplies. The balance-of-payments improvement might also be more readily sustained.

2. Growth based on unemployment or underemployment in his second submodel seems perfectly reasonable, although it does not necessarily follow that export expansion will channel resources into the more highly productive sector. But what is not evident in this submodel as well as in the one just discussed is why this growth has to come from exports. Surely if there are idle resources, expansionary domestic fiscal policy could work to produce growth just as well as exports, balance-of-payments considerations aside. And at full employment, other stimuli besides increased exports could bring greater growth. Thus, if exports actually turn out in an individual case to have been the catalyst to growth, it must mean that alternative stimuli were not necessary or feasible. Exports, in other words, could be a sufficient, but not a necessary, condition for growth.

3. Since all of Kindleberger's submodels except the first one are based essentially upon microeconomic relationships, the workings of these submodels cannot be comprehended fully without detailed knowledge of the relative availability of productive factors, the connections between factor and product markets, and the conditioning characteristics of entrepreneurial behavior. It would appear particularly important, moreover, for the analytical development and relevancy of the model to make allowance for the initial policy environment at home and abroad and the adaptations of policy which must occur for the changes in trade to be transformed into greater domestic growth. There is, finally, no explicit reference made concerning the extent to which the other countries, presumably with balance-of-payments deficits, can speed up their own investment and technological progress and therefore reverse their

relatively unfavorable position.

   It should be evident from the foregoing discussion that Kindleberger's contribution is an important one for the analysis of export-led
growth. Although not articulated in great detail, [7] the model is nonetheless of very considerable value in suggesting a number of alternative
hypotheses that can serve as the basis for further research.

THE LAMFALUSSY MODEL

   Because of its acknowledged derivation from Kindleberger's
work, we may next consider the growth model developed by A. Lamfalussy in order to provide insight into the differences in the postwar
growth performance of the United Kingdom as compared to the member
countries of the Common Market. [8] Lamfalussy assumed explicitly that
all the countries concerned had either finished or were actively in
the process of liberalizing their import controls and tariffs, and that
the goals of government policy were to promote full employment and
stimulate growth without inflation and external disequilibrium. [9] An increase in domestic income as a consequence of growth will of course
lead to an induced increase in imports. Exports must obviously be
expanded sufficiently, therefore, in order at least to maintain external
balance. Otherwise, external disequilibrium would necessitate government policies to restrict home demand, with the result that the level of
employment and the rate of growth might be adversely affected.

   The achievement of equilibrium, or, better yet, a surplus, in the
balance of payments was of great importance according to Lamfalussy
because it thereby enabled the government to follow expansionist policies which encouraged domestic investment. Moreover, the increase
in exports would itself stimulate investment because of accelerator effects. These increases in investment would have the consequence of
increasing internal demand and, at the same time, would expand productive capacity and productivity. If money wages were then assumed to be
increasing at the same rate in all of the relevant countries, the increase
in productivity in the given country would result in a relatively less
rapid increase or in greater stability of its domestic prices and an improvement in its international competitive position. So long as exports
kept rising, there would thus be a self-reinforcing tendency for a country
to maintain its competitive position and to continue its rapid rate of
economic growth.

   In order to demonstrate the foregoing relationships more clearly,
Lamfalussy set up the following model in which I = investment; S =

savings; Y = national income; X = exports of goods and services; M =

imports of goods and services; $y = \dfrac{\Delta Y}{Y_{t-1}}$; y_p = the rate of growth of

labor productivity per unit of time, defined as $y - \dfrac{\Delta L}{L_{t-1}}$, with L being

the number of hours effectively worked; and $\dfrac{I}{Y}$, $\dfrac{S}{Y}$, and $\dfrac{X - M}{Y}$ being,

respectively, the investment, savings, and balance of payments ratios:[10]

Investment function

$$\frac{I}{Y} = ay + \alpha \qquad\qquad (a > 0;\ 1 > \alpha > 0) \qquad\qquad (1)$$

Savings function

$$\frac{S}{Y} = by + \beta \qquad\qquad (b > 0;\ 1 > \beta > 0) \qquad\qquad (2)$$

Productivity function

$$y_p = p\,\frac{I}{Y} + \pi \qquad\qquad (p > 0;\ 1 > \pi > 0) \qquad\qquad (3)$$

Balance-of-payments function

$$\frac{X - M}{Y} = c(y_p - \gamma) \qquad\qquad (c > 0) \qquad\qquad (4)$$

Equilibrium condition

$$\frac{S}{Y} = \frac{I + X - M}{Y} \qquad\qquad\qquad (5)$$

The investment function is evidently of the accelerator type, which postulates that the investment ratio depends on the rate of growth in income.[11] The constant term α refers to the autonomous component of the investment ratio which is independent of the rate of growth of income and which is undertaken for innovational purposes rather than for the expansion of capacity.

The savings function postulated depends also on the rate of growth in income. It is thus different from the more common formulation employed in growth models of a constant savings ratio which is independent of the rate of growth of income. Lamfalussy's justification for a variable savings ratio stemmed, first, from his definition of savings and his assumptions concerning household behavior. That is, if consumption in time t depended upon the level of income in t-1 because of habit, inertia, or prudence, a higher rate of growth of income would increase the savings ratio.[12] Second, business savings were taken to be based upon the share of profits in national income, which was considered a function of the investment share and thus of the rate of growth. Finally, more rapid growth was considered to generate an excess of tax receipts over public expenditures on the assumption that there was an institutional time lag before public expenditures policies designed to reduce public savings could be adopted and implemented.

The rate of growth of labor productivity is taken to be a linear function of the investment ratio and of the constant π, which represents the autonomous increase in productivity.

The balance-of-payments function is based upon the idea that in a world in which trade was being liberalized, the relation between the development of merchandise and service exports and imports would be determined by the variations of relative unit labor costs. In particular, the balance-of-payments surplus (deficit) ratio is taken to be a linear function of the difference between the rate of increase in labor productivity and a constant, γ. This constant is defined as $\dfrac{w_n}{w_e / y_{pe}}$, where w_n is the rate of increase in money wages in the given country, w_e that of money wages abroad, and y_{pe} the rate of increase of foreign labor productivity. Thus, in order for a country to achieve a balance-of-payments surplus, the rate of increase in its labor productivity must more than offset the rate of increase in its money wages relative to the rate of increase in foreign unit labor costs. An unchanged γ is taken to represent a perfectly elastic domestic supply of labor, an assumption which is relaxed (as noted below).

The equilibrium condition in equation (5) refers to the economy as a whole and, it should be noted, is not merely an identity. What is of interest in the model is the value of y, the rate of growth of income, when the system is in equilibrium. This works out as:[13]

$$y = \frac{\alpha + c(p\alpha + \pi - \gamma) - \beta}{b - a(1 + cp)} \tag{6}$$

In interpreting equation (6), it is evident that the equilibrium rate of growth will be higher: The higher is the level of the autonomous component of the investment ratio (α) and the greater the acceleration coefficient (a); the lower the savings terms (β and b); the greater is technical progress (π) and the impact of investment upon productivity (p); and the higher is the balance-of-payments effect (c) of the difference between domestic productivity and the ratio of the rate of change in domestic money wages to foreign unit labor costs. It is this latter effect which represents the particular contribution of exports to domestic growth.[14]

After setting forth his model, Lamfalussy proceeded to point
out certain drawbacks in it: (1) It may not be legitimate to have domestic money wages determined independently of the rate of growth of the
economy; (2) the supply of labor may not be perfectly elastic as assumed,
in which case the rate of increase in productivity will determine the
rate at which the productive capacity of the economy can develop as well
as play a role in the determination of the balance-of-payments condition
and of effective demand; and (3) instead of savings having a negative influence on the rate of growth, as can be seen in equation (6) in the values
of β and b, they might rather, in the growth context at least, be considered to have a stimulating effect on the economy.

In considering the foregoing points, Lamfalussy placed greatest
emphasis upon the implications for his model which followed from relax-
ing the assumption of a perfectly elastic supply of labor. Observation of
the growth experience of the 1950's revealed that the rate of increase in
productivity was slower than the rate of increase in income in the most
rapidly growing countries, such as Germany and Italy. This was due to
the growth of employment and thus in the total number of hours worked.
One could specify, accordingly, a functional relationship between the rate
of increase in productivity and in income, such as $y_p = f(y)$ which is
represented as follows:[15]

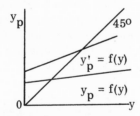

In terms of the model, this relationship could be described by substituting the investment function (1) into the productivity function (3) to
obtain the expression: $y_p = pay + p\alpha + \pi$.

The positive intercept in this expression would be due to the influence of the autonomous component of the investment ratio (α), technical progress (π), and p, the investment-productivity coefficient, which
will be larger or smaller depending upon the orientation of investment
toward capital deepening or widening. Because of differences in inst-
tutions, behavioral patterns, and economic structure, the functions
would vary from one country to another. Thus, a function such as y_p

would have a flatter slope for countries (e.g., Italy) in which employment was growing relatively fast and investment was, consequently, capital widening, a steeper slope such as y'_p for countries (e.g., France)
in which employment was growing more slowly and investment was,
consequently, relatively more capital deepening. The diagram implies
therefore that, everything else equal, a tightened labor market might
result in a higher intercept and a steeper slope, as illustrated by a shift
from y_p to y'_p. This would have a substantial effect in reducing the rate
of increase of income in the country formerly moving along y_p.[16]

The implications of relative labor scarcity can also be considered
in terms of the increases which will occur in money wages and the consequent impact upon the competitive position of the country. Thus, if γ
increases, the economy would experience a diminution in its equilibrium
rate of growth and a worsening in its balance of payments. Increased
money wages might reduce the share of profits in national income and
hence lead to a fall in the savings ratio. The savings ratio might be
lowered further if domestic prices rose and households responded by increasing their consumption. Actually, these reductions in the savings
terms, β and b, in equation (6), could serve to offset the rise in γ as home
demand was substituted for external demand. If, however, the inflationary effect predominated and resulted in a marked balance-of-payments
deficit, the government might be forced to introduce policies to restrict
domestic demand. Such policies might well have the effect of reducing
the autonomous component of the investment ratio (α), and, in terms of
the foregoing diagram, cause the productivity function to shift its intercept downward. At the same time, the slope of the function might become
steeper if there is a reduction in the rate of increase in employment.
This would mean essentially that the rate of increase in income would be
diminished because there is less labor available for the given rate of increase in productivity. It might thus be necessary to maintain the restrictive domestic policies, in which case the economy might find itself truly
in a vicious circle due to its inability to restore its international competitive position.

The outcome will depend importantly upon the reaction of entrepreneurs who would be motivated to undertake labor-saving investments
and adopt other measures of rationalization of their operations. Such increases in p and π might be sufficient to offset the fall in α. In terms of
the diagram, the productivity function might shift upward and become
steeper compared to its earlier position where labor was more plentiful.
But in any case, the relative scarcity of labor would be overcome and a
new, though perhaps lower, equilibrium rate of growth attained.

Lamfalussy concluded the discussion of his model by noting that the issue involved was by no means simply one of the effects of variations in domestic policy upon investment and thus upon the productivity of labor. Rather, as disturbances were introduced into the model, the precise chronology of events would become crucially important and the equations of the model would have to be able to handle these rather complex phenomena. Moreover, he pointed out the probable necessity of introducing a specific function for wage determination that would reflect the state of the labor market. But, as he noted, the fact that this function might be nonlinear, that the constants of the model should perhaps be treated as variables, and that time should enter into each function might well make the analysis sufficiently more complex as to run the risk of diminishing returns for the added effort required.

The preceding discussion of Lamfalussy's model was of necessity somewhat lengthy in order to do justice to the structure and characteristics of the model, and to focus upon the qualifications connected particularly with labor-supply conditions that Lamfalussy himself felt to be important in using the model analytically. Although, as noted, he anticipated a number of the important limitations of the model, there are a few additional points which are worth mentioning:

1. The fact that Lamfalussy chose to frame the dependent variables of his models in terms of ratios rather than levels is bothersome. This is because the theoretical relationships between the dependent variable ratios and the independent variables of the model do not always have a clear economic meaning. Also, because of the way in which the model has been written, it cannot be transformed into levels without changing the structure and thus the interpretation of the individual relationships.

2. There may be some difficulty in treating both the private and public components of investment in equation (1) within a relatively simple accelerator framework. Some parts of private investment, even in the manufacturing sector, will certainly not conform to simple accelerator effects. This will be true also of substantial parts of public investment, especially in the nonmanufacturing sectors. Lamfalussy's investment function may thus abstract from some important determinants of investments with respect to particular sectors of the economy. [17]

3. A corollary to the foregoing point is that the determination of y_p, the rate of change of labor productivity, in equation (3) refers apparently to the economy as a whole, whereas it may vary considerably depending upon the sector and the type of investment being considered. Equation (3) assumes, moreover, that investment is the major determination of y_p, whereas such factors as changes in organization which may require relatively little investment or the realization of increasing returns could

be of equal or even greater importance in individual industries. The formulation of y_p is important, finally, in equation (4) for the balance of payments inasmuch as it is related there to the rate of change in wages, w_n. The more broadly conceived are the concepts of comparative changes in productivity and wages, the less relevance they may have for the determination of the net balance-of-payments ratio. The various points thus raise the crucial question of whether Lamfalussy's macroeconomic growth model is entirely suitable for the analysis of export-led growth in particular. Rather, some type of a more disaggregated model might be preferred in order more clearly to identify the sectors especial-ly important in foreign trade and reasons for differences in their contributions to exports and imports and thus to the balance of payments.

4. A further difficulty with equation (4) is the extent to which merchandise and service exports and imports can be assumed to vary only with the rate of change in comparative unit labor costs, for these items may certainly be influenced significantly as well by changes in foreign and domestic incomes. It may be noted, further, that the balance-of-payments ratio in equation (4) is cast in real terms. There is a difficulty here in that the numerator of this ratio is a monetary phenome-non typified by changes in foreign claims or debt. [18] It is thus evident that interest rate and other capital account considerations are being ex-cluded from the model. This may, consequently, limit to a certain ex-tent the analytical usefulness of the model.

Lamfalussy's model is definitely an important contribution to the theory of growth in an open economy, for it encompasses many of the most significant aggregative forces which affect a country's economic growth and balance of payments. It is perhaps open to question, however, as to whether this type of aggregative model can identify the differences among and within sectors that contribute in particular to export-led growth. We shall have occasion to say more on this matter in the following chapter.

THE BECKERMAN MODEL

The occasion for presentation of W. Beckerman's model of export-led growth was his review of the massive Twentieth Century Fund study, Europe's Needs and Resources. [19] In making their growth projections for 1970, the authors of this study relied upon a "conver-gence" model according to which there was "some long run historical rate of growth from which substantial deviations must be of a temporary nature." Beckerman observed, however, that Europe's over-all growth during the second half of the 1950's actually exceeded the 1955-70 pro-

jected rate by nearly 1 per cent, and that, contrary to the Twentieth
Century Fund assumptions, there was substantial dispersion of the
growth rates of individual countries around the over-all average. As a
consequence according to Beckerman, a "divergence" rather than a
"convergence" theory of the growth process seemed more appropriate
to explain the relative growth experience of countries in Europe during
the 1950's.[20]

Beckerman's interpretation of this experience was that rapid
growth depended upon confident expectations concerning future demand
prospects both domestically and in foreign markets. Entrepreneurs
were thus motivated to increase their investment rates and take other
steps to expand their rates of productivity increase per unit of input.
A favorable initial position of international price competitiveness which
permitted rapid growth would tend, consequently, to be perpetuated or
maybe even accentuated by the increases in investment and productivity.
Some countries would therefore experience significantly more rapid
growth as compared to other countries in which foreign trade prices
especially were uncompetitive and might become increasingly so.

In order to clarify the foregoing relationships, Beckerman set
up the following model in which X = exports, O = labor productivity,
W = money wages, P = domestic prices, P_f = foreign prices, and x, o,
w, and p represent the proportionate rates of change in the variables
per unit of time for a given country:[21]

Export equation	$x = a + b(1 - P/P_f)$	$(b > 0)$	(1)
Productivity equation	$o = c + dx$	$(d > 0)$	(2)
Wage equation	$w = m + no$	$(1 > n > 0)$	(3)
Price equation	$p = w - o$		(4)

Beckerman stated that the constant term in equation (1) can be
taken to represent the rate of increase in world trade. Thus, if for a
given country $P/P_f < 1$, its exports will rise faster than world trade.[22]
It is assumed in equation (2) that o is positively correlated with the rate
of increase in output, which is in turn correlated with x.[23] That the
relation between o and x may not be proportional can be allowed for in
the size of d in equation (2). It is assumed that in equation (3) $n < 1$.
Equation (4) is designed to measure the "wage drift" on the (implicit)
assumption of constant distributive shares.

From (3) and (4), it follows that:

$$p = m + o(n - 1) \qquad\qquad (5)$$

From (1) and (2) for a given country,

$$o = (c + ad) + bd(1 - P/P_f) \qquad\qquad (6)$$

Thus, if a given country has a competitive advantage in trade $(P/P_f <1)$, its rate of productivity growth, o, will exceed the average rate $(c + ad)$ by $bd(1 - P/P_f)$. Since by assumption in equation (5), $n <1$, p will rise less (fall more), the greater is o. It follows therefore that an initial disparity in relative prices will tend to become accentuated and will bring about a growing disparity in relative growth rates.

While Beckerman was concerned primarily with the forces of divergence in his model of export-led growth, he nevertheless gave some attention as well to forces which might cause growth rates to converge. He stated in particular that convergence might come about through a rise in the constant term, m, in the wage equation (3) in the faster growing country. That is if we regard m "as partly a weighted average of w in preceding periods" and note that w will be greater the greater is o in the faster-growing country, then w will tend to rise even more in this country because of an increasing m. [24]

In a comment on Beckerman's model, Bela Balassa has argued, however, that equation (3) and its alternative formulations have "stacked the cards" against a convergent solution of the model. [25] This is because the wage relationship is linked to the growth of productivity with an apparent disregard of "the possible impact of inter-country and intertemporal differences in the elasticity of labour supply on wage-changes." [26] Balassa thus suggested that the wage equation (3) be rewritten as $w = m - nU$, where U = unemployment as a percentage of the labor force. [27]

According to his interpretation, the rate of increase of wages will rise as U falls, and at some value of U, will exceed the rate of increase in productivity. The consequent rise in prices will reduce the rate of increase of exports in the faster-growing country and raise this rate to the benefit of the slower-growing country. Disparities in rates of growth will therefore be reduced and the conventional balance-of-payments mechanism of adjustment will become operative.

In replying to Balassa, Beckerman argued that the empirical evidence contradicted Balassa's main point in that during the 1950's wages rose fastest in those European countries where productivity rose fastest. This was in spite of the relatively high levels of unemployment in these countries. [28] Beckerman, nevertheless, acknowledged the possible converging effect of reductions in unemployment. He stated that the unemployment factor could be introduced in his equation (3) by redefining m "as partly a weighted average of past rates of increase in money wages." [29] Beckerman thus intended that labor market conditions be reflected in m, along with other significant factors affecting the rate of increase of wages. [30]

In a rejoinder to Beckerman, Balassa expressed doubts as to the convergence properties of the model as modified in cases where exports and productivity grew at constant rates and at steadily diverging rates. [31] But Beckerman allayed such doubts in a subsequent rebuttal in which he demonstrated algebraically and arithmetically the convergence characteristics of his model in examples of the cases mentioned. [32] Balassa acknowledged this demonstration in a further note, but added that he would not necessarily consider Beckerman's interpretation of m in the wage equation (3) to be realistic. [33] It is thus evident that the controversy between the two authors was not resolved with regard to the empirical significance and the method of conceptualizing the effects of unemployment upon the rate of increase in wages.

An additional point of difference apparently still remaining between the two authors concerned the implications of introducing oscillation possibilities into the model. Such possibilities may arise, according to Beckerman, due to upward (downward) movements in m which, by affecting the rate of increase of exports, will dampen (improve) entrepreneurial expectations about demand and thus lead to a fall (rise) in the rate of increase in output and productivity. Countries could thus oscillate between "virtuous" and "vicious" circles of economic growth through changes in their export competitiveness. [34]

In Beckerman's view, an oscillating model would of necessity involve important time lags. Thus, the slowing down in the growth rate of one country would not be matched necessarily by an instantaneous increase in the growth rate of the other country. Under these conditions the oscillating model therefore implies a slower average rate of growth for all countries than would otherwise be the case. Balassa argued, however, that the outcome need not necessarily follow the foregoing pattern. [35] Rather, the outcome might well be inflationary if policies are introduced to expand domestic demand to compensate for the falling off in exports in the one country while both exports and domestic demand may be booming in the other country.

The foregoing discussion has concentrated on the nature and workings of the Beckerman model of export-led growth and on the major points in the dialogue concerning the model between Beckerman and Balassa. While certain other points were raised in this dialogue, they were considered for present purposes to be of secondary importance and thus were not discussed. With regard to the model as outlined above, therefore, the following comments can be offered:

1. As has been noted, Beckerman based his model upon the responses which entrepreneurs made to favorable demand expectations at home and abroad by increasing their investments and taking other steps to raise productivity. His model is thus demand-oriented. It might be just as reasonable to argue, however, that autonomous forces on the supply side lay behind entrepreneurial investment and output decisions. The direction of causality in the model is consequently open to differences in interpretation. It might be possible, accordingly, to develop alternative hypotheses along the lines, for example, suggested above in Kindleberger's submodels 2 and 4. This situation of having alternative hypotheses could conceivably be resolved by empirical analysis of the factors influencing investment decisions. But, unfortunately, Beckerman was not very explicit in his productivity equation (2) concerning the route by which output, exports, investment, and productivity were related. He left unanswered, moreover, the questions of how "technical dynamism" and investment worked together in increasing productivity, and whether this technical dynamism was concentrated in some sectors or spread evenly among all sectors of the economy.

2. The statement of the model would have been clearer if Beckerman had related the investment and savings process more directly to the balance of payments and pointed out the importance of a favorable balance-of-payments position to domestic expansionary policies with respect especially to investment. Closely related to the point just made is that Beckerman does not mention the source of a given country's initial export competitiveness. The consideration of such underlying factors as the exchange rate valuation and the wage level and elasticity of the labor supply would have provided additional insight into the enabling characteristics of the expansion, acceleration, and possibly the retardation of exports from a given country.

3. The aforementioned controversy with regard to the wage equation (3) involves both conceptual and empirical questions. Beckerman's emphasis was upon the rate of increase in productivity, while Balassa emphasized the level of (and rate of change in) unemployment as the major determining factor(s) in the rate of change in wages. Since Beckerman admitted the importance of unemployment in wage determina-

tion, the question then becomes one of finding for wage changes the relationship which best suits the remaining equations of the model and which may provide the best empirical representation of what actually has happened in individual countries. The difficulty with Beckerman's suggestion to consider the m term in equation (3) as partly a weighted average of past rates of wage increase is that it introduces into the model a time lag of undetermined length and weight distribution, thus rendering it difficult to retain generality in the model's analytical framework. It also subsumes, as was noted above, not only the effects of unemployment but, in addition, certain institutional factors affecting wage formation. The alternative is of course to introduce unemployment and other factors explicitly into the model. However, this might necessitate additional definitional or behavioral equations.[36] It is therefore difficult to resolve this question of the form of the wage equation and ultimately the form of the entire model until various formulations have been tested empirically.

4. On the question of introducing oscillation possibilities into the model, Beckerman correctly emphasizes, in my opinion, the deflationary implications resulting from lags in entrepreneurial response. Balassa is by no means incorrect when he stresses the combined inflationary effect of domestic expansionary policy in the given country to compensate for its falling off of exports and of the export and domestic boom that occurs in the other country. The important point is, however, that the given country may be forced to reduce its rate of growth because of deterioration in its balance of payments. Unless it has a surfeit of foreign-exchange reserves or is prepared to devalue, a compensating policy of domestic expansion would have of necessity to be restrained.

Beckerman's model has the virtue of simplicity in focusing on the productivity and wage determinants of prices and thus of export competitiveness. There is an important drawback in the model, however, in its explicit demand orientation since export-led growth could stem just as well from changes on the supply side. The simplicity of the model has a price, moreover, insofar as it leaves certain points vague, necessitates the introduction of unverified empirical assumptions, and subjects some parameters of the model to differences in interpretation. The empirical analysis of the following chapter will hopefully shed light on some of the foregoing considerations.

CONCLUSION

Having completed our review of the Kindleberger, Lamfalussy, and Beckerman-(Balassa) models of export-led growth, we could now attempt a synthesis of the major elements of these models into a more comprehensive and systematic model of export-led growth. But since many of the issues raised in the preceding discussion are empirical rather than theoretical in nature, it may be more fruitful at this stage to examine the empirical implications of the existing models. Thus, in the next chapter we shall focus attention on the relationships contained in the Lamfalussy and Beckerman models in particular in the light of Italian postwar growth experience.

CHAPTER **4** ESTIMATES OF THE
LAMFALUSSY AND
BECKERMAN MODELS

The purpose of this chapter is to determine the extent to which
the Lamfalussy and Beckerman models can be utilized in the understanding and "explanation" of the postwar Italian growth experience.
Kindleberger's model, which was discussed in the preceding chapter,
will not be treated directly here since its formulation was not readily
amenable to empirical specification.

It is important to point out that both Lamfalussy and Beckerman
intentionally simplified their models in order to concentrate attention
theoretically upon the variables and relationships which they felt to be
of central importance in the analysis of a country's growth. Since the
models were thus theoretical rather than econometric in construction,
it is necessary for purposes of the empirical investigation to make certain adaptations in them and to introduce additional variables in an attempt to provide a better explanation of the observed variation in the
dependent variables specified. In the following sections there will be
presented, accordingly, lists of the variables used and the empirical
estimations of various versions of the individual equations of the two
models. Some brief remarks on the applicability of the models to
Italy's postwar growth experience will then be offered in the final section.

ESTIMATION OF THE LAMFALUSSY MODEL

The procedure followed with respect to the Lamfalussy model
was, first, to estimate the simple version of each equation, using the
most highly aggregative data available. Additional variables were then
introduced, the form of some equations altered, and alternative specifications formulated in the light of analytical considerations and data
availability.

As stated in the preceding chapter, the equations of Lamfalussy's
model were as follows:

Investment function

$$\frac{I}{Y} = ay + \alpha \qquad\qquad (a > 0;\ 1 > \alpha > 0) \qquad\qquad (1)$$

Savings function

$$\frac{S}{Y} = by + \beta \qquad\qquad (b > 0;\ 1 > \beta > 0) \qquad\qquad (2)$$

Productivity function

$$y_p = p\frac{I}{Y} + \pi \qquad\qquad (p > 0;\ 1 > \pi > 0) \qquad\qquad (3)$$

Balance-of-payments function

$$\frac{X - M}{Y} = c\,(y_p - \gamma) \qquad\qquad (c > 0) \qquad\qquad (4)$$

Equilibrium condition

$$\frac{S}{Y} = \frac{I + X - M}{Y} \qquad\qquad (5)$$

The following variables were used in the different versions of the individual equations:

Equation (1) - Investment Function

$\frac{I}{Y}$ = Ratio of gross domestic investment to GNP in 1954 lire.

$(\frac{I}{Y})'$ = Ratio of gross investment to GNP in 1954 lire, net of investment in dwellings and public administration.

y = Rate of change in GNP in 1954 lire.

y' = Rate of change in GNP in 1954 lire, net of investment in dwellings and public administration.

C = Index of capacity utilization in industry, 1954 = 100.

i = Long-term rate of interest on Government bonds (Titoli di Stato).

Equation (2) - Savings Function

$\frac{S}{Y}$ = Ratio of savings (i.e., gross investment plus the balance on current account) to GNP in 1954 lire.

y = Rate of change in GNP in 1954 lire.

$(\frac{S}{Y})_{-1}$ = Savings ratio lagged one year.

$\frac{W}{P}$ = Ratio of total wages to total profits in current lire.

Equation (3) - Productivity Function

y_p = Rate of change in labor productivity for all employed labor in the economy as a whole.

y'_p = Rate of change in labor productivity in industry.

$\frac{I}{Y}$ = Ratio of gross investment to GNP in 1954 lire.

$(\frac{I}{Y})''$ = Ratio of gross investment to GNP in 1954 lire, net of investment in forestry, and fishing; dwellings; public administration; and other service industries.

$(\frac{I}{Y})''_{-1}$ = Investment ratio lagged one year.

Equation (4) - Balance-of-Payments Function

$\frac{X - M}{Y}$ = Ratio of current account balance to GNP in 1954 lire.

$\frac{X}{Y}$ = Ratio of merchandise exports to GNP in 1954 lire.

$(\frac{X}{Y})_{-1}$ = Export ratio lagged one year.

$\frac{M}{Y}$ = Ratio of merchandise imports to GNP in 1954 lire.

$(\frac{M}{Y})_{-1}$ = Import ratio lagged one year.

$y_p - \gamma$ = Rate of change in labor productivity in manufacturing in Italy less the ratio of the rate of change in Italian wages in manufacturing to the rate of change in unit labor costs in the other industrial countries.

$c_{I, W}$ = Rate of change in the ratio of relative unit labor costs in manufacturing in Italy and the other major industrial countries.

t_W = Rate of change in world exports, excluding Italian exports, in 1953 dollars.

y'' = Rate of change in consumption plus investment in 1954 lire.

$p_{I, W}$ = Rate of change in the ratio of relative GNP prices in Italy and the other major industrial countries.

The annual data which were used for the calculations are reproduced in Table 20 of Appendix I. The regression results for the various formulations of the individual equations are shown below. All the equations refer to the period of 1951-63, except (3b) and (3c) which refer to the period of 1954-63. The standard errors are shown in parentheses beneath the regression coefficients, and the corrected coefficients of determination ($\bar{R}^2$) and the Durbin-Watson (D.W.) statistic where appropriate,[1] are indicated to the right of each result.

Equation (1) - Investment Function, 1951-63

(1a) $\dfrac{I}{Y} = .20 + .23y$ $\qquad r^2 = .03$ D.W. $= .21$
$\qquad\qquad\quad (.40)$

(1b) $\dfrac{I}{Y} = .29 - .03\,y + .04\,C - 1.78\,i$ $\quad \bar{R}^2 = .02$ D.W. $= .27$
$\qquad\qquad\quad (.42)\quad (.20)\quad (1.24)$

(1c) $\left(\dfrac{I}{Y}\right)' = .15 + .23\,y'$ $\qquad r^2 = .08$ D.W. $= .62$
$\qquad\qquad\quad (.23)$

(1d) $\left(\dfrac{I}{Y}\right)' = -.25 - .04\,y' + .40\,C$ $\qquad \bar{R}^2 = .61$ D.W. $= 2.22$
$\qquad\qquad\quad (.16)\quad (.10)$

(1e) $\left(\dfrac{I}{Y}\right)' = -.11 - .09\,y' + .32\,C - .88\,i$ $\quad \bar{R}^2 = .66$ D.W. $= 1.63$
$\qquad\qquad\quad (.15)\quad (.10)\quad (.54)$

Equation (2) - Savings Function, 1951-63

(2a) $\dfrac{S}{Y} = .17 + .62\,y$ $\qquad r^2 = .12$ D.W. $= .33$
$\qquad\qquad\quad (.47)$

(2b) $\dfrac{S}{Y} = .03 + .31\,y + .80\left(\dfrac{S}{Y}\right)_{-1}$ $\quad \bar{R}^2 = .88$
$\qquad\qquad\quad (.17)\quad (.10)$

(2c) $\dfrac{S}{Y} = .12 + .21\,y + .97\left(\dfrac{S}{Y}\right)_{-1} - .22\,\dfrac{W}{P}$
$\qquad\qquad\quad (.19)\quad (.17)\quad\quad (.19)$
$\qquad\qquad\qquad\qquad\qquad\qquad\qquad\quad \bar{R}^2 = .88$

Equation (3) - Productivity Function

(3a) $y_p = -.02 + .34\dfrac{I}{Y}$ $\quad$ (1951-63) $\quad r^2 = .13$ D.W. $= 1.69$
$\qquad\qquad\quad (.26)$

(3b) $y'_p = .09 - .27\left(\dfrac{I}{Y}\right)''$ $\quad$ (1954-63) $\quad r^2 = .06$ D.W. $= 1.73$
$\qquad\qquad\quad (.37)$

(3c) $y'_p = .13 + 1.30\left(\dfrac{I}{Y}\right)'' - 1.95\left(\dfrac{I}{Y}\right)''_{-1}$ $\quad \bar{R}^2 = .36$ D.W. $= 2.43$
$\qquad\qquad\quad (.69)\qquad\quad (.78)$

Equation (4) - Balance-of-Payments Function, 1951-63

(4a) $\quad \dfrac{X - M}{Y} = -.01 + .15 \, (y_p - \gamma)$ $\qquad r^2 = .14$ D.W. $= .59$
$\qquad\qquad\qquad (.12)$

(4b) $\quad \dfrac{X}{Y} = .11 + .08 \, t_W$ $\qquad\qquad\qquad r^2 = .01$ D.W. $= .09$
$\qquad\qquad\quad (.25)$

(4c) $\quad \dfrac{X}{Y} = .12 + .20 \, t_W - .63 \, c_{I,\,W}$ $\qquad \bar{R}^2 = .37$ D.W. $= .66$
$\qquad\qquad\quad (.20) \qquad (.21)$

(4d) $\quad \dfrac{X}{Y} = .02 + .08 \, t_W + .16 \, c_{I,\,W} + 1.20 \, (\tfrac{X}{Y})_{-1}$ $\quad \bar{R}^2 = .98$
$\qquad\qquad\quad (.04) \qquad (.06) \qquad\quad (.07)$

(4e) $\quad \dfrac{M}{Y} = .07 + 1.38 \, y''$ $\qquad\qquad\qquad r^2 = .39$ D.W. $= 1.07$
$\qquad\qquad\quad (.53)$

(4f) $\quad \dfrac{M}{Y} = .09 + 1.05 \, y'' + 1.12 \, p_{I,\,W}$ $\qquad \bar{R}^2 = .62$ D.W. $= 1.55$
$\qquad\qquad\quad (.41) \qquad (.37)$

(4g) $\quad \dfrac{M}{Y} = -.01 + .50 \, y'' + .21 \, p_{I,\,W} + .97 \, (\tfrac{M}{Y})_{-1}$ $\quad \bar{R}^2 = .94$
$\qquad\qquad\quad (.18) \qquad (.19) \qquad (.13)$

It may be useful in considering the foregoing results to explain
briefly the individual equations. Equation (1a) is a representation of
Lamfalussy's investment equation (1) and says that the investment ratio
depends positively on the rate of change in GNP. This is a type of accelerator relationship as was noted in the preceding chapter. Since
there is reason to believe that the response of investment to changes
in GNP may vary depending upon changes in the utilization of productive capacity, a measure of capacity utilization in industry was also introduced into equation (1b). This was designed to represent for the
economy as a whole a "flexible" accelerator while the rate of change
in GNP was taken to reflect the ordinary accelerator in the more usual
sense. Also included in equation (1b) was the long-term rate of
interest on Government bonds (Titoli di Stato), which was expected to
be negative in sign.

Turning then to the results of equations (1a) and (1b), there was
evidently no relationship between the aggregate investment ratio and
the independent variables specified. This is perhaps not surprising
since the investment and GNP variables in these equations include the
influence of autonomous public investment decisions especially in the[2]
agricultural sector, dwellings, transportation, and communication.
While such autonomous investment might be presumed to be reflected
in the constant term of the equation, it was felt, nonetheless, that a
somewhat more disaggregated specification might be more appropriate.
Hence in equations (1c)-(1e) investment and GNP net of dwellings and
public administration were employed as the basis for specification.

It is evident that this change resulted in making the index of capacity utilization in industry statistically significant. It thus appeared that a flexible accelerator was at work during the period under study. The coefficient of the long-term rate of interest had the correct sign in equation (1e) but was not statistically significant.[3]

Equation (2a) represents Lamfalussy's savings equation (2) and says that the savings ratio depends positively on the rate of change in GNP. For want of a more accurate measure of the effects on current savings of past period aggregative consumption and savings behavior, the lagged savings ratio was introduced in equation (2b). In order to assess the impact on the savings ratio of changes in distributive shares, $\frac{W}{P}$, the ratio of total money wages to total profits, was introduced into equation (2c). This was a highly imperfect measure of distributive shares, however, since the denominator included substantial returns accruing to self-employed individuals and family units.

It is evident from the results that only the lagged savings ratio, $(\frac{S}{Y})_{-1}$, turned out to be statistically significant. The inclusion in equation (2c) of $\frac{W}{P}$ did not effect any improvement. These results tell us that certain past period behavior phenomena subsumed in $(\frac{S}{Y})_{-1}$ were important determinants of the current savings ratio. But this is unfortunately not saying a great deal because these phenomena have not been specified concretely.

Equation (3a) is a representation of Lamfalussy's productivity equation (3) and says that y_p, the rate of change in labor productivity, depends positively on the investment ratio for the economy as a whole. This relationship was also formulated on a less aggregative basis for industry only in equation (3b). The effect of the lagged investment ratio for industry was tested in equation (3c). It is evident that the results for all three versions of the productivity equation were unsatisfactory.[4]

It is well known of course that the factors influencing the rate of change in productivity are rather complex. These factors are also, perhaps in considerable part, difficult to measure by means of relatively simple formulations. This is the case to the extent that they may involve qualitative improvements in factor inputs, organizational changes, the adoption of new technology, and increasing returns rather than conventional inputs of labor and capital. Further progress here thus appears contingent upon the availability of more detailed and reliable estimates of productivity and its determinants.[5]

Equation (4a) represents Lamfalussy's balance-of-payments equa tion and says that the current account balance ratio depends positively on the difference between the rate of change in domestic productivity and γ, which is the rate of change in domestic money wages divided by the rate of change in foreign unit labor costs. As noted in the previous chapter, it seems unlikely that the current account balance ratio and its component export and import ratios would be affected solely by or even directly by the rate of change in relative unit labor costs. It therefore appeared more appropriate to consider separately the factors determining the merchandise export and import ratios.

Thus, in order to make allowance for income and price factors, the merchandise export ratio was taken in equations (4b) and (4c) to depend positively on t_W, the rate of change in total world exports exclusive of Italian exports, and negatively upon $c_{I,W}$, the rate of change in relative unit labor costs. The form of these equations was patterned after the export relationships which were reported in Chapter 2, with the difference that the dependent variable here was expressed as a ratio and the independent variables in terms of rates of change. In Chapter 2 all the variables were expressed in levels.

The merchandise import ratio in equations (4e) and (4f) was assumed to be related positively to y'', the rate of change in income measured here as consumption plus investment, and to $p_{I,W}$, the rate of change in relative GNP prices. These equations were modeled after the ones presented for imports also in Chapter 2 and they reflect the same differences just mentioned with respect to exports. It should be noted that the rate of change in unit labor costs used above for the export ratio equations might have been used here as well in order to follow the Lamfalussy model more closely. The reason for not doing so was that it was negatively correlated with the rate of change in relative GNP prices.[6] This latter variable thus seemed more appropriate as a means of focusing upon the general inflationary forces affecting imports.

A problem arises in assessing the determinants of the export and import ratios in the manner so far indicated. This is because there is nothing in the current explanatory variables introduced which distinguishes how the export and import ratios have changed relative to their level in the previous period. The lagged export and import ratios were therefore introduced as noted in equations (4d) and (4g).

It is evident from the results of equation (4a) that the current account balance ratio version of the Lamfalussy model was not statistically significant. The rate of change in relative unit labor costs, $c_{I,W}$, was statistically significant in the export ratio equation (4c), as

were the rates of change in GNP and in relative GNP prices in the
import ratio equation (4f). The inclusion of the lagged ratios in equations (4d) and (4g) yielded coefficients close to unity, which indicated
that the current values of the ratios could be fairly well approximated
by the lagged values and that the current explanatory variables would
be relevant then only for the year-to-year change.

It is noteworthy, therefore, that the inclusion of the lagged export ratio changed the sign of $c_{I,W}$ from negative in equation (4c) to
positive in (4d). It will be recalled from Chapter 2 that equation (5)
for Italy's exports of manufactures yielded similarly insignificant results using the level of relative unit labor costs. It would appear,
therefore, that the results of equation (4c) are open to question. The
inclusion of the lagged import ratio in equation (4g) mainly affected
$p_{I,W}$ by reducing its regression coefficient and increasing its standard
error. Current $\frac{M}{Y}$ was still influenced positively, although to a lesser
extent than in equation (4f), by y'' the rate of change in consumption
plus investment.

In considering the foregoing results, it is clear from equations
(1a), (2a), (3a), and (4a) that Lamfalussy's basic model was not at all
closely approximated by the data utilized. This was a consequence apparently of the level of aggregation of the model, the way in which the
individual equations were formulated, [7] and the lack of adequate data
relating particularly to productivity and its determinants. A few
improvements were effected in the process of identifying important
additional variables and integrating them into the model. But the fact
remains that the results were on the whole rather limited with respect
to providing a satisfactory explanation of the Italian postwar growth
experience.

What the results did show was that during the 1951-63 period
the investment ratio, net of investment in dwellings and public administration, was explained in part by variations in industry capacity utilization; that the savings ratio was influenced by consumption and savings
behavior in past periods; that the merchandise export ratio may possibly have been responsive to the rate of change in relative unit labor
costs; and that the merchandise import ratio varied in response to the
rate of change in GNP and possibly relative GNP prices. While these
findings are not without interest, it is difficult to interrelate them in
the absence of a satisfactory explanation of the rate of change in labor
productivity. The need for additional research on the determinants of
productivity is therefore obvious. When more is known about these
determinants, which no doubt vary among as well as within different
economic sectors, we may then be able to construct and utilize aggre-

gative growth models with greater confidence and precision for individual nations.

ESTIMATION OF THE BECKERMAN MODEL

The estimation procedure with respect to the Beckerman model was basically similar to that followed in the Lamfalussy model. That is, the simple version of each equation was first estimated and additional variables were then introduced, with alterations being made and alternative formulations specified for the individual equations. In order to deal with the problem of simultaneity among the equations, both single-stage and two-stage least squares estimates were computed for each equation.

As noted in the previous chapter, the equations of Beckerman's model were as follows:

Export equation	$x = a + b(1 - P/P_f)$	$(b > 0)$	(1)
Productivity equation	$o = c + dx$	$(d > 0)$	(2)
Wage equation	$w = m + no$	$(1 > n > 0)$	(3)
Price equation	$p = w - o$		(4)

The following variables were used in the different versions of the individual equations:

Equation (1) - Export Equation

x = Rate of change in total Italian exports in 1953 dollars.

$(1 + P_F - P_I)$ = A linear approximation to $(1 - P_I/P_F)$, which is an expression for unity minus the GNP price index of Italy relative to that of the major industrial countries.

t_W = Rate of change in world exports, excluding Italian exports, in 1953 dollars.

Equation (2) - Productivity Equation

o = Rate of change in labor productivity in Italian industry based on Banca d'Italia data.

x = Rate of change in total Italian exports in 1953 dollars.

Equation (3) - Wage Equation

w_m = Rate of change in average annual wages of workers in Italian industry based on Banca d'Italia data.

w'_m = Rate of change in average hourly wages of workers in Italian manufacturing based on Banca d'Italia data.

w''_m = Rate of change in average hourly wages of workers in Italian manufacturing based on OECD data.

o = Rate of change in labor productivity in Italian industry based on Banca d'Italia data.

o' = Rate of change in labor productivity in Italian manufacturing based on Banca d'Italia data.

o'' = Rate of change in labor productivity in Italian manufacturing based on OECD data.

$\frac{U}{L}$ = Unemployment as a percentage of Italy's total labor force.

p_I = Rate of change in Italy's GNP price deflator.

Equation (4) - Price Equation

p_I = Rate of change in Italy's GNP price deflator.

w_m = Rate of change in average annual wages of workers in Italian industry based on Banca d'Italia data.

o = Rate of change in labor productivity in Italian industry based on Banca d'Italia data.

w_g = Rate of change in average annual compensation of government employees.

The annual data underlying the calculations are reproduced in Table 21 of Appendix I. The regression results for the various formulations of the individual equations are shown below, using the same format as in the presentation of the estimates of the Lamfalussy model. All the results indicated refer to the period of 1954-63, except for equation (3d), which covers the period of 1952-63. [8]

Equation (1) - Export Equation, 1954-63

(1a) Single-stage estimate

$$x = -1.25 + 1.37 \ (1 + P_F - P_I) \qquad r^2 = .30 \quad D.W. = 1.94$$
$$(.75)$$
$$x = -1.60 + 1.65 \ (1 + P_F - P_I) + 1.18 \ t_W \quad \bar{R}^2 = .58 \quad D.W. = 1.70$$
$$(.55) (.41)$$

(1b) Two-stage estimate

$$x = -.89 + 1.52 (1 + P_F - P_I) + .96 t_W$$
$$\quad\quad (1.27) \quad\quad\quad\quad (.55) \quad \bar{R}^2 = .12 \quad D.W. = 2.08$$

Equation (2) - Productivity Equation, 1954-63

(2a) Single-stage estimate

$$o = .03 + .18 x \quad\quad\quad\quad\quad r^2 = .50 \quad D.W. = 1.43$$
$$\quad\quad (.06)$$

(2b) Two-stage estimate

$$o = .02 + .20 x \quad\quad\quad\quad\quad r^2 = .45 \quad D.W. = 2.58$$
$$\quad\quad (.08)$$

Equation (3) - Wage Equation

(3a) Single-stage estimate, 1954-63

$$w_m = .02 + 1.10 o \quad\quad\quad\quad r^2 = .90 \quad D.W. = .67$$
$$\quad\quad\quad (.13)$$

$$w_m = .05 + 1.65 o - 1.03 \frac{U}{L} \quad\quad \bar{R}^2 = .89 \quad D.W. = 1.19$$
$$\quad\quad\quad (.49) \quad\quad (.87)$$

$$w_m = .01 + .82 o - .44 \frac{U}{L} + 2.05 p_I \quad \bar{R}^2 = .99 \quad D.W. = 2.54$$
$$\quad\quad\quad (.20) \quad\quad (.30) \quad\quad (.27)$$

(3b) Two-stage estimate, 1954-63

$$w_m = .11 - .51 o - .41 \frac{U}{L} + 2.17 p_I \quad \bar{R}^2 = .84 \quad D.W. = 2.42$$
$$\quad\quad\quad (.49) \quad\quad (.33) \quad\quad (.43)$$

(3c) Single-stage estimate, 1954-63

$$w'_m = .12 - .66 o' \quad\quad\quad\quad\quad r^2 = .09 \quad D.W. = .86$$
$$\quad\quad\quad (.74)$$

$$w'_m = .17 - .34 o' - 1.18 \frac{U}{L} \quad\quad \bar{R}^2 = .33 \quad D.W. = 1.08$$
$$\quad\quad\quad (.61) \quad\quad (.52)$$

$$w'_m = .05 + .13 o' - .53 \frac{U}{L} + 1.50 p_I \quad \bar{R}^2 = .92 \quad D.W. = 2.90$$
$$\quad\quad\quad (.22) \quad\quad (.19) \quad\quad (.21)$$

(3d) Single-stage estimate, 1952-63

$$w''_m = .10 - .52 o'' \quad\quad\quad\quad\quad r^2 = .04 \quad D.W. = .46$$
$$\quad\quad\quad (.84)$$

$$w''_m = -.01 + .31\, o'' \qquad\qquad + 2.08\, p_I \qquad \bar{R}^2 = .82 \quad D.W. = 1.72$$
$$\qquad\quad (.36) \qquad\qquad\qquad\quad (.29)$$

$$w''_m = .06 + .12\, o'' - .65\, \frac{U}{L} + 1.71\, p_I \qquad \bar{R}^2 = .94 \quad D.W. = 2.92$$
$$\qquad\quad (.22) \quad\ (.15) \qquad (.19)$$

Equation (4) – Price Equation, 1954-63

(4a) Single-stage estimate

$$p_I = .02 + .379\, w_m - .381\, o \qquad\qquad \bar{R}^2 = .85 \quad D.W. = 2.13$$
$$\qquad\quad (.066) \qquad (.198)$$

$$p_I = .02 + .25\, w_m - .46\, o + .08\, w_g \qquad \bar{R}^2 = .83 \quad D.W. = 1.94$$
$$\qquad\quad (.21) \qquad (.24) \qquad (.13)$$

$$p_I = .02 + .38\, (w_m - o) \qquad\qquad\qquad r^2 = .88$$
$$\qquad\quad (.05)$$

$$p_I = .02 + .35\, (w_m - o) + .03\, w_g \qquad \bar{R}^2 = .83$$
$$\qquad\quad (.10) \qquad\qquad (.07)$$

(4b) Two-stage estimate

$$p_I = .02 + .08\, w_m - .42\, o + .19\, w_g \qquad \bar{R}^2 = .58 \quad D.W. = 2.02$$
$$\qquad\quad (.45) \qquad (.40) \quad\ (.27)$$

$$p_I = .01 + .27\, (w_m - o) + .08\, w_g \qquad \bar{R}^2 = .63 \quad D.W. = 1.90$$
$$\qquad\quad (.18) \qquad\qquad (.13)$$

As was the case in discussing the results of the Lamfalussy model, it may be useful here also to explain the individual equations briefly. The first step of equation (1a) represents Beckerman's export equation (1) and says that x, the rate of change in total Italian exports, depends positively on unity plus the difference between the level of foreign and domestic prices. This slight alteration was made in order to express Beckerman's equation (1) in linear form. In order to take account of the effect of changes in world income as well as relative prices, t_w, the rate of change in total world exports excluding those from Italy, was introduced into equation (1a).

The fact that the constant term was negative in the simple regression results of equation (1a) is of some interest since Beckerman had intended that this term represent the rate of increase in world trade. It is evident, however, that the explicit introduction of the rate of increase in

world trade had a positive and significant effect and improved the fit
of this equation. It thus appeared that both Italy's relative price advantage and the rate of change in world demand were important determinants of the rate of change in total Italian exports.[9] These results, it
may be noted, are consistent with those obtained in estimating the
elasticities of demand for Italy's exports in Chapter 2 above.[10]

Equation (2a) is Beckerman's productivity equation (2) and says
that o, the rate of change in labor productivity, depends positively on
x, the rate of change in exports. While the results of this equation appear plausible, it will be recalled that Beckerman intended that the rate
of change in exports be interpreted as a surrogate measure of the rate
of change in total output. That this is only an approximation at best is
indicated by the fact that in the period 1951-63 the simple correlation between the rate of change in exports and the rate of change in output
was .75 for real GNP and .69 for manufacturing production.

It is also of interest to point out that generally poor results,
which are not reported here, were obtained when the rate of change in
productivity was correlated directly with various formulations of lagged
rates of change in output and in exports and with different measures of
gross investment. In effect, then, the same puzzle concerning the explanation of changes in productivity that emerged in estimating equation
(3) of the Lamfalussy model is still with us.

The first step in equation (3a) represents Beckerman's wage
equation (3) and says that w_m, the rate of change in money wages, depends positively on o, the rate of change in labor productivity. The
second step of equation (3a) contains a measure of the percentage rate
of unemployment, $\frac{U}{L}$. This was introduced in order to test the conten-
tion that the rate of change in wages would vary inversely with the percentage rate of unemployment. The rate of change in prices, p_I, was
introduced in the third step of equation (3a) in order to pick up any remaining general demand influences and certain special factors affecting
wages such as cost-of-living escalator arrangements.

It will be noted that equation (3a) is based upon annual wage and
labor productivity data for workers in industry as prepared and published by the Banca d'Italia. Given that the Banca d'Italia and the Organization for European Cooperation and Development (OECD) also publish
wage and productivity series on a hourly basis for manufacturing alone,
it was thought to be of interest to see what differences, if any, would
result if these series were used. Hence equation (3c) was estimated
using Banca d''Italia data on hourly wages and productivity in manufac-

turing, and equation (3d) was estimated using OECD data.

Looking at the results for these three equations, Beckerman's views concerning the impact of changes in productivity were apparently borne out by equation (3a). In addition, the rate of change in prices turned out to be statistically significant. The level of unemployment had the correct sign but was not statistically significant. In contrast, however, it is evident from equations (3c) and (3d) that Balassa's views concerning unemployment were reinforced. That is, the level of unemployment was statistically significant in both equations together with the rate of change in prices. The rate of change in productivity had the expected sign but was not statistically significant.[11]

We thus have a situation in which the acceptance or rejection of the hypothesis concerning the wage impact of changes in productivity and the existing level of unemployment depends on the data utilized for the statistical analysis. If, as might be argued, both the productivity and unemployment estimates are unreliable, it would seem impossible at the present time to resolve the question of the importance of each factor in the Italian case.[12] In any event, all three estimates provide a clear indication that changes in wages moved in close harmony with changes in the price level, although it is not completely clear here which is cause and which is effect.[13]

Equation (4a) represents Beckerman's price equation (4). It will be recalled from the preceding chapter that Beckerman made an implicit assumption in writing this equation without a coefficient that distributive shares were unchanged. For purposes of the empirical analysis, this equation was estimated in two ways, first with separate coefficients for w and o and then with a single coefficient for (w - o). In addition, a constant term was introduced in order to represent the trend effects on the rate of change in prices of other things besides wages in industry. Finally, there was introduced into the equation a variable, w_g, which measured the change in the average annual compensation of government employees. This was designed to measure the separate influence on the price level of autonomously determined wages in the nonproduction sectors.

The statistical results showed that the coefficients of the rates of change in money wages and labor productivity were each about .38. This was also the case therefore for the coefficient of the difference between these two variables, (w - o). The fact that this coefficient was less than one is indicative of an increase in the share of income going to wages. This seems to be consistent with the limited data available on the wage share, especially after 1959.[14] No improvement was effected in the results by introducing w_g, which turned out to be highly correlated with w_m. The size of the constant term was indicative of the existence of other unspecified forces making for an annual rise of 2 per cent in the rate of change in prices.[15]

When taken individually, the results of equations (1a), (2a), (3a), and (4a) provided some measure of support for the Beckerman model in its amended form. All of these equations, however, were estimated using ordinary single-stage least squares procedures. Since it was clear from the model that the variables in the individual equations were interrelated, it was thought desirable to reestimate the equations in order to take account of the simultaneity involved. Two-stage least squares estimates were thus made of each equation. The results are shown in equations (1b), (2b), (3b), and (4b).

It is evident from these results that the adjustments made for simultaneity by the computation of the two-stage least squares estimates had on the whole a marked effect in reducing the regression coefficients and increasing their standard errors. In deciding whether to use the ordinary or the two-stage least squares estimates, it is important to note that the Beckerman model as a whole was not completely specified. Consequently, the multiple regressions computed to obtain values of the individual endogenous variables for use in the second-stage regressions yielded relatively low R^2's and relatively high standard errors for the coefficients of the exogenous variables.[16] The second-stage estimates were thus bound to turn out poorly and accordingly should be discounted to a great extent.

If the single-stage least squares estimates are accepted, then it may be concluded that the Beckerman model as amended provided a reasonable description of Italy's growth experience from 1954-63. It should be emphasized at the same time, however, that the statistical results were by no means definitive and that the variables of the model were not completely specified. The lack, in particular, of reliable measures of productivity and the inability to specify its determinants posed serious difficulties in interpretation. A final judgment concerning the Beckerman model must be held in abeyance, therefore, pending the availability of better and more complete statistical information and the further clarification of the determinants of changes in productivity.

CONCLUSION

One of the chief drawbacks mentioned in the preceding chapter's discussion of Lamfalussy's model was the highly aggregative character of the model. This drawback was indeed evident in the present chapter insofar as the statistical results of the highly aggregative and simple versions of the individual equations were relatively poor. Somewhat better results were obtained, in contrast, especially for the investment equation, when the focus was on investment in industry and upon variations in capacity utilization. This suggests that it would be fruitful to extend this analysis further in order to determine whether the relationship observed was typical for all or only for some of the important component sectors of Italian manufacturing that contributed significantly to the export expansion of the postwar period.

A more disaggregated approach would also be helpful in adding substance to the Beckerman model. This is the case especially if additional insights can be obtained with regard to the productivity and price determinants in the individual industries whose performance was subsumed in the statistical results presented above.

In the next chapter, therefore, there will be presented a statistical analysis by industry of the changes in exports and imports, the determinants of investment expenditures, and the developments in productivity and prices.

CHAPTER **5** FOREIGN TRADE AND GROWTH
IN MANUFACTURING, 1951-63

We shall pursue in this chapter a more disaggregated approach
to the relations between foreign trade and postwar economic growth in
Italy by concentrating upon the main branches of manufacturing activity.
Our interest will be, in particular, to identify the manufacturing industries which have been important in Italy's foreign trade and, in this
light, to draw attention to some of the economic characteristics which
these industries have displayed in their over-all postwar development.

ITALY'S FOREIGN TRADE IN MANUFACTURES, 1951-63

The composition of Italy's foreign trade in manufactured goods
in the postwar period can be assessed from the sixteen-industry breakdown shown in Table 6. It may be useful in interpreting this table to
single out industries 1-5 as representing the "more traditional" lines
and industries 7-12 the "newer" lines of manufacturing activity subject
to rapid technological change. Thus, the first group consists of foodstuffs, beverages, tobacco, textiles, clothing, shoes, and leather,
while the second group embodies metallurgy, machinery and metal products, vehicles, chemicals and synthetic fibers, and petroleum and
coal derivatives.

Taking 1951-53 as the base for comparison, the more traditional
industries accounted in these years for 44.4 per cent of exports as
against 47.6 per cent for the newer industries. The two groups accounted
individually for the same share of imports, 45.9 per cent. In 1961-63,
however, the shares in exports and imports of the more traditional industries were 32.4 and 28.8 per cent, respectively, as compared to 59.9
and 61.7 per cent for the newer industries. These marked changes in
the industrial composition of Italy's foreign trade can also be illustrated
by the fact that the newer industries accounted for close to 60 per cent
of the absolute increase in exports between 1951-53 and 1961-63 and
more than two-thirds of the absolute increase in imports.

It is of interest to compare the changes in the industrial composition of foreign trade with the changes in value added by industry.

Table 6

Italy: Percentage Distribution of Exports and Imports of
Manufactured Goods (in 1959 Lire) by Industry, 1951–53 and 1961–63

	Percentage Distribution of Exports		Percentage Distribution of Imports	
	Average Value 1951–53	Average Value 1961–63	Average Value 1951–53	Average Value 1961–63
1. Foodstuffs	11.6%	4.8%	19.1%	12.5%
2. Beverages	2.5	1.3	.4	.4
3. Tobacco	.8	.4	.6	.8
4. Textiles	23.5	17.8	22.3	11.7
5. Clothing, shoes, and leather	6.0	8.1	3.5	3.4
6. Furniture and wood	2.0	1.2	3.8	3.2
7. Metallurgy	4.6	4.4	10.6	16.7
8. Machinery and metal products	20.7	22.9	21.4	21.4
9. Vehicles	6.5	11.0	2.6	6.0
10. Stone, clay, and glass products	2.7	2.7	2.1	2.4
11. Chemicals and synthetic fibers	5.4	12.0	5.1	11.9
12. Petroleum and coal derivatives	7.7	6.8	4.1	3.3
13. Rubber	1.6	1.6	.4	.6
14. Paper and paper products	1.1	.5	1.9	3.0
15. Films and printed materials	.3	.8	.1	.2
16. Other manu- factures	3.0	3.7	2.0	2.5
Total	100.0%	100.0%	100.0%	100.0%
Value (Billions of 1959 Lire)	Ł650.1	Ł2,665.5	Ł832.8	Ł2,773.1

Source: Derived from Appendix I, Tables 24–28.

Thus, according to Table 7, the share in value added of the traditional industries was 36.9 per cent in 1951-53 and 28.4 per cent in 1959-61. The observed shift in foreign trade toward the newer industries was therefore reflected in the changing importance of these industries in domestic production. It appears from lines 15 and 16 in Table 7, moreover, that a sizable proportion of the increased contribution during the period of the manufacturing sector to real gross domestic product was attributable to the expansion of the newer industries.

A further indication of the relations between changes in foreign trade and production for individual industries during the period is provided by Table 8. As we would expect, production in the newer industries increased significantly more than for "all manufacturing". The only exception here was machinery and metal products. The converse was true for the traditional industries, except beverages. Looking at exports and production over-all, it is noteworthy that the percentage increase in exports was almost double that in production. This was due in greatest part to the expansion of exports in the newer industries, particularly vehicles and chemicals and synthetic fibers. The export expansion in the traditional industries was in contrast considerably smaller, except for clothing, shoes, and leather. The percentage increases which were equally striking for imports over-all and for the main growth industries will be commented upon below.

It is evident from Table 9 that some important changes took place during the period in the foreign trade orientation of the individual industries. These changes can be seen more clearly from the beginning and end of period ratios of exports to production and imports to production which appear in this table. It should be emphasized that these ratios are only rough approximations. This is because the export and import price indexes used to deflate the value figures had to be estimated for the early years. Also, it should be pointed out that the value of production for each industry was estimated by multiplying the value recorded in the 1959 input-output table by the annual index of manufacturing production for that industry.

In any event, as we would expect from Tables 6-8, the ratios calculated in Table 9 are indicative of some remarkable changes in the foreign trade orientation of individual industries on both the export and import sides. The most striking changes in the export ratios were in textiles; clothing, shoes, and leather; machinery and metal products; vehicles; chemicals and synthetic fibers; rubber; and other manufactures. It thus seems clear that the expansion of these particular industries has been linked significantly with their developments in exports in the postwar period.

Table 7

Italy: Percentage Distribution of Value Added by
Manufacturing Industry, 1951-53 and 1959-61

Industry	1951-53	1959-61
1. Foodstuffs and beverages	17.6%	14.3%
2. Tobacco	1.4	1.0
3. Textiles	13.4	9.5
4. Clothing, shoes, and leather	4.5	3.6
5. Furniture and wood	4.6	4.3
6. Metallurgy	8.6	8.7
7. Machinery, metal products, and vehicles	24.1	29.1
8. Stone, clay, and glass products	3.9	4.4
9. Chemicals and synthetic fibers	10.2	12.4
10. Petroleum and coal derivatives	2.7	3.5
11. Paper	1.9	1.6
12. Rubber	1.8	1.3
13. All other	5.3	6.3
Total[a]	100.0%	100.0%
14. Value added in manufacturing (Billions of current Lire)	Ł3,177	Ł5,652
15. Value added in manufacturing (Billions of 1954 Lire)	2,942	5,711
16. Total gross domestic product (Billions of 1954 Lire)	9,980	15,750
15 ÷ 16	29.5%	36.3%

[a]Based on values in current lire.
Source: Derived from Istituto Nazionale per lo Studio della Congiuntura (ISCO), Quadri della contabilita nazionale italiana per il periodo
1950-1964 (Rome, 1965).

The increases in imports in relation to production noted already
in Table 8 show up clearly also in Table 9. These increases were marked
across all industries with the exception of petroleum and coal derivatives.
What is interesting and important about these changes is that the imports
in question are made up in large measure of intermediate products and
machinery and equipment of various kinds. The intermediate products
imported are of course processed further domestically. They are then
sold at home and in export markets as objects of final demand for con-

Table 8

Italy: Percentage Increases in Production,
Exports, and Imports by Industry, 1951-63

Industry	Percentage Increase, 1951-63[a]		
	Production	Exports	Imports
1. Foodstuffs	69.7%	66.5%	138.7%
2. Beverages	215.8	102.4	296.3
3. Tobacco	53.3	129.3	681.3
4. Textiles	39.6	171.0	130.3
5. Clothing, shoes, and leather	110.1	563.4	439.0
6. Furniture and wood	88.1	108.2	289.9
7. Metallurgy	203.5	354.6	626.4
8. Machinery and metal products	122.4	373.8	486.7
9. Vehicles	394.2	670.5	1,092.4
10. Stone, clay, and glass products	256.2	357.2	650.0
11. Chemicals and synthetic fibers	315.4	1,070.4	925.5
12. Petroleum and coal derivatives	477.1	788.3	179.0
13. Rubber	140.9	311.8	1,164.7
14. Paper and paper products	144.1	- .8	646.4
15. Films and printed materials	171.6[b]	2,184.6	1,114.3
16. Other manufactures	171.6[b]	494.5	508.7
17. All manufacturing	171.6	336.8	364.5

[a]Based upon changes in the indexes of manufacturing production
(1953 = 100) and in the value of exports and imports in 1959 lire.
[b]Assumed to be the same as for "all manufacturing."
Source: Derived from Appendix I, Tables 24-27.

sumption and investment purposes or as more highly processed intermediate goods for input purposes elsewhere in the production process.
By the same token, imports of machinery and equipment for investment purposes serve to expand productive capacities of all kinds to
serve the domestic and foreign markets.

Some indication is given in Table 10 of the relative importance
by industry of use of the manufactured goods imports of various kinds
for 1959. It should be mentioned that the classifications of imports by
sector of origin and sector of use were based upon the 33-sector input-
output table of the Italian economy that was published in early 1965.

Table 9

Italy's Merchandise Exports and Imports by Industry as a
Percentage of Production, 1951-53 and 1961-63

	Exports ÷ Production		Imports ÷ Production	
	Average 1951-53	Average 1961-63	Average 1951-53	Average 1961-63
1. Foodstuffs	4.1%	4.6%	8.8%	12.3%
2. Beverages	17.0	15.8	3.4	4.7
3. Tobacco	7.8	11.9	7.3	22.2
4. Textiles	19.9	45.3	24.4	31.0
5. Clothing, shoes, and leather	5.8	17.9	4.3	7.8
6. Furniture and wood	3.8	5.6	9.1	15.3
7. Metallurgy	7.0	10.3	20.6	40.3
8. Machinery and metal products	10.1	22.6	13.3	21.9
9. Vehicles	9.7	18.8	5.0	10.4
10. Stone, clay, and glass products	6.3	8.7	5.7	8.0
11. Chemicals and synthetic fibers	7.1	17.3	8.7	17.9
12. Petroleum and coal derivatives	21.9	22.2	16.7	11.3
13. Rubber	9.6	17.7	2.9	6.6
14. Paper and paper products	4.9	3.6	10.3	24.9
15. Films and printed materials	.7	4.4	.5	1.4
16. Other manufactures	13.8	29.5	11.9	21.0

Source: Derived from Appendix I, Tables 29 and 30.

Table 10

Percentage Distribution of Italy's Merchandise Imports by Sector of Origin and Use, 1959

| Sector of Origin | Total Manufactures | Sector of Use | | | | Value[a] (Billions of Lire) |
		Other Productive Sectors	Consumption	Gross Investment	Total	
1. Foodstuffs	56.0%	2.7%	41.2%	- %	100.0%	256.4
2. Beverages	24.4	2.9	72.5	.2	100.0	7.8
3. Tobacco	110.5	-	4.3	-22.1	100.0[b]	7.8
4. Textiles	84.0	.2	15.7	-	100.0	64.0
5. Clothing, shoes, and leather	46.8	.4	52.8	-	100.0	26.2
6. Furniture and wood	91.0	6.0	1.7	1.3	100.0	70.2
7. Metallurgy	92.3	7.2	-	.4	100.0	204.7
8. Machinery and metal products	15.2	8.2	11.3	65.2	100.0	332.6
9. Vehicles	29.8	19.2	14.7	36.2	100.0	48.7
10. Stone, clay, and glass products	35.7	27.0	19.7	17.6	100.0	42.9
11. Chemicals and synthetic fibers	79.2	6.4	14.5	-	100.0	188.1
12. Petroleum and coal derivatives	22.1	69.3	8.6	-	100.0	55.2
13. Rubber	55.3	39.9	.8	4.1	100.0	6.6
14. Paper and paper products	76.6	18.6	4.7	-	100.0	59.0
15. Films and printed materials	5.5	18.0	76.5	-	100.0	4.0
16. Other manufactures	16.5	13.3	65.1	5.1	100.0	11.7

[a]Includes indirect taxes on imports. [b]Reflects a 1.7 billion lire reduction in inventories and .6 billion of imports re-exported.

Source: Based upon the 33-sector input-output table in Appendix 2 of Istituto Centrale di Statistica, Primi studi sulle interdi-pendenze settoriali dell'economia italiana (Tavola economica, 1959), Note e Relazioni, No. 27 (Rome, January, 1965).

The sectors of use were aggregated for present purposes into total
manufacturing, other productive sectors, consumption, and investment.

According to Table 10, the main types of imports that went in
large proportion directly into consumption consisted of foodstuffs;
beverages; clothing, shoes, and leather; films and printed materials;
and other manufactures. Nevertheless, fairly substantial amounts of
these imports were in the form of intermediate products intended for
further processing in the manufacturing sector.[1] The chief industries
characterized by intermediate product imports were textiles; furniture
and wood; metallurgy; chemicals and synthetic fibers; rubber; and paper
and paper products.[2] Imports of investment goods were concentrated,
as would be expected, in machinery and metal products and vehicles.[3]

While information is not available for Italy concerning the import content of exports, the data in Tables 8-10 suggest that this content must be fairly important for a substantial number of export industries. This would be all the more true particularly if account is taken
of the importation of capital goods for investment purposes. The relatively high ratios of imports to production observed in Table 9 for
several industries must therefore be viewed in part as a consequence
of the favorable export performance of these same industries as well
as other related ones.

SOME INDIVIDUAL INDUSTRY TESTS OF
AN ACCELERATOR RELATIONSHIP

It will be recalled from the preceding chapter that some evidence of an accelerator relationship was found in testing equation (1e)
of the Lamfalussy model. This was the equation in which the investment ratio, exclusive of investment in dwellings and public administration, was regressed against the rate of change in GNP, an index of
capacity utilization in industry, and the long-term interest rate. It
may also be remembered that in the discussion of the Beckerman model
in Chapter 4, great emphasis was placed upon entrepreneurial expectations concerning demand as a primary determinant of investment. Given
the importance of investment in these models, it was considered interesting and worthwhile in following the more disaggregated approach in
the present chapter to see to what extent investment expenditures could
be explained at the individual industry level. We shall be especially
interested in this regard in those industries which have been observed
to have relatively high ratios of exports to production. The reason for
this is to establish whether exports may have stimulated investment in

these industries.

In approaching this task, one is faced by the existence in the literature of a number of different models purporting to explain investment expenditures in industry. I have chosen the one which Gardner Ackley used in estimating his econometric model of Italian postwar growth. This relationship was of the form:

$$i_t = \alpha y_{t-1} - \beta K_{t-1},$$

where i is net investment, y is sales, and K the capital stock. This is an accelerator type of relationship in which the lagged level of sales (or output) enters positively and the size of the existing capital stock at the beginning of the period negatively into the determination of investment. [4]

The above equation is of course only one possible interpretation of investment and is perhaps subject to the criticism that lagged sales may not be a good proxy for expected future sales which in fact may shape investment decisions. However, if there happens to be a lag in effecting these decisions, the explanation of current investment expenditures which is our object may nevertheless be closely approximated by the use of lagged sales as an explanatory variable. An alternative which would give more explicit consideration to expected future sales is to use a weighted average of lagged and current sales. This is what was done in the present study, as will be noted shortly.

Because data on the existing capital stock were not available by sector, the foregoing equation could not be estimated directly. Fortunately, however, when expressed in first differences, we arrive at a form of the equation which can be estimated with available data on investment. That is, if

$$\Delta i_t = \alpha \Delta y_{t-1} - \beta \Delta K_{t-1} \quad \text{and since } \Delta K_{t-1} = i_{t-1},$$

the equation can be written as:

$$\Delta i_t = \alpha \Delta y_{t-1} - \beta i_{t-1}.$$

This says that the change in current investment expenditures will depend positively upon the change in lagged sales and negatively upon the level of lagged investment expenditures. The equation was not fitted exactly in this form, however, since it was desired to attempt to take expected future sales into account. In the absence of direct information on expectations and thus of the proper lag structure, the basic equation was fitted with three alternative measures of the change in sales:

$$\triangle y_t, \quad (.5 \triangle y_t + .5 \triangle y_{t-1}), \quad \text{and} \quad (.33 \triangle y_t + .67 \triangle y_{t-1}).$$

Also, since information on depreciation was not available, it was necessary to measure the changes in investment on the basis of gross investment.[5]

Since we are interested mainly in the influence of exports on investment and growth in individual industries, the question arises as to why export sales were not distinguished separately in the foregoing relationship. Thus, we could have proceeded from the data underlying Tables 7 and 9 above to obtain estimates of production and exports in constant lire. Assuming inventories to be unchanged for lack of information, domestic sales would simply be the difference between production and exports. The changes in domestic sales and in export sales might accordingly have been introduced into the estimating equation as separate explanatory variables. Unfortunately, however, data on total investment expenditures by individual industries were not available on an annual basis for the period under study. Our procedure for evaluating the influence of export sales on industry investment and growth had perforce to be roundabout.

The only available data that were suitable for our purposes were partial in nature. These data were collected by the Istituto Centrale di Statistica (ISTAT) on a sample basis covering firms in all lines of economic activity for the period 1951-61. The ISTAT sample for individual industries included the largest firms up to the cut-off point, generally, where 50 per cent of the employees in each industry were covered. Firms were included only if they had been in existence continually during the entire period. In addition to the industry totals, the data were broken down according to firms with sales of above and below 1 billion lire in 1958.[6] While ISTAT has published data subsequent to 1961, they were based on a new sample without providing any link with the old sample. It was therefore impossible to bring the data more up to date on a continuous basis.[7]

Some indication of the representativeness of the ISTAT sample can be obtained from Table 11 in which the value added by industry according to the ISTAT sample is shown as a percentage of the total value added for that industry for 1951-53 and 1959-61. The percentage coverage of the ISTAT sample was evidently the smallest in foodstuffs and beverages; clothing, shoes, and leather; and furniture and wood. These are industries in which the average size of firms is, of course, relatively small. But the clothing, shoes, and leather industry con-

Table 11

ISTAT Sample Value Added by Industry as a Percentage of
Total Value Added, 1951-53 and 1959-61

Industry	Average 1951-53	1959-61
1. Foodstuffs and Beverages	20.9%	24.2%
2. Tobacco	80.4	85.3
3. Textiles	58.3	59.9
4. Clothing, shoes, and leather	19.6	21.5
5. Furniture and wood	12.9	13.9
6. Metallurgy	63.0	66.2
7. Machinery, metal products, and vehicles	55.9	54.0
8. Stone, clay, and glass products	58.4	56.4
9. Chemicals and synthetic fibers	50.6	48.8
10. Petroleum and coal derivatives	44.7	30.4
11. Paper	58.7	76.6
12. Rubber	88.9	113.5
13. All other	32.7	32.6
Total manufacturing industry	45.8	47.2

Source: Sample value added data are from Istituto Centrale di Statistica (ISTAT), Il valore aggiunto delle imprese nel periodo 1951-1959, Note e Relazioni, No. 18 (Rome, March, 1962) and Annuario Statistico Italiano. Total value added data are from Istituto Nazionale per lo Studio della Congiuntura (ISCO), Quadri della contabilita nazionale italiana per il periodo 1950-1964 (Rome, 1965).

tains nevertheless a fairly large number of firms that carry on a sizable export business. Thus, the ISTAT data may not be entirely representative to the extent that small-sized firms specializing in production for export were excluded from the sample because they were not in existence continually during the entire 1951-61 period.

The coverage in most of the other major industries was between 50 and 60 per cent at the beginning and end of the sample period. However, the coverage in petroleum and coal derivatives fell from 44.7 to 30.4 per cent. This was due most likely to the expansion of firms that were newly created during the period. The coverage in paper and rubber increased substantially, moreover, by the end of the period. The fact

Table 12

Italy: Percentage Distribution by Industry of
Gross Fixed Investment of ISTAT Sample Firms, 1951-53 and 1959-61

	Average	
Industry	1951-53	1959-61
301. Foodstuffs and beverages	9. 8%	7.6%
302. Tobacco	1. 3	1.0
303. Silk, cotton, and synthetic fiber textiles	6. 7	6.1
304. Woolen textiles	2. 3	1.7
305. Hard fiber and other textiles	2. 2	2.0
306. Clothing and accessories	. 2	.4
307. Shoes	. 2	.1
308. Leather	. 3	.3
309. Furniture	. 1	.1
310. Wood	. 5	.7
311. Metallurgy	22. 6	17.8
312. Nonelectrical machinery and metal products	5. 1	6.3
313. Electrical machinery	2. 4	2.8
314. Precision instruments	. 9	1.6
316. Vehicles	9. 9	13.2
317. Stone, clay, and glass products	4. 6	6.6
318. Chemicals	13. 6	16.1
319. Petroleum and coal derivatives	6. 6	2.4
320. Rubber	2. 0	2.6
321. Synthetic fibers	3. 8	5.2
322. Paper	2. 7	2.4
323. Graphic arts and printed materials	1. 4	2.0
324. Photographs, films, and recordings	. 2	.1
325. Other manufactures	. 6	.9
Total ISTAT sample	100. 0%	100.0%

Gross fixed investment (Billions of
    current lire)

A. ISTAT sample	Ł 263.9	Ł 531.1
B. Total manufacturing and construction	533.3	994.7

Table 12 (cont'd)

Industry	Average 1951-53	1959-61
C. Total gross investment	2,071.7	4,442.0
A ÷ B	49.4%	53.4%
A ÷ C	12.7	12.0

Source: Based on Appendix I, Tables 6 and 31.

that rubber coverage exceeded 100 per cent in 1959-61 was probably due to the inclusion of firms in this industry that should have been in some other industry such as chemicals and synthetic fibers.

The relative importance by industry of the gross fixed investment of the ISTAT sample firms for 1951-53 and 1959-61 is shown in Table 12. The firms covered in the traditional industries (301-308) accounted for 23.0 per cent of the total sample investment in 1951-53 and 19.2 per cent in 1959-61. The corresponding percentages for the firms in the newer industries (311-319 and 321) were 69.5 per cent in 1951-53 and 72.0 in 1959-61. It can be seen from the information shown at the bottom of Table 12 that gross fixed investment by the ISTAT sample firms amounted in 1951-53 to 49.4 per cent of total investment in manufacturing and construction and 12.7 per cent of total investment in all sectors. The comparable percentages for 1959-61 were 53.4 and 12.0.

The foregoing discussion thus gives some idea of the partial nature of the ISTAT sample data and suggests that there may possibly be a question about the representativeness and over-all significance of these data. This is because of the exclusion of the relatively small firms as well as the firms that were newly created and operated on a substantial scale during part of 1951-61. The use of the ISTAT data might be justified, nevertheless, if it is legitimate to assume that the relatively largest firms, in the major industries at least, accounted for most of the export activity. As far as the newly created firms are concerned, their exclusion is not necessarily crucial for our purposes. The reason for this is that their creation might be looked upon as an investment undertaken in response to the favorable home and foreign market conditions extant during the period under study. Thus, if our tests of the accelerator hypothesis hold for the ISTAT sample firms, they might be applicable a fortiori to the newly created firms not covered.

The data used for the analysis are recorded in Tables 31 and 32 of Appendix I. Gross fixed investment, which was given for each industry in current lire in the ISTAT source, was deflated by the GNP implicit price index for investment in industry as a whole. Sales, which were also given for each industry, were deflated by the whole-sale price index corresponding to the particular industry. First, differences were then computed for gross fixed investment and for sales. Weighted first differences were also computed for sales with equal weights given to Δy_t and Δy_{t-1} and weights of .33 to Δy_t and .67 to Δy_{t-1}. This was done for the aforementioned purpose of introducing some element of expectations concerning sales into the relationship. While there were eleven observations in total, the regressions had to be calculated using only nine observations for 1953-61 due to the use of lagged first differences in the sales variable.

Each industry regression was computed in step-wise fashion without a constant term for the three alternative measures of the change in sales.[8] The results are indicated in Table 13 according to the best (or least poor) fit obtained with respect to the three sales variables used. The standard errors are shown beneath their respective regression coefficients, and the coefficients of determination corrected for degrees of freedom are shown in the last column of the table.[9] It will be noted that more industries were identified separately in Table 13 than was the case in the preceding tables in this chapter. This was because the ISTAT data used here were based upon the more disaggregated official industry classification.

The results for foodstuffs and beverages (301) and tobacco (302) were not statistically significant. There was some indication in the textiles industry (303-305) that the sales variable accounted for half or more of the variation in changes in investment. Lagged investment was not significant, although it carried the expected sign in the cases of woolen textiles (304) and hard fiber and other textiles (305).[10] None of the results for the clothing, shoes, and leather industries (306-308) was significant. There was a modest indication of the relationship in the furniture industry (309), but none in the wood industry (310).

The results for the metallurgy industry (311) were suggestive though not significant. What stands out most clearly in the results as a whole is the strong support evidenced for the relationship in nonelectrical machinery and metal products (312),[11] precision instruments (314), and vehicles (316). The results for electrical machinery (313) also certainly looked plausible. The sales variable came through strongly in the chemical industry in the simple regression, but not in the multiple

Table 13

Regression Results for Changes in Gross Fixed Investment
by Manufacturing Industry in Italy, 1953–61

Industry	Δy_t	$(.5\,\Delta y_t + .5\,\Delta y_{t-1})$	$(.33\,\Delta y_t + .67\,\Delta y_{t-1})$	Lagged Investment i_{t-1}	r^2 or $\bar{R}^2$
301. Foodstuffs and beverages			-.05 (.10)	.16 (.21)	.00
302. Tobacco			.10 (.09)	-.11 (.13)	.26
303. Silk, cotton, and synthetic fiber textiles	.09 (.04)				.49
	.09 (.10)			.01 (.11)	.42
304. Woolen textiles			.06 (.02)		.67
			.09 (.03)	-.09 (.08)	.62
305. Hard fiber and other textiles	.25 (.11)			-.32 (.18)	.60
306. Clothing and accessories	.04 (.02)				.16
	.03 (.05)			.04 (.20)	.04
307. Shoes	.00 (.05)			.08 (.20)	.00
308. Leather	.05 (.03)				.25
	.07 (.07)			-.06 (.24)	.12
309. Furniture			.21 (.10)	-.31 (.18)	.50

(cont'd)

Table 13 (cont'd)

		Change in Sales			
Industry	Δy_t	$(.5 \, \Delta y_t + .5 \, \Delta y_{t-1})$	$(.33 \, \Delta y_t + .67 \, \Delta y_{t-1})$	Lagged Investment i_{t-1}	r^2 or $\bar{R}^2$
310. Wood			-.03 (.12)	.12 (.20)	.00
311. Metallurgy			.40 (.23)	-.42 (.32)	.46
312. Nonelectrical machinery and metal products		.34 (.10)		-.46 (.22)	.80
313. Electrical machinery		.23 (.12)		-.58 (.38)	.67
314. Precision instruments			.46 (.11)	-1.36 (.48)	.83
316. Vehicles		.37 (.07)		-.48 (.15)	.86
317. Stone, clay, and glass products		.15 (.05)			.18
		.09 (.19)		.06 (.19)	.09
318. Chemicals		.13 (.04)			.74
		.21 (.19)		-.11 (.27)	.65
319. Petroleum and coal derivatives	.10 (.06)			-.16 (.09)	.51
320. Rubber		.23 (.04)		-.28 (.10)	.88

Table 13 (cont'd)

Industry	Δy_t	Change in Sales		Lagged Investment i_{t-1}	r^2 or $\bar{R}^2$
		$(.5\Delta y_t + .5\Delta y_{t-1})$	$(.33\Delta y_t + .67\Delta y_{t-1})$		
321. Synthetic fibers	.39 (.08)			-.42 (.14)	.91
322. Paper	-.15 (.12)			.25 (.19)	.25
323. Graphic arts and printed materials			.12 (.19)	-.14 (.43)	.00
324. Photographs, films, and recordings	-.23 (.99)			-.05 (.17)	.29
325. Other manufactures			.09 (.11)	-.06 (.29)	.07

regression. Reasonable, though not significant, results were obtained for petroleum and coal derivatives (319). The relationship was also supported strongly in rubber (320) and synthetic fibers (321). None of the remaining results (322-325) was significant.

What is interesting about these results is that the industries in which the accelerator hypothesis was borne out to the greatest extent were in general the ones which according to Tables 7 and 8 realized the most substantial increases in production between 1951 and 1963. These were also the industries which figured importantly in the expansion of Italy's export trade and as was shown in Table 9, experienced sizable increases in the proportion of production that was exported.

Thus, since exports were a rapidly rising component of total sales in a number of industries in which the accelerator hypothesis appeared to work, it seems reasonable to conclude that export sales must have provided a major stimulus to investment and growth in these industries. Since these were the industries, furthermore, which were responsible in large part for the increased share of the manufacturing sector in total gross domestic product, exports can be seen to have played a significant role indeed in Italy's postwar economic growth.

POSTWAR DEVELOPMENTS IN PRODUCTIVITY BY INDUSTRY

If we were to follow the logical development of both the Lamfalussy and Beckerman models, the next step would be an examination of the factors influencing productivity on the individual industry level. Such an investigation was attempted using the ISTAT sample data by industry for 1951-61 and relating changes in output per employee and lagged investment expenditures. However, the results for every industry but one were not statistically significant and thus are not reported here. The lack of success in the preceding chapter in relating productivity and investment in the aggregate was therefore borne out on the individual industry level.

We are fortunately not completely in the dark here due to Graziani's work which was noted in the preceding chapter. Some insights into the development of productivity are available from total productivity indexes that he calculated for individual industries for 1953-59 using the same ISTAT data referred to above in connection with investment expenditures. His results are summarized in Table 14.

It is interesting that in the textiles industry nearly 90 per cent of the increase in value added was attributed to an increase in productivity. The fact that the increase attributed to greater employment was negative means that capital must have been substituted for labor in this industry on a large scale. In the foodstuffs, metal and machinery, and chemical industries, about half of the percentage increase in value added was attributed to an increase in productivity. Wood was clearly the laggard industry in terms of productivity increase.

These total productivity indexes for individual industries have of course the well-known difficulty that the increase in productivity comes out as a residual after allowance is made for the increases in labor and capital inputs. It would of course be of great interest to examine such factors as the improved quality of inputs, economies of scale, improved technology, and changes in organization that may be reflected importantly in the measured productivity residual. But such a task is beyond the scope of the present study. What seems clear in any event is that these factors, as distinguished from the conventionally measured inputs of labor and capital, have been significant in the over-all development especially of the textile, metal and machinery, and chemical industries, all of which have figured importantly in Italy's export trade in the postwar period.

Table 14

Percentage Distribution of the Increase in Value Added by Industry Attributed to Labor, Capital, and the Increase in Productivity, 1953-59

Industry[a]	Increase in Value Added Due to:				Percentage Increase in Value Added
	Greater Number of Employees	New Investment	Increase in Productivity	Total	
Foodstuffs	15.7%	39.6%	44.7%	100.0%	77.6%
Textiles	- 9.3	22.7	86.6	100.0	42.9
Wood	46.9	25.5	27.6	100.0	41.6
Metal and Machinery	11.2	33.6	55.2	100.0	64.9
Chemicals	5.8	46.9	47.3	100.0	73.4

[a]The individual industry components based on the official ISTAT classification as noted in Table 13 were as follows: foodstuffs, 301; textiles, 303-305; wood, 309-310; metals and machinery, 311-316; chemicals, 318-322.

Source: Derived from Augusto Graziani, Sviluppo del mezzogiorno e produttivita delle risorse (University of Naples, Cassa Per Il Mezzogiorno, Centro Edizioni Scientifiche Italiane Napoli, 1964), p. 108.

POSTWAR DEVELOPMENTS IN UNIT LABOR COSTS
AND PRICES BY INDUSTRY

We shall examine in this section the developments in unit labor costs and prices for the individual manufacturing industries. The focus on unit labor costs is for the purpose of identifying on the individual industry level the wage-productivity movements that were so important in the discussion and estimation of the Lamfalussy and Beckerman models on the aggregative level. It will be recalled from Chapter 1 especially that the rapid development of productivity as compared to wages in manufacturing during the period was reflected in a comparative stability of wholesale prices and in a declining of export prices, at least until 1962. What we wish to see now for individual industries are the productivity and price experiences that lay behind the substantial increases in exports which took place in the postwar period.

The ISTAT sample data already described were used for the calculation of unit labor costs in each industry for the period 1951-61. Wages per employee were calculated for this purpose by dividing expenditures on personnel by the number of employees. Production was computed as the algebraic sum of the data given for net sales and inventory change and was then divided by the number of employees to obtain production per employee. The division of wages per employee by production per employee thus yielded unit labor costs for each industry. The wholesale, export, and import price indexes for 1951-63 were taken without change from regularly published ISTAT sources with the exception of the early years which had to be estimated in part.

Before proceeding with the discussion in detail, it is worthwhile to reiterate the imperfections in the data used. We have already discussed the problems of coverage of the ISTAT sample data. The point made earlier that the analysis is not seriously handicapped by the exclusion of firms that were newly created during the 1951-61 period applies in the present context as well. That is, if we observe substantial reductions in industry unit labor costs for the ISTAT sample firms, it would be reasonable to expect that the same or perhaps even greater reductions would be typical of the newly created firms which could take advantage of the most up-to-date methods of production.

Problems of coverage and representativeness are also at issue in the construction of the wholesale, export, and import price indexes. This is especially the case in machinery and vehicles where a meaningful price index poses grave difficulties in formulation and interpretation. These indexes will have to suffice for present purposes, however, since no better ones are available.

All the data expressed on the base 1953 = 100 are listed in Tables 10, 26, 27, and 34 of Appendix I and are depicted in Appendix III on semilogarithmic graphs. In discussing these graphs it may be useful to divide the industries, as we did before, into the more traditional (301-310) and the newer lines (311-321) of production.

Considering first the traditional industries, it is evident that unit labor costs remained either close to the base value or tended to rise in foodstuffs and beverages (301); tobacco (302); woolen textiles (304); clothing and accessories (306); and furniture and wood (309 and (310). These costs fell in contrast in cotton and silk textiles (303); hard fiber and other textiles (305); shoes (307); and leather (308). Wholesale prices were comparatively steady or rose somewhat for all of the industries, except leather.

The export price index for foodstuffs, beverages, and tobacco decreased between 1953 and 1956, rose slightly in 1957, and remained thereafter more or less unchanged. Export prices for textiles showed a marked and continuous drop throughout the period except for 1963, while those for clothing, shoes, and leather fell steadily after 1956. The export price index for furniture and wood rose during this period in contrast to all of the others noted.

The import price index for foodstuffs, beverages, and tobacco fluctuated slightly, for the most part, around the base value, except for 1963 when it increased. The fact that import prices of textiles declined sharply is noteworthy especially since, as noted above, a substantial proportion of textiles imports consisted of intermediate product inputs used in the textile industry itself. The import price index of clothing, shoes, and leather was steady for most of the period, but fell considerably in 1962-63, while that for furniture and wood increased above the base level after 1954 and remained relatively high.

It is difficult to draw conclusions concerning unit labor costs and prices for these industries in view of the relatively small coverage of the ISTAT data (especially for foodstuffs and beverages, clothing, shoes, and tobacco, and furniture and wood) and in view of the fact that these data excluded firms that were created after 1951. In any event, there did not appear to be much relationship between unit labor costs and prices of foodstuffs. The downward movement of unit labor costs in shoes and leather showed up to some extent in wholesale prices and also in export prices. The tendency for higher unit labor costs in furniture and wood was fairly closely reflected in higher wholesale and import prices. The decline in unit labor costs in textiles was reflected somewhat in wholesale prices but perhaps more so in the very substantial decline in export prices. It is noteworthy that the downward movement of both export and import prices diverged considerably from the wholesale price of textiles after 1959.

Turning to the newer lines of industry, unit labor costs fell substantially in metallurgy (311); precision instruments (314); vehicles (316); and synthetic fibers (321). These costs fell moderately in non-electrical and electrical machinery (312 and 313); stone, clay, and glass products (317); and chemicals (318). There was some tendency for unit labor costs to rise in the firms covered in petroleum and coal derivatives (319), while there was relatively little movement in rubber (320) until 1959, after which time costs fell considerably.

The wholesale and import price indexes for metallurgy moved closely together, while the export price index was on the whole unchanged after 1954. Similarity in the upward movements of the wholesale and import price indexes for machinery and metals was also evident. The export price index moved downward in contrast from 1953 to 1958 but rose somewhat thereafter. It can be seen that the wholesale and export price indexes for vehicles both moved downward until 1956 and fluctuated around this level in subsequent years, whereas the import price index, except for the sharp and probably aberrant increase in 1957, fluctuated around the base period level.

The wholesale price index for stone, clay, and glass products stayed close to the base level until 1961 and then increased, whereas the export price index fell sharply after 1957. The import price index fluctuated more or less steadily around the base value. In chemicals, the wholesale price index moved down somewhat during the period, whereas there was a truly remarkable fall in the export and import price indexes. The wholesale price index for petroleum and coal derivatives increased from 1953-57 and then fell slightly in contrast to the fairly substantial declines which took place in both the export and import price indexes. In rubber, the wholesale price index moved moderately downward as compared to upward trends in export and import prices. The fairly substantial decline in the wholesale prices of synthetic fibers was generally reflected in the export price index and to a lesser extent in the import price index.

As far as unit labor costs and prices were concerned, the most pronounced downward relationships between unit labor costs and export prices were evidenced in vehicles; chemicals; and synthetic fibers. The relationships were more ambiguous in machinery and metals;

stone, clay, and glass products; and petroleum and coal derivatives.
It is especially worth noting that as compared to the wholesale price
indexes, there was a substantially greater decline in the export prices
of vehicles; stone, clay, and glass products; chemicals; petroleum and
coal derivatives; and synthetic fibers. Thus it appears that unit labor
costs were sometimes but not always a reliable indicator of price movements, while wholesale prices did not in some cases accurately reflect
the direction of movements in export prices and in other cases did not
fall by anywhere near the same magnitude as export prices. [12]

We can conclude from the foregoing discussion and the data por-
trayed in the figures in Appendix III that the industries which contributed significantly to the expansion of exports exhibited in most cases
significant declines in their unit labor costs and export prices in the
period under study. The increase which was noted earlier in this chapter in the export dependence of these industries can thus be seen to have
been firmly grounded in the productivity increases and associated improvements in price competitiveness which these industries experienced.

CONCLUSION

The focus in this chapter has been on the foreign trade and
growth experience of individual manufacturing industries in the postwar
period. It was shown first that there were marked changes in the industrial composition of Italy's foreign trade in favor of the newer industries. Among these industries were metallurgy; machinery and metal
products; vehicles; chemicals and synthetic fibers; and petroleum and
coal derivatives. Although the relative importance of textiles, taken
to be one of the traditional industries, decreased during the period, it
remained nevertheless as one of the major industries on both the export
and import sides.

It was next shown that the newer industries increased significantly
their share in total value added in manufacturing during the period. The
shifts in the industrial composition of foreign trade were thus a reflec-
tion of comparable shifts in the industrial composition of domestic production. It was shown further that production in the newer industries
increased, in general, substantially more than the average for all industries, while the converse was true for the traditional industries. The
over-all increase in exports during the period was about double that in pro-
duction--due in great measure to the expansion of exports in the newer
industries. A pronounced increase took place therefore in the foreign
trade orientation of individual industries during the period. This was

seen expecially clearly in the beginning and end-of-period ratios of
exports to production and imports to production that were calculated.

The fact that the ratio of imports to production in several industries increased as much as, and in some cases more than, the export
ratio was explained mainly by the interdependence between imports and
exports. That is, imports in many industries consisted of intermediate
product inputs and of capital goods for use and investment in industries
that were reliant upon export markets as well as upon the home market.
In other words, the import content of exports was judged to be important in many industries.

Indirect evidence of the stimulus provided to investment expenditures by export sales was furnished by the results of the tests of an
accelerator hypothesis for individual industries. The equation tested
was one in which changes in investment expenditures were to be explained by changes in sales and lagged investment. Statistically significant results were obtained for the majority of the industries that
contributed significantly to exports in the postwar period. It was concluded therefore that, data limitations notwithstanding, exports were
an important stimulus to investment and thus to the growth of these industries in the period under study. Moreover, since these were the
industries that contributed significantly to the increased share of manufacturing in Italy's gross domestic product in the postwar period, it
would appear in this light that the role of exports in the growth of the
Italian economy was a notable one indeed.

No direct relationship was found between investment and the
change in output per man at the individual industry level. This finding
was similar to the one reached in examining this relationship in the
aggregate in the preceding chapter. That the increases in productivity
in individual industries may thus have been due in large measure to
factors other than investment was consistent with the findings of Graziani
that were noted in Table 14. The investigation of these productivity
determinants which are reflected in the residuals in Graziani's indexes
would certainly be worthwhile.

The experiences of individual industries with regard to their
unit labor costs and prices, which were examined at some length, disclosed significant declines in unit labor costs and export prices in a
number of the important export industries. It was also shown in several cases that export prices declined more and at times moved in a
divergent manner as compared to wholesale prices.

The general conclusion which can be drawn therefore from the evidence presented in this chapter is that the growth of the manufacturing sector and of the important manufacturing industries in Italy was closely linked with the involvement of these industries in foreign trade in the postwar period. This was evident from the examination of the foreign trade and production relationships and the behavior of investment in individual industries. It can be inferred, furthermore, from the developments in the productivity and prices of these industries that their foreign trade performance had a solid foundation in improvements in their price competitiveness.

CHAPTER 6 CONCLUSIONS

Having examined at some length in the preceding two chapters the question of whether exports can be assigned a special role in post-war Italian economic growth, it seems fitting to consider our findings within the broader context of the discussion in Chapters 1 and 3 especially.

It will be recalled from Chapter 1 that even though we concentrated our attention on the statistical record of Italian growth from 1950 onward, the years immediately preceding were very special and important in nature. This was because the authorities had on the whole succeeded by 1950 with their policies to stabilize the domestic economy and reconstitute the stock of official foreign-exchange reserves. Were this not accomplished, the growth performance of the 1950's would certainly have been much less impressive. As things turned out, these policies were continued with apparently considerable success until the beginning of the 1960's, when Italy in effect reached conditions approaching full employment. At this time (1962-63), inflation and balance-of-payments difficulties appeared on a significant scale for the first time in the postwar period.

Following the introduction of restrictive domestic policies in 1963, the growth of the economy was sharply curtailed in 1964 and continued more or less unchanged at this rate in 1965. Since Italy's experience before 1963 thus appears to be qualitatively and quantitatively different from that after 1963, it may be fruitful for analytical purposes to treat the individual periods separately. It will be remembered in this regard that we focused in our discussion in Chapter 1 on a number of factors which were important in explaining Italy's unusual growth from 1950-63.

The first of these factors noted was the freeing of substantial amounts of resources for domestic use following World War II as a consequence of reduced Government expenditures that were made possible by cutbacks in military, colonial, and debt servicing requirements. This strengthened both the balance of payments and the domestic economy since nonessential imports could be reduced and wartime excess capacity diverted to serve domestic and export markets. A second important

development was the liberalization of foreign trade which took place
in Italy and in the other industrial countries. This had the effect, together with the growth of foreign incomes, of encouraging Italy's export expansion. At the same time, Italy's own import liberalization
exposed her domestic economy to widespread competition in manufacturing industries especially.

It was next emphasized that the rapid postwar growth was predicated on an elastic supply of labor. The increase of employment opportunities in the industrial and tertiary sectors made possible the
absorption of large numbers of the new labor force entrants as well as
workers from agriculture and from the ranks of the unemployed. Wage
increases were thus moderate throughout the period until 1962-63.
There was also substantial evidence of technological progress which
was made possible in the process of converting to a peacetime economy
and in the development of completely new lines of production. The
importance of the manufacturing sector thus increased substantially
and there were clear indications of significant rises in productivity.

The important factors in Italy's postwar development until the
beginning of the 1960's thus stemmed from the combination of favorable
domestic and foreign demand conditions with an elastic labor supply
and a large, comparatively untapped reservoir of technological opportunities. As we have noted, this development would have been far less
impressive were it not for the success realized in the implementation
of policies designed to achieve monetary stabilization and to build up
the level of official foreign-exchange reserves. Distributional factors
were also very important since substantial savings were needed to help
finance the growing investment demands. It was a remarkable achievement indeed that such rapid growth could be achieved over more than a
decade without any major disturbances to domestic stability and the
balance of payments.

It was shown in Chapter 1 and especially in Chapter 2 that in
considerable measure the large increase in exports during the postwar
period could be attributed to an improvement in Italy's international
competitive position in terms of price as well as nonprice factors.
The question for analysis then was to determine the extent and the process by which these developments in exports were linked to domestic
economic growth. The way chosen to deal with this question was to
set the analysis in the framework suggested by recent contributions in
the literature that have stressed the idea of "export-led" growth.

Of the three models which were examined in Chapter 3, only

Lamfalussy's provided a fairly explicit statement of the important relationships which the foregoing discussion suggested. It will be recalled
that Lamfalussy assumed in his model that trade liberalization was
occurring at home and abroad and that governments were striving to
promote full employment and to stimulate growth without inflation and
external disequilibrium. Under the circumstances of rising domestic
income and imports, export expansion was crucial if external imbalance
was to be avoided. If exports were not expanded sufficiently, government policies of restraint would be needed. Such restrictive policies
might well have an adverse effect on domestic employment and the rate
of growth. External equilibrium or, better yet, an external surplus was
therefore desirable since expansionist domestic policies could be pur-
sued particularly with regard to investment.

Lamfalussy also considered the possibility that exports might
stimulate investment because of accelerator effects. Internal demand
might thus be increased, and productive capacity and productivity expanded as well. Given foreign unit labor costs and relatively elastic
labor market conditions at home, the increase in productivity would
lead to an improvement in the given country's international competitive
position. So long as the increase in exports was sustained and wage increases moderated, the country would be able to maintain its international competitive position and its rapid rate of economic growth.

The Lamfalussy model thus appeared to contain most of the
elements which the previous discussion suggested were important in
Italy's postwar growth experience. The next object then was to determine if the facts of Italy's growth experience were consistent with the
relationships hypothesized in the model. Since it was Lamfalussy's intention that his model be used to elucidate mainly theoretical matters, it
was necessary to make a number of adaptations in it and to introduce
additional variables for purposes of empirical investigation.

The attempt to fit Italian data to Lamfalussy's basic model was
unsuccessful on the whole. This was apparently due to the level of aggregation of the model, the particular ways in which his equations were
formulated, and the absence of data--especially on productivity and its
determinants. Some improvements in the estimations were effected in
the investment equation by introducing a flexible accelerator and in the
savings and export and import equations by considering other variables.
But the investigation was stymied because no satisfactory explanation
of the rate of change in productivity could be obtained. It was concluded
therefore that the results of the statistical estimations of the Lamfalussy
model were rather limited with respect to explaining the Italian postwar
growth experience.

In contrast to the Lamfalussy model, the model developed by Beckerman was less explicit on the role of exports in the growth process. Rather than focusing on the usual macroeconomic relationships involving savings, investment, and the balance of payments, Beckerman chose to concentrate more directly on the interdependencies involving exports, relative prices, productivity, and wages. The relations involving exports and the balance of payments and exports and the rate of economic growth were thus only implicit in Beckerman's model. The productivity and wage relationships occupied a central position in his model, however, just as they did in the Lamfalussy model.

Briefly stated, Beckerman's model stressed the importance of confident expectations concerning the prospects for home and foreign demand as providing the framework in which rapid economic growth would occur. Entrepreneurs were motivated under such conditions to expand investment and to undertake activities designed to increase productivity. If a given country had a favorable initial position with respect to its international competitiveness, its economic growth could be sustained and perhaps increased by virtue of its investments and increases in productivity. So long as productivity increased faster than wages, the given country's international competitive position would be improved and hence it would experience significantly more rapid growth as compared to countries in a less favorable competitive position.

As was the case with Lamfalussy's model, it was also necessary to amend the Beckerman model in a number of different ways for purposes of empirical analysis. The single stage least squares estimates of the individual amended equations turned out on the whole to provide a reasonable approximation to Italy's growth experience from 1954-63, which was the period for which comparable data were available. These results were by no means definitive, however, due to certain unresolved statistical problems and inadequate specifications and data especially for productivity and its determinants. We thus ran again into the same stumbling block on which the estimation of the Lamfalussy model foundered.

One of the chief drawbacks which was noted in discussing and estimating the Lamfalussy model was its highly aggregative character. Since more plausible results were obtained for the investment equation in particular by focusing upon investment in industry and variations in industry capacity utilization, this suggested that further disaggregation might be useful. Disaggregation also seemed fruitful in the case of the Beckerman model as a means of getting at the productivity and price determinants in the individual manufacturing industries. Chapter 5 was devoted therefore to an analysis of the foreign trade and growth experience of individual industries in the postwar period.

It was observed first in Chapter 5 that there was a marked shift in the industrial composition of Italy's foreign trade in the post-war period toward the newer industries that were subject to rapid technological development. These included such industries as metallurgy; machinery and metal products; vehicles; chemicals and synthetic fibers; and petroleum and coal derivatives. It was then established that the contribution of these industries to total value added in manufacturing increased significantly during the period. Since exports from these industries expanded, in general, considerably more than production, there was a substantial increase in their foreign trade orientation as measured by the ratio of exports to production and of imports to production. This latter increase was considered in large part to reflect the relatively high import content of exports.

One of the basic hypotheses of the export-led growth models was that investment depended upon changes in demand, both home and foreign. This hypothesis was tested at the individual industry level by relating changes in investment expenditures to changes in sales and lagged investment. It was noteworthy that statistically significant results were obtained for most of the industries that contributed importantly to the postwar expansion in exports. It was concluded, therefore, that exports were important in stimulating investment and growth in these industries. Finally, since the contribution of these industries had resulted in an increased share of manufacturing in total gross domestic product, there seemed little doubt of the important role that exports played in stimulating Italy's over-all economic growth in the postwar period.

Attempts to explain the observed changes in productivity at the individual industry level on the basis of investment expenditures were unsuccessful. This corroborated the same lack of success experienced in the more highly aggregative estimations noted earlier. It was concluded, therefore, that factors other than investment were responsible in large part for the increases in productivity in individual industries and in the aggregate. The examination, finally, of unit labor costs and prices showed significant declines in these costs and in export prices in a number of the important export industries. It thus appeared that the foreign trade performance of these industries was solidly grounded in improvements in their price competitiveness.

The results of Chapter 5 seem clearly to have established the

importance of exports in shaping the structure and development of
Italy's manufacturing industries in the postwar period. These results
are indicative, therefore, of the need for disaggregation to approximate
more closely the relationships which the more highly aggregative
models suggested. There is an additional need, moreover, to deal
with one of the major problems which the present study has left unresolved. This has to do with the factors determining changes in productivity. This problem is of course not a unique one posed by the present
study. It has been given considerable attention in recent years by theo-
rists and empirical researchers, but thus far our knowledge is seriously
incomplete. New theoretical developments and better data on measured
productivity will hopefully reduce our area of ignorance before too long.

In concentrating our attention mainly on the period ending in
1963, it will be recalled that it was in this year that the cumulative inflationary pressures became serious and that a sizable deficit occurred
in Italy's balance of payments. As the monetary restraint introduced in
1963 became more widely felt and expectations became less favorable,
the rate of increase in domestic economic activity dropped considerably
in 1964 and 1965 as compared to earlier years. This resulted in 1964
in a reduction in imports, and in 1965 imports were slightly below the
level of the preceding year. But fortunately exports increased considerably both in 1964 and 1965, as did net receipts on services and capital
flows. The balance of payments thus moved into substantial surplus
in these years.

How do these events of recent years fit into the models of export-led growth that have been discussed? The inflationary pressures
and balance-of-payments difficulties could be interpreted by means of
Lamfalussy's balance-of-payments equation (4) via the impact on the
rate of increase in domestic wages. In the simple model, the balance-
of-payments effect would impart a diminished or perhaps even a negative influence upon the rate of economic growth. The slowdown in 1964
and 1965 could be interpreted especially through the investment equation (1) and the productivity equation (3). The balance-of-payments improvement noted would appear in equation (4). The net outcome for the
rate of growth would thus reflect the weakened investment effect and
the strengthened balance-of-payments effect. If one looks at the actually
recorded rates of increase in GNP in 1964 and 1965, the export stimulus was of obvious importance as compared to investment, which actually fell in absolute terms in 1964.

The fact that the Lamfalussy model can be interpreted so as to
incorporate these recent events is an indication of the model's interest
and relevancy from a theoretical point of view. But as we have shown,

since most of the essential relationships of the model are oversimplified or unclear on both theoretical and empirical grounds, the model would thus have to be considerably expanded and clarified in order to be of greater use in the analysis of economic growth.

We have seen that in contrast to the Lamfalussy model which is an explicit model of economic growth, the Beckerman model focuses more directly on the interrelationships involving the rates of change of exports, productivity, wages, and the price level. Since investment, saving, and the balance of payments enter into the Beckerman model only indirectly, it is therefore not possible to determine in this model the rate of economic growth. It is also important to note that if exports and domestic output do not move together, the Beckerman model may conceivably yield misleading results as far as growth is concerned.

These gaps in the Beckerman model are serious, for our purpose, in the sense that the model does not provide a completely satisfactory interpretation of the events of recent years. One could say that the inflationary forces of 1963 were represented in an increase in money wages that was in excess of productivity and that Italy's exports thus became less competitive. But this fails to take into account the changes in the distribution of income in favor of wages which resulted in an increase in demand both for domestic goods and imports. It was perhaps more this latter factor rather than the supposed decline in competitiveness per se that created the balance-of-payments difficulties in 1963.

The slowdown of 1964 and 1965 also does not fit well into the Beckerman model. This is because the increase in competitiveness and therefore in exports in these years was due in considerable part to a weakening in home demand and a shift, therefore, by producers from domestic sales to export sales. Thus, one of the basic assumptions of Beckerman's productivity equation (2) was not fulfilled in that the rate of change in exports could not be taken as a proxy for the rate of change in total output in 1964 and 1965. Growth in these years was in fact sustained in part by exports, although at significantly lower levels than previously. But this growth was not "export-led," at least in the sense that Beckerman's model would have it.

The data available in the first quarter of 1966 indicated that the rate of economic activity had picked up noticeably in Italy at the end of 1965 after nearly a two-year lull. The relatively substantial balance-of-payments surpluses of 1964 and 1965 should therefore provide the authorities, just as in the 1950's, with some freedom from external constraints and hence permit them to encourage more rapid domestic expansion than might otherwise be possible. It is unlikely, however, that Italy will be able to sustain, for any extended period of time, rates of growth comparable to those of the 1950's. The main reason for this is that labor resources available for employment in the industrial sector are now in much more limited supply than was formerly the case. In order for rapid growth to occur, the orientation of investment in industry would have to become more labor-saving in character and further advantage would have to be taken of unexploited technological and organizational improvements. It might therefore be possible in these ways to compensate for the limitations on labor supply.

There is no way of predicting whether these changes can be made readily and therefore if, after a two-year pause, Italy will continue again to grow rapidly on the basis of a strong export performance. Much may depend, moreover, on what happens in the other industrial countries with which Italy competes in foreign trade. It is quite possible, in other words, that factor availabilities and increases in productivity may become more favorable elsewhere than in Italy. If this indeed happens, Italy's postwar economic growth until 1963, which was stimulated importantly by its export trade, will go down in history as a truly remarkable performance, but one that it may not necessarily be able to repeat--at least in the near future.

APPENDIXES

APPENDIX I

STATISTICAL APPENDIX

Table 1

Italy: National Product and Expenditure at Current Prices, 1950-64
(Billions of Lire)

	1950	1951	1952	1953	1954	1955	1956	1957	1958	1959	1960	1961	1962	1963	1964
1. Private consumption	6,206	7,047	7,651	8,343	8,655	9,213	9,885	10,428	10,908	11,356	12,235	13,305	15,006	17,543	18,918
2. Public consumption	973	1,183	1,431	1,475	1,620	1,785	2,024	2,156	2,447	2,649	2,896	3,175	3,645	4,536	5,115
3. Gross-fixed-capital formation	1,527	1,860	2,101	2,254	2,454	2,750	3,046	3,434	3,481	3,786	4,441	5,099	5,846	6,641	6,525
4. Changes in stocks	123	223	- 10	30	35	190	105	84	95	149	305	295	300	225	150
5. Exports of goods and services	972	1,287	1,186	1,406	1,530	1,722	1,998	2,450	2,521	2,801	3,411	3,908	4,357	4,845	5,559
6. Total use of resources	9,801	11,600	12,359	13,508	14,294	15,660	17,058	18,552	19,452	20,741	23,288	25,782	29,154	33,790	36,267
7. Imports of goods and services	1,033	1,437	1,569	1,677	1,678	1,853	2,173	2,560	2,338	2,451	3,351	3,760	4,365	5,461	5,317
8. Gross national product at market prices	8,768	10,163	10,790	11,831	12,616	13,807	14,885	15,992	17,114	18,290	19,937	22,022	24,789	28,329	30,950
9. Gross domestic product at factor cost[a] of which:	7,728	8,928	9,439	10,496	11,090	12,134	12,997	14,002	15,013	15,961	17,497	19,211	21,621	24,491	27,051
10. Agriculture, forestry, and fishing	2,234	2,332	2,352	2,678	2,666	2,820	2,736	2,837	3,011	3,033	2,993	3,297	3,668	3,797	3,964
11. Mining and quarrying	84	101	112	116	132	154	181	195	184	189	195	200	200	210	
12. Manufacturing	2,428	3,114	3,113	3,305	3,503	3,816	4,064	4,362	4,602	4,987	5,668	6,300	7,043	8,096	
13. Construction	240	306	399	534	632	756	837	978	1,072	1,177	1,276	1,430	1,711	1,966	
14. Public utilities	673	761	861	959	1,033	1,141	1,260	1,339	1,413	1,513	1,717	1,891	2,123	2,401	
15. Other (commerce, banking, public administration, and miscellaneous services)	2,069	2,314	2,602	2,904	3,124	3,447	3,919	4,291	4,731	5,062	5,648	5,993	6,876	8,021	

aNet of adjustments for duplications for the industry groups. bPartly estimated.

Sources: Organization for European Cooperation and Development, Statistics of National Accounts, 1951-1961 (Paris, 1964); Istituto Centrale di Statistica, Annuario statistico italiano (various issues); and Banca d'Italia, Assemblea generale ordinaria dei participanti, Anno 1964 (LXXI) (Rome, 1965).

Table 2

Italy: National Product and Expenditure at 1954 Prices, 1950-64
(Billions of Lire)

	1950	1951	1952	1953	1954	1955	1956	1957	1958	1959	1960	1961	1962	1963	1964
1. Private consumption	7,223	7,563	7,865	8,469	8,655	8,982	9,333	9,707	9,953	10,492	11,211	12,078	12,963	14,174	14,514
2. Public consumption	1,127	1,270	1,474	1,481	1,620	1,666	1,776	1,850	2,081	2,160	2,293	2,405	2,561	2,858	2,890
3. Gross-fixed-capital formation	1,729	1,890	2,095	2,265	2,454	2,706	2,927	3,196	3,241	3,568	4,122	4,634	5,046	5,342	4,844
4. Changes in stocks	133	212	- 10	30	35	189	103	81	95	158	319	307	298	221	147
5. Exports of goods and services	1,027	1,143	1,127	1,397	1,530	1,732	1,942	2,379	2,474	2,884	3,430	3,996	4,421	4,708	5,225
6. Total use of resources	11,239	12,078	12,551	13,642	14,294	15,275	16,081	17,213	17,844	19,262	21,375	23,420	25,289	27,303	27,620
7. Imports of goods and services	1,160	1,234	1,396	1,637	1,678	1,814	2,058	2,310	2,285	2,511	3,437	3,967	4,560	5,523	5,197
8. Gross national product at market prices	10,079	10,844	11,155	12,005	12,616	13,461	14,023	14,903	15,559	16,751	17,938	19,453	20,729	21,780	22,423
9. Gross domestic product at factor cost[a] of which:	8,724	9,471	9,758	10,712	11,090	11,847	12,315	12,882	13,671	14,635	15,718	16,897	17,837[b]	18,721[b]	
10. Agriculture, forestry, and fishing	2,391	2,502	2,551	2,848	2,666	2,830	2,782	2,774	3,134	3,217	3,055	3,281	3,314	3,242	
11. Mining and quarrying	67	82	99	117	132	158	206	231	237	253	267	284	285	272	
12. Manufacturing	2,452	2,802	2,872	3,153	3,503	3,818	4,063	4,344	4,508	5,041	5,755	6,336	6,957	7,520	
13. Construction	284	353	451	556	632	700	731	822	882	968	1,012	1,108	1,208	1,267	
14. Public utilities	776	867	910	974	1,033	1,107	1,169	1,219	1,279	1,343	1,486	1,613	1,741	1,875	
15. Other (commerce, banking, public administration, and miscellaneous services)	2,754	2,865	2,875	3,064	3,124	3,234	3,364	3,492	3,631	3,813	4,143	4,275[b]	4,332[b]	4,545[b]	

[a]Net of adjustments for duplication for the industry groups. [b]Partly estimated.
Sources: Same as Table 1.

Table 3

Italy: Percentage Distribution of National Product and Expenditure at 1954 Prices, 1950-64

	1950	1951	1952	1953	1954	1955	1956	1957	1958	1959	1960	1961	1962	1963	1964
1. Private consumption	71.7%	69.7%	70.5%	70.5%	68.6%	66.7%	66.6%	65.1%	64.0%	62.6%	62.5%	62.1%	62.5%	65.1%	64.7%
2. Public consumption	11.2	11.7	13.2	12.3	12.8	12.4	12.7	12.4	13.4	12.9	12.8	12.4	12.4	13.1	12.9
3. Gross-fixed-capital formation	17.2	17.4	18.8	18.9	19.5	20.1	20.9	21.4	20.8	21.3	23.0	23.8	24.3	24.5	21.6
4. Change in stocks	1.3	2.0	- .1	.2	.3	1.4	.7	.5	.6	.9	1.8	1.6	1.4	1.0	.7
5. Exports of goods and services	10.2	10.5	10.1	11.6	12.1	12.9	13.8	16.0	15.9	17.2	19.1	20.5	21.3	21.6	23.3
6. Total use of resources	111.5	111.4	112.5	113.6	113.3	113.5	114.7	115.5	114.7	115.0	119.1	120.4	122.0	125.3	123.1
7. Imports of goods and services	-11.5	-11.4	-12.5	-13.6	-13.3	-13.5	-14.7	-15.5	-14.7	-15.0	-19.1	-20.4	-22.0	-25.3	-23.1
8. Gross national product at market prices	100.0%	100.0%	100.0%	100.0%	100.0%	100.0%	100.0%	100.0%	100.0%	100.0%	100.0%	100.0%	100.0%	100.0%	100.0%
9. Gross domestic product at factor cost of which:	100.0%	100.0%	100.0%	100.0%	100.0%	100.0%	100.0%	100.0%	100.0%	100.0%	100.0%	100.0%	100.0%	100.0%	
10. Agriculture, forestry, and fishing	27.4	26.4	26.1	26.6	24.0	23.9	22.6	21.5	22.9	22.0	19.4	19.4	18.6	17.3	
11. Mining and quarrying	.8	.9	1.0	1.1	1.2	1.3	1.7	1.8	1.7	1.7	1.7	1.7	1.6	1.5	
12. Manufacturing	28.1	29.6	29.4	29.4	31.6	32.2	33.0	33.7	33.0	34.4	36.6	37.5	39.0	40.2	
13. Construction	3.3	3.7	4.6	5.2	5.7	5.9	5.9	6.4	6.5	6.6	6.4	6.6	6.8	6.8	
14. Public utilities	8.9	9.2	9.3	9.1	9.3	9.3	9.5	9.5	9.4	9.2	9.5	9.5	9.8	10.0	
15. Other (commerce, banking, public administration, and miscellaneous services)	31.6	30.2	29.5	28.6	28.2	27.3	27.3	27.1	26.6	26.1	26.4	25.3	24.3	24.3	

Source: Derived from Table 2.

125

Table 4

Italy: Annual Rates of Change in National Product and Expenditure at 1954 Prices, 1951-64

	1951	1952	1953	1954	1955	1956	1957	1958	1959	1960	1961	1962	1963	1964
1. Private consumption	4.7%	4.0%	7.7%	2.2%	3.8%	3.9%	4.0%	2.5%	5.4%	6.9%	7.7%	7.3%	9.3%	2.4%
2. Public consumption	12.7	16.1	.5	9.4	2.8	6.6	4.2	12.5	3.8	6.2	4.9	6.5	11.6	1.1
3. Gross-fixed-capital formation	9.3	10.8	8.1	8.3	10.3	8.2	9.2	1.4	10.1	15.5	12.4	8.9	5.9	- 9.3
4. Change in stocks	59.4	-104.7	400.0	16.7	440.0	-45.5	-21.4	17.3	66.3	101.9	-3.8	-2.9	-25.8	-33.5
5. Exports of goods and services	11.3	- 1.4	24.0	9.5	13.2	12.1	22.5	4.0	16.6	18.9	16.5	10.6	6.5	11.0
6. Total use of resources	7.5	3.9	8.7	4.8	6.9	5.3	7.0	3.7	7.9	11.0	9.6	8.0	8.0	1.2
7. Imports of goods and services	6.4	13.1	17.3	2.5	8.1	13.5	12.2	-1.1	9.9	36.9	15.4	14.9	21.1	- 5.9
8. Gross national product at market prices	7.6	2.9	7.6	5.1	6.7	4.2	6.3	4.4	7.7	7.1	8.4	6.6	5.1	3.0
9. Gross domestic product at factor cost of which:	8.6	3.0	9.8	3.5	6.8	4.0	4.6	6.1	7.1	7.4	7.5	5.6	5.0	
10. Agriculture, forestry, and fishing	4.6	2.0	11.6	-6.4	6.2	- 1.7	- .3	13.0	2.6	- 5.0	7.4	1.0	- 2.2	
11. Mining and quarrying	22.4	20.7	18.2	12.8	19.7	30.4	12.1	2.6	6.8	5.5	6.4	.4	- 4.6	
12. Manufacturing	14.3	2.5	9.8	11.1	9.0	6.4	6.9	3.8	11.8	14.2	10.1	9.8	8.1	
13. Construction	24.3	27.8	23.3	13.7	10.8	4.4	12.4	7.3	9.8	4.5	9.5	9.0	4.9	
14. Public utilities	11.7	5.0	7.0	6.1	7.2	5.6	4.3	4.9	5.0	10.6	8.5	7.9	7.7	
15. Other (commerce, banking, public administration, and miscellaneous services)	4.0	.3	6.6	2.0	3.5	4.0	3.8	4.0	5.0	8.7	3.2	1.3	4.9	

Source: Derived from Table 2.

Table 5

Italy: Contribution by Sector to the Rate of Increase in Gross National Product at 1954 Prices, 1951-64

	1951	1952	1953	1954	1955	1956	1957	1958	1959	1960	1961	1962	1963	1964
1. Private consumption	3.4	2.8	5.4	1.5	2.6	2.6	2.7	1.7	3.5	4.3	4.8	4.6	5.9	1.6
2. Public consumption	1.4	1.9	.1	1.2	.3	.8	.5	1.5	.5	.8	.6	.8	1.4	.2
3. Gross investment excluding dwellings	2.0	- .9	1.1	.8	2.3	.3	1.0	.3	2.1	4.3	2.3	1.2	.6	-3.0
4. Dwellings	.3	.7	.7	.8	1.0	.7	.8	.1	.4	-	.5	.9	.5	.3
5. Exports of goods and services	1.2	- .1	2.4	1.1	1.6	1.6	3.1	.6	2.6	3.2	3.1	2.2	1.4	2.4
6. Total use of resources	8.3	4.4	9.7	5.4	7.8	6.0	8.1	4.2	9.1	12.6	11.3	9.7	9.8	1.5
7. Imports of goods and services	- .7	-1.5	-2.1	- .3	-1.1	-1.8	-1.8	.2	-1.4	-5.5	-2.9	-3.1	-4.7	1.5
8. Gross national product at market prices	7.6	2.9	7.6	5.1	6.7	4.2	6.3	4.4	7.7	7.1	8.4	6.6	5.1	3.0

Source: Derived from Table 2.

Table 6

Italy: Gross Investment by Sector and Saving at Current Prices, 1950-64
(Billions of Lire)

	1950	1951	1952	1953	1954	1955	1956	1957	1958	1959	1960	1961	1962	1963	1964[a]
1. Agriculture, forestry, and fishing	180	265	270	310	337	372	373	404	414	450	538	528	587	633	553
2. Mining and quarrying	36	51	61	55	50	60	70	65	62	86	105	121			
3. Manufacturing and construction	395	497	568	535	550	630	705	836	742	772	978	1,234	2,821	3,172	2,884[a]
4. Public utilities	424	439	472	508	564	581	668	661	700	789	973	1,136	1,541	1,884	2,197
5. Dwellings	230	304	386	466	579	715	827	974	998	1,069	1,101	1,236			
6. Public administration and other service industries	262	304	344	380	374	392	403	494	565	620	746	844	897	952	891[a]
7. Total fixed investment	1,527	1,860	2,101	2,254	2,454	2,750	3,046	3,434	3,481	3,786	4,441	5,099	5,846	6,641	6,525
8. Total excluding dwellings	1,297	1,556	1,715	1,788	1,875	2,035	2,219	2,460	2,483	2,717	3,340	3,863	4,305	4,757	4,328
9. Increases in stocks	123	223	- 10	30	35	190	105	84	95	149	305	295	300	225	150
10. Total gross investment (= 7 + 9)	1,650	2,083	2,091	2,284	2,489	2,940	3,151	3,518	3,576	3,935	4,746	5,394	6,146	6,866	6,675
11. Foreign balance on goods and services and factor income	- 61	- 150	- 383	- 271	- 148	- 131	- 175	- 110	183	350	60	148	- 8	- 616	242
12. Saving (= 10 + 11)	1,589	1,933	1,708	2,013	2,341	2,809	2,976	3,408	3,759	4,285	4,806	5,542	6,138	6,250	6,917
as percentage of GNP:															
7. Total fixed investment	17.4%	18.3%	19.5%	19.1%	19.5%	19.9%	20.5%	21.5%	20.3%	20.7%	22.3%	23.2%	23.6%	23.4%	21.1%
8. Fixed "productive" investment	14.8	15.3	15.9	15.1	14.9	14.7	14.9	15.4	14.5	14.9	16.8	17.5	17.4	16.8	14.0
12. Saving	18.1	19.0	15.8	17.0	18.6	20.3	20.0	21.3	22.0	23.4	24.1	25.2	24.8	22.1	22.3

[a] Partly estimated
Sources: Same as Table 1.

Table 7

Italy: Gross Investment by Sector and Saving at 1954 Prices, 1950-64
(Billions of Lire)

	1950	1951	1952	1953	1954	1955	1956	1957	1958	1959	1960	1961	1962	1963	1964[a]
1. Agriculture, forestry, and fishing	207	277	271	305	337	361	354	373	379	415	491	473	499	499	401
2. Mining and quarrying	39	50	59	54	50	59	67	60	58	81	97	109			
3. Manufacturing and construction	427	486	553	531	550	618	676	776	690	725	906	1,103	2,543	2,736	
4. Public utilities	458	429	461	509	564	588	660	638	679	784	969	1,116			
5. Dwellings	288	323	401	483	579	701	789	896	918	983	983	1,071	1,236	1,341	1,408
6. Public administration and other service industries	310	325	350	383	374	379	381	453	517	580	676	762[a]	768[a]	766	
7. Total fixed investment	1,729	1,890	2,095	2,265	2,454	2,706	2,927	3,196	3,241	3,568	4,122	4,634	5,046	5,342	4,844
8. Total excluding dwellings	1,441	1,567	1,694	1,782	1,875	2,005	2,138	2,300	2,323	2,585	3,139	3,563	3,810	4,001	3,436
9. Increases in stocks	133	212	- 10	30	35	189	103	81	95	158	319	307	298	221	147
10. Total gross investment (= 7 + 9)	1,862	2,102	2,085	2,295	2,489	2,895	3,030	3,277	3,336	3,726	4,441	4,941	5,344	5,563	4,991
11. Foreign balance on goods and services and factor incomes	- 133	- 91	- 269	- 240	- 148	- 82	- 116	69	189	373	- 7	29	- 139	- 815	28
12. Saving (= 10 + 11)	1,729	2,011	1,816	2,055	2,341	2,813	2,914	3,346	3,525	4,099	4,434	4,970	5,205	4,748	5,019
as percentage of GNP:															
7. Total fixed investment	17.2%	17.4%	18.8%	18.9%	19.5%	20.1%	20.9%	21.4%	20.8%	21.3%	23.0%	23.8%	24.3%	24.5%	21.6%
8. Fixed "productive" investment	14.3	14.5	15.2	14.8	14.9	14.9	15.2	15.4	14.9	15.4	17.5	18.3	18.4	18.4	15.3
12. Saving	17.2	18.5	16.3	17.1	18.6	20.9	20.8	22.5	22.7	24.5	24.7	25.5	25.1	21.8	22.3

[a]Partly estimated.
Sources: Same as Table 1.

Table 8

Italy: Industrial Production and Primary Production, 1951-64
(1953 = 100)

	1951	1952	1953	1954	1955	1956	1957	1958	1959	1960	1961	1962	1963	1964
A. Industrial Production														
1. Extractive industries	69	84	100	110	123	140	157	162	175	185	196	204	196	209
2. Manufacturing	88	91	100	109	120	128	137	142	159	183	201	220	239	240
a . Foodstuffs and beverages	93	98	100	108	123	121	119	131	148	146	150	158	165	168
b . Tobacco	92	96	100	108	111	116	120	123	128	131	138	143	141	149
c . Textiles	100	93	100	103	94	100	110	105	115	127	126	135	140	130
d . Leather	90	102	100	106	100	106	116	123	139	147	162	165	176	164
e . Shoes	85	97	100	105	102	109	126	136	143	157	170	171	185	178
f . Wood	87	103	100	91	93	99	107	108	129	138	152	159	157	156
g . Furniture	81	93	100	106	114	108	110	116	127	138	143	146	156	159
h . Metallurgy	91	101	100	119	148	162	183	171	184	228	248	260	275	269
i . Engineering goods	96	102	100	101	112	117	129	128	137	164	189	196	214	187
(1) Nonelectrical machinery	102	106	100	100	110	116	127	123	132	154	173	176	195	172
(2) Electrical machinery	107	107	100	99	100	96	100	98	96	98	120	122	129	103
(3) Precision instruments	89	99	100	118	153	180	217	241	274	398	479	531	566	521
j . Vehicles	72	81	100	105	124	146	156	171	189	228	256	301	355	321
k . Stone, clay, and glass products	80	85	100	108	130	142	153	162	180	209	227	268	284	301
l . Chemicals	86	83	100	122	135	148	154	176	212	254	294	336	364	397
m . Petroleum and coal products	60	79	100	122	132	147	159	180	194	228	256	304	347	409
n . Rubber	95	89	100	117	122	113	118	117	135	173	191	189	229	223
o . Synthetic fibers	124	79	100	128	138	159	171	183	238	284	326	420	478	569
p . Paper	90	88	100	104	114	126	138	140	157	175	192	207	220	216
3. Electricity and gas	91	95	100	108	114	121	126	133	142	160	171	183	200	210
4. General index	88	91	100	109	120	128	137	142	159	181	199	218	235	237
B. Primary Production														
5. Crops	n.a.	85	100	93	102	99	100	114	117	109	116	117	122	125
6. Animal products	n.a.	103	100	103	102	106	113	115	122	129	132	132	129	136
7. Forest products	99	110	100	98	93	84	81	74	76	71	76	70	67	75
8. General index	88	91	100	95	102	100	102	113	117	112	120	121	122	127

Source: Istituto Centrale di Statistica, Annuario statistico italiano (various years) and Banca d'Italia, Assemblea generale ordinario dei
participanti, Anno 1964 (LXXI) (Rome, 1965).

Table 9

Italy: Implicit Price Deflators for National Product and Expenditure, 1950-64
(1954 = 100)

	1950	1951	1952	1953	1954	1955	1956	1957	1958	1959	1960	1961	1962	1963	1964
1. Private consumption	85.9	93.2	97.3	98.5	100.0	102.6	105.9	107.5	109.7	108.3	109.2	110.2	115.8	123.8	130.3
2. Public consumption	86.4	93.1	97.1	99.6	100.0	107.2	113.9	116.5	117.6	122.6	126.3	132.0	142.3	158.7	177.0
3. Gross-fixed-capital formation	88.4	98.4	110.2	99.5	100.0	101.6	104.1	107.5	107.4	106.1	107.8	110.0	115.9	124.3	134.7
4. Changes in stocks	92.5	105.2	100.0	100.0	100.0	100.5	101.9	103.7	100.0	94.3	95.6	96.1	100.7	101.8	102.0
5. Exports of goods and services	94.6	112.6	105.2	100.6	100.0	99.4	102.8	102.9	101.9	97.1	99.4	97.8	98.6	102.9	106.4
6. Total use of resources	87.2	96.0	98.5	99.0	100.0	102.5	106.1	107.8	109.0	107.7	108.9	110.1	115.3	123.8	131.3
7. Imports of goods and services	89.0	116.5	112.4	102.5	100.0	102.1	105.6	110.9	102.3	97.6	97.5	94.8	95.7	98.9	102.3
8. Gross national product at market prices	87.0	93.7	96.7	98.5	100.0	102.6	106.1	107.3	110.0	109.2	111.1	113.2	119.6	130.1	138.0
9. Gross domestic product at factor cost of which:	88.5	94.2	96.7	97.9	100.0	102.4	105.5	108.6	109.8	109.0	111.3	113.7	121.2	130.8	
10. Agriculture, forestry, and fishing	93.5	93.2	92.3	94.1	100.0	99.7	98.4	102.4	96.1	94.4	98.0	103.5	110.7	117.1	
11. Mining and quarrying	125.3	123.1	113.1	99.1	100.0	97.4	87.8	84.3	77.6	74.6	73.0	70.4	70.4	77.2	
12. Manufacturing	99.1	111.1	108.4	104.8	100.0	100.0	104.0	100.4	102.1	99.0	98.5	99.4	101.2	107.7	
13. Construction	84.5	86.7	88.5	96.1	100.0	108.1	114.5	119.0	121.6	121.6	126.1	129.1	141.6	155.2	
14. Public utilities	86.7	87.8	94.6	98.5	100.0	103.1	107.8	109.8	110.5	112.7	115.5	117.2	121.9	128.1	
15. Other (commerce, banking, public administration, and miscellaneous services)	75.1	80.8	90.5	94.8	100.0	106.6	116.5	122.9	130.3	132.8	136.3	140.2	158.7	176.5	

Sources: Same as Table 1, and derived in part from Tables 1 and 2.

Table 10

Italy: Wholesale Prices, 1951-64
(1953 = 100)

	1951	1952	1953	1954	1955	1956	1957	1958	1959	1960	1961	1962	1963	1964
1. General index	106.3	100.4	100.0	99.1	100.0	101.7	102.7	100.9	97.9	98.8	99.0	102.0	107.3	110.9
By class of product:														
2. Agricultural products	n.a.	n.a.	100.0	101.0	102.8	109.4	105.8	107.6	100.3	102.0	103.8	112.8	119.8	119.7
3. Nonagricultural products	n.a.	n.a.	100.0	99.0	99.3	99.8	101.9	99.0	97.2	97.9	97.7	99.2	104.0	108.5
By use of product:														
4. Consumer goods	107.8	98.4	100.0	99.9	99.2	100.3	100.5	100.5	97.0	97.8	97.6	101.9	107.7	111.3
5. Investment goods	109.0	112.6	100.0	97.3	101.4	103.2	105.7	101.6	100.2	101.7	103.6	104.6	109.1	112.2
6. Auxiliary materials	110.4	107.9	100.0	97.9	101.9	100.0	110.7	102.0	98.2	98.7	97.3	96.4	100.3	103.9
By industry group:[a]														
7. Foodstuffs and beverages	97.4	95.3	100.0	99.9	99.9	98.7	98.2	98.2	96.8	97.8	96.6	97.5	105.0	
8. Tobacco	100.1	94.4	100.0	101.3	104.1	104.0	103.8	103.8	108.1	111.1	106.7	107.7	116.8	
9. Textiles	130.8	108.0	100.0	99.6	97.0	94.8	98.6	92.6	89.2	93.4	93.0	97.6	101.0	
10. Clothing and accessories	107.7	97.5	100.0	98.9	98.3	97.6	101.4	98.2	97.4	100.0	100.1	104.1	101.0	
11. Shoes	115.4	102.9	100.0	98.3	94.5	93.4	95.1	95.8	97.4	101.1	98.9	103.1	106.4	
12. Leather	130.1	104.5	100.0	90.2	82.4	82.8	89.1	87.0	101.7	102.1	98.7	94.7	90.0	
13. Furniture	86.3	99.4	100.0	101.1	103.8	105.1	108.0	110.1	111.4	112.1	111.3	118.1	124.7	
14. Wood	86.3	99.4	100.0	101.5	112.7	115.7	115.8	113.8	112.3	112.7	116.1	117.2	118.2	
15. Metallurgy	125.8	137.0	100.0	95.2	105.6	111.0	111.6	96.7	97.0	101.6	100.5	97.6	95.9	
16. Nonelectrical machinery	106.1	103.9	100.0	98.3	99.4	95.4	102.4	103.0	101.3	101.4	104.7	108.4	116.1	
17. Electrical machinery	100.1	103.9	100.0	96.1	96.1	98.6	98.1	96.1	97.5	100.7	102.5	106.1	111.7	
18. Precision instruments	106.1	103.9	100.0	96.5	98.1	99.9	103.2	99.1	97.8	99.3	100.5	101.5	104.6	
19. Vehicles	97.6	101.4	100.0	97.8	94.6	93.9	96.4	97.0	94.9	94.9	94.8	94.9	95.4	
20. Stone, clay, and glass products	114.3	95.2	100.0	100.8	102.0	100.8	102.6	101.5	98.7	99.5	104.7	105.2	116.2	
21. Chemicals	114.4	108.8	100.0	97.8	97.4	97.6	96.0	94.8	92.3	89.8	88.8	88.3	91.5	
22. Petroleum and coal derivatives	114.3	95.2	100.0	112.6	112.9	123.8	131.3	123.4	119.2	116.5	112.2	112.9	113.3	
23. Rubber	126.2	106.8	100.0	97.8	97.4	97.6	96.0	94.8	92.3	89.8	88.8	88.3	91.5	
24. Synthetic fibers	157.6	118.3	100.0	99.0	94.7	89.6	85.6	85.2	83.5	84.2	83.3	84.9	88.2	
25. Paper			100.0	101.0	103.4	103.5	109.4	104.2	96.4	99.7	105.7	104.6	110.2	

[a] The wholesale price indexes by industry group were adapted from the ISTAT source noted below, following the classification of Augusto Graziani, Sviluppo del mezzogiorno e produttività delle risorse, University of Naples, Centro di specializzazione e ricerche economico agrarie per il Mezzogiorno (Naples: Edizioni Scientifiche Italiane Napoli, 1964), pp. 105-07. The same classification was followed insofar as possible in extending these indexes back to 1951 and 1952.

Source: Istituto Centrale di Statistica, Annuario statistico italiano (various issues).

Table 11

Italy: Consumer Price and Cost-of-Living Indexes, 1951-64
(1953 = 100)

	1951	1952	1953	1954	1955	1956	1957	1958	1959	1960	1961	1962	1963	1964
A. Consumer Prices														
1. General index	n.a.	n.a.	100.0	103.0	105.2	108.8	110.2	113.3	112.8	115.4	117.8	123.3	132.5	140.3
2. Food products	n.a.	n.a.	100.0	104.0	106.4	111.2	111.1	115.0	112.3	113.4	113.8	118.8	128.6	135.1
3. Nonfood products	n.a.	n.a.	100.0	n.a.	n.a.	n.a.	n.a.	103.9	103.0	103.6	103.5	108.8	115.4	121.9
4. Services	n.a.	n.a.	100.0	n.a.	n.a.	n.a.	n.a.	121.5	126.8	135.6	146.3	153.5	164.6	177.3
B. Cost of Living														
5. General index[a]	94.2	98.2	100.0	102.8	105.7	111.0	113.1	118.4	117.9	121.1	124.6	131.9	141.8	149.1
6. Food	94.0	97.9	100.0	103.0	105.7	105.7	110.3	110.5	115.3	111.7	114.5	120.7	130.1	136.5
7. Clothing	112.2	103.2	100.0	101.4	101.1	100.8	103.5	104.0	103.7	106.1	106.6	110.9	117.9	124.5
8. Housing	71.5	90.7	100.0	106.4	121.5	156.4	186.6	218.5	277.3	319.8	362.8	407.0	447.7	478.9

[a]The index for 1938 = 1 was converted to a 1953 base and linked with the new index for 1961 = 100 at 1963.

Source: Istituto Centrale di Statistica, Annuario statistico italiano (various issues).

133

Table 12

Italy: Annual Rates of Change in Implicit Price Deflators
for National Product and Expenditure, 1951-64

	1951	1952	1953	1954	1955	1956	1957	1958	1959	1960	1961	1962	1963	1964
1. Private consumption	8.5%	4.4	1.2	1.5	2.6	3.3	1.5	2.0	-1.3	.8	.9	5.1	6.9	5.3
2. Public consumption	7.8	4.3	2.6	.4	7.2	6.3	2.3	.9	4.3	3.0	4.5	7.8	11.5	11.5
3. Gross-fixed-capital formation	11.3	12.0	-9.7	.5	1.6	2.5	3.3	-.1	-1.2	1.6	2.0	5.4	7.2	8.4
4. Changes in stocks	13.7	-4.9	-	-	.5	1.4	1.8	-3.6	-5.7	1.4	.5	4.8	1.1	.2
5. Exports of goods and services	19.0	-6.6	-4.4	-.6	.6	3.4	.1	1.0	-4.7	2.4	-1.6	.8	4.4	3.4
6. Total use of resources	10.1	2.6	.5	1.0	2.5	3.5	1.6	1.1	-1.2	1.1	1.1	4.7	7.4	6.1
7. Imports of goods and services	30.9	-3.5	-8.8	-2.4	2.1	3.4	5.0	-7.8	-4.6	-.1	-2.8	.9	3.2	3.4
8. Gross national product at market prices	7.7	3.2	1.9	1.5	2.6	2.4	1.1	2.5	-.7	1.7	1.9	5.7	8.8	
9. Gross domestic product at factor cost of which:	6.4	2.7	1.2	2.3	2.4	3.0	2.9	1.1	-.7	2.1	2.2	6.6	7.9	6.1
10. Agriculture, forestry, and fishing	-.3	-1.0	2.0	6.3	-.3	1.3	4.1	-6.2	-1.8	3.8	5.6	7.0	5.8	
11. Mining and quarrying	-1.8	-8.1	-12.4	.9	-2.6	-9.9	-4.0	-7.9	-3.9	-2.1	-3.6	-	9.7	
12. Manufacturing	12.1	-2.4	-3.3	-4.6	-	-	.4	1.7	-3.0	-.5	-.9	1.8	5.4	
13. Construction	2.6	2.1	8.6	4.1	8.1	5.9	3.9	2.2	-	-	2.4	9.7	9.6	
14. Public utilities	1.3	7.7	4.1	1.5	3.1	4.6	1.9	.6	2.0	2.5	1.5	4.0	5.1	
15. Other (commerce, banking, public administration, and miscellaneous)	7.6	12.0	4.8	5.5	6.6	9.3	5.5	6.0	1.9	2.6	2.9	13.2	11.2	

Source: Derived from Table 9.

134

Table 13

Italy: Annual Rates of Change in Wholesale Price, Consumer Price, and Cost-of-Living Indexes, 1952-64

	1952	1953	1954	1955	1956	1957	1958	1959	1960	1961	1962	1963	1964
A. Wholesale Prices													
1. General index	-5.6	- .4	- .9	.9	1.7	1.0	-1.7	-3.0	.9	.2	3.0	5.2	3.4
By class of product:													
2. Agricultural products	n.a.	n.a.	1.0	2.7	6.4	-3.3	-1.7	-6.8	-1.7	1.8	8.7	6.2	- .1
3. Nonagricultural products	n.a.	n.a.	-1.0	.3	.5	1.1	-2.8	-1.8	.7	- .2	1.5	4.8	4.3
By use of product:													
4. Consumer goods	-8.7	1.6	- .1	- .7	1.1	.2	-	-3.5	.8	- .2	4.4	5.7	3.3
5. Investment goods	3.3	-11.2	-2.7	4.2	1.8	2.4	-3.9	-1.4	1.5	1.9	1.0	4.3	2.8
6. Auxiliary materials	-2.3	-7.3	-2.1	4.1	-1.9	10.7	-7.9	-3.7	.5	-1.4	- .9	4.0	3.6
B. Consumer Prices													
7. General index	n.a.	n.a.	3.0	2.1	3.4	1.3	2.8	- .4	2.3	2.1	4.7	7.5	5.9
8. Food products	n.a.	n.a.	4.0	2.3	4.5	- .1	3.5	-2.3	.8	.4	4.4	8.2	5.1
9. Nonfood products	n.a.	n.a.	n.a.	n.a.	n.a.	n.a.	n.a.	- .9	.6	- .1	5.1	6.1	5.6
10. Services	n.a.	n.a.	n.a.	n.a.	n.a.	n.a.	n.a.	4.4	6.9	7.9	4.9	7.2	7.7
C. Cost of Living													
11. General index	4.2	1.8	2.8	2.8	5.0	1.9	4.7	- .4	2.7	2.9	5.9	7.5	5.1
12. Food	4.1	2.1	3.0	2.6	-	4.4	.2	4.3	-3.1	2.5	5.4	7.8	4.9
13. Clothing	-8.0	-3.1	1.4	- .3	- .3	3.5	.5	- .3	2.3	.5	4.0	6.3	5.6
14. Housing	26.9	10.3	6.4	14.2	28.7	19.3	17.1	26.9	15.3	13.4	12.2	10.0	7.0

Source: Derived from Tables 10 and 11.

Table 14

Italy: Labor Force, Employment, Unemployment, Net Emigration, and Workers Employed Temporarily Abroad, 1951-64
(Thousands)

	1951	1952	1953	1954	1955	1956	1957	1958	1959	1960	1961	1962	1963	1964
1. Labor force [a]	18,900	19,055	19,250	19,430	19,530	19,615	19,720	19,865	19,994	20,066	20,005	19,978	20,134	20,130
2. Employment: [a]														
a. Agriculture	6,800	6,730	6,650	6,570	6,480	6,390	6,300	6,250	6,066	6,028	5,689	5,474	5,295	4,967
b. Industry	5,505	5,619	5,768	5,926	6,059	6,180	6,320	6,380	6,928	7,201	7,466	7,693	7,986	7,996
c. Other	4,695	4,791	4,957	5,119	5,286	5,440	5,600	5,750	5,883	6,001	6,140	6,200	6,349	6,618
Total	17,000	17,140	17,375	17,615	17,825	18,010	18,220	18,380	18,877	19,230	19,295	19,367	19,630	19,581
3. Unemployed [b]	1,900	1,915	1,875	1,815	1,705	1,605	1,500	1,485	1,117	836	710	611	504	549
4. Net emigration	206	181	122	144	178	190	178	116	112	192	177	137	56	
5. Workers employed temporarily abroad									419	429	537	526	515	430
6. Percentage unemployed	10.1%	10.0%	9.7%	9.3%	8.7%	8.2%	7.6%	7.5%	5.6%	4.2%	3.5%	3.1%	2.5%	2.7%
7. Percentage distribution of employment:														
a. Agriculture	40.0%	39.3%	38.3%	37.3%	36.4%	35.5%	34.6%	34.0%	32.1%	31.3%	29.5%	28.3%	27.0%	25.4%
b. Industry	32.4	32.8	33.2	33.6	34.0	34.3	34.7	34.7	36.7	37.5	38.7	39.7	40.7	40.8
c. Other	27.6	27.9	28.5	29.1	29.6	30.2	30.7	31.3	31.2	31.2	31.8	32.0	32.3	33.8
Total	100.0%	100.0%	100.0%	100.0%	100.0%	100.0%	100.0%	100.0%	100.0%	100.0%	100.0%	100.0%	100.0%	100.0%

[a] Excludes workers abroad. [b] Includes unemployed and persons in search of their first job.

Sources: Labor force and employment estimates to 1957 from Associazione per lo sviluppo dell'industria nel Mezzogiorno (SVIMEZ), L'aumento dell' occupazione in Italia dal 1950 al 1957 (Rome, 1959); 1958 estimate by the Banca d'Italia; later estimates and remaining data from Istituto Centrale di Statistica, Annuario statistico italiano (various years).

Table 15

Italy: Wages and Productivity, 1951-64

	1951	1952	1953	1954	1955	1956	1957	1958	1959	1960	1961	1962	1963	1964
1. Minimum contractual wage rates, including family allowances (1953 = 100):														
a. Agriculture	85.9	90.3	100.0	105.1	108.5	112.3	123.5	132.6	136.4	137.7	148.2	172.7	191.5	209.7
b. Industry	84.6	94.0	100.0	103.1	107.2	113.0	117.1	123.4	125.3	129.2	134.2	145.1	160.7	184.2
c. Transport	84.7	94.9	100.0	101.5	106.3	112.2	115.2	120.3	126.2	126.6	135.2	147.5	156.1	178.4
d. Commerce	85.9	94.0	100.0	102.2	105.4	112.0	116.4	122.9	126.4	129.0	135.5	142.3	155.8	171.3
2. Hourly earnings in manufacturing (1953 = 100):														
a. OECD	93.0	97.7	100.0	103.5	109.9	117.0	122.2	128.1	131.6	138.0	147.4	169.6	198.7	222.2
b. Banca d'Italia			100.0	103.4	109.8	117.0	122.4	127.5	130.6	137.3	146.9	169.4	197.0	217.9
3. Output per manhour in manufacturing (1953 = 100):														
a. OECD	89.0	90.0	100.0	106.9	115.6	123.5	130.4	138.7	152.4	162.9	171.8	185.5	195.4	209.6
b. Banca d'Italia			100.0	108.2	119.7	127.7	135.4	144.6	160.7	175.8	184.0	198.9	210.1	222.6
4. Industry (1953 = 100):														
a. Income per worker			100.0	105.6	114.2	118.3	124.3	133.5	137.9	148.7	158.8	184.4	220.4	
b. Output per employee			100.0	108.3	115.8	121.3	127.6	132.2	143.2	154.9	164.0	174.0	181.0	

Sources: Rows 1a. - 1d. from Istituto Centrale di Statistica, Annuario statistico italiano; rows 2a. and 3a. from Organization for Economic Cooperation and Development, General Statistics and Main Economic Indicators; rows 2b., 3b., and 4a.-b. from Banca d'Italia, Assemblea generale ordinaria dei partecipanti (various issues).

Table 16

Value, Quantum, and Unit Value of Total World and Italian Exports, 1950-64
(Billions of Dollars)

	1950	1951	1952	1953	1954	1955	1956	1957	1958	1959	1960	1961	1962	1963	1964
A. Total world exports:[a]															
1. Value (at current prices)	54.6	74.2	71.6	72.6	75.1	81.6	90.7	97.1	92.4	97.8	108.9	114.0	119.7	130.4	145.9
2. Quantum (at 1953 prices)	61.3	68.7	68.2	72.6	75.9	82.4	89.8	94.2	92.4	98.8	110.0	114.0	119.7	129.1	148.9
3. Unit value (1953 = 100)	89	108	105	100	99	99	101	103	100	99	99	100	100	101	102
B. Total Italian exports:															
4. Value (at current prices)	1.2	1.6	1.4	1.5	1.6	1.9	2.2	2.5	2.5	2.9	3.7	4.2	4.7	5.1	6.0
5. Quantum (at 1953 prices)	1.4	1.6	1.4	1.5	1.7	2.0	2.3	2.7	2.8	3.5	4.2	5.0	5.7	5.9	6.8
6. Unit value (1953 = 100)	87	104	97	100	97	94	92	95	91	83	87	84	83	86	88
C. World exports of manufactures:[b]															
7. Value (at current prices)	19.9	28.2	29.4	30.7	31.6	34.5	39.3	43.1	42.2	45.1	51.3	53.4	56.9	61.4	69.7
8. Quantum (at 1958 prices)	24.8	29.9	30.1	32.7	34.1	36.8	40.4	42.9	42.2	45.1	50.4	51.9	55.2	59.5	66.8
9. Unit value (1958 = 100)	81	94	98	94	92	93	97	100	100	100	102	103	103	104	105
10. Unit labor cost (1953 = 100)[c]	87	93	100	100	101	101	105	109	109	107	109	113	116	118	118
D. Italian exports of manufactures:															
11. Value (at current prices)	.8	1.2	.9	.9	1.0	1.2	1.4	1.6	1.7	2.0	2.7	3.1	3.5	3.9	4.7
12. Quantum (at 1958 prices)	.8	.9	.8	.8	.8	1.1	1.4	1.6	1.7	2.2	2.8	3.4	3.9	4.1	4.8
13. Unit value (1958 = 100)	101	122	112	116	112	107	101	104	100	93	96	92	89	94	97
14. Unit labor cost (1953 = 100)	105	104	109	100	97	95	95	94	92	86	85	86	91	102	106

[a]Excluding the exports of Italy and the Sino-Soviet Bloc. [b]Includes the United States, West Germany, United Kingdom, France, Japan, Belgium-Luxembourg, Canada, Netherlands, Switzerland, and Sweden. The unit value indexes for 1950-58 were weighted by the value of each country's exports in 1953; the value of exports in 1959 was used to weight the indexes for 1959-64. [c]Covers all the countries in footnote b., except Switzerland.

Sources: Total world and total Italian exports from Organization for European Economic Cooperation and Development, Statistical Bulletins, Foreign Trade, Series A, Overall Trade by Countries and Main Economic Indicators. World and Italian exports of manufactures from the United Nations, Monthly Bulletin of Statistics.

138

Table 17

Value, Quantum, and Unit Value of Italian Imports, 1951-64[a]
(Billions of Lire)

	1951	1952	1953	1954	1955	1956	1957	1958	1959	1960	1961	1962	1963	1964
A. Total imports:														
1. Value (at current prices)	1,354	1,460	1,513	1,524	1,696	1,984	2,296	2,010	2,106	2,953	3,264	3,792	4,712	4,520
2. Quantum (at 1954 prices)	1,177	1,291	1,450	1,524	1,671	1,895	2,084	2,072	2,334	3,318	3,752	4,363	5,361	4,978
3. Unit value (1954 = 100)	115.1	113.1	104.3	100.0	101.4	104.7	110.2	97.0	90.2	89.0	87.0	87.2	87.9	90.8
B. Consumer goods imports:														
4. Value (at current prices)	697	685	701	648	712	819	921	844	929	1,256	1,306	1,484	2,042	1,980
5. Quantum (at 1954 prices)	607	636	695	648	743	876	967	940	1,089	1,474	1,597	1,776	2,341	2,155
6. Unit value (1954 = 100)	114.4	107.3	100.3	100.0	95.6	93.0	94.7	89.9	85.5	85.9	82.4	85.1	88.3	91.9
C. Investment goods imports:														
7. Value (at current prices)	317	421	437	480	543	633	744	633	656	1,057	1,267	1,534	1,770	1,565
8. Quantum (at 1954 prices)	296	361	406	480	494	526	594	584	622	990	1,198	1,462	1,695	1,394
9. Unit value (1954 = 100)	106.6	116.2	107.2	100.0	109.5	119.5	124.6	108.6	105.9	107.8	106.9	107.8	106.0	112.3
D. Auxiliary materials imports:														
10. Value (at current prices)	340	354	375	396	441	532	631	533	521	640	691	774	900	975
11. Quantum (at 1954 prices)	274	294	349	396	434	493	523	548	623	854	957	1,125	1,325	1,417
12. Unit value (1954 = 100)	123.6	120.2	107.2	100.0	101.4	107.1	120.1	97.4	83.8	75.5	72.7	69.6	68.6	68.8

[a]There are minor discrepancies in the quantum and unit value series due mainly to rounding.

Sources: The data for 1951-58 are unofficial ISTAT estimates; the data for subsequent years are from Istituto Centrale de Statistica (ISTAT), Annuario statistico italiano.

139

Table 18

Italy: Balance of Payments, 1950-64
(Millions of Dollars)

	1950	1951	1952	1953	1954	1955	1956	1957	1958	1959	1960	1961	1962	1963	1964
1. Imports (f.o.b.)	1,364	1,919	2,125	2,212	2,218	2,450	2,815	3,249	2,896	2,993	4,204	4,659	5,459	6,842	6,444
2. Exports	1,203	1,644	1,379	1,473	1,582	1,777	2,083	2,480	2,523	2,860	3,570	4,103	4,581	4,984	5,876
3. Trade balance	- 161	- 275	- 746	- 739	- 636	- 673	- 732	- 769	- 373	- 133	- 634	- 556	- 878	-1,858	- 568
4. Services	71	48	153	321	420	462	462	599	670	693	731	792	878	872	1,002
5. Goods and services	- 90	- 227	- 593	- 418	- 216	- 211	- 270	- 170	297	560	97	235	0	- 986	434
6. Unilateral transfers	272	286	248	202	139	136	176	203	267	195	220	273	294	285	262
7. CURRENT BALANCE	182	59	- 345	- 216	- 77	- 75	- 94	33	564	755	317	508	294	- 701	696
8. Capital movements plus errors and omissions	- 222	64	213	133	69	155	129	136	157	49	125	69	- 244	- 551	78
9. OVER-ALL BALANCE	- 40	123	- 132	- 83	- 8	80	35	169	721	804	442	577	50	-1,252	774
10. Monetary movements:															
a. Official reserves (increase = -)	- 13	- 50	25	- 118	- 180	- 250	- 97	- 225	- 764	- 877	- 127	- 340	- 22	432	- 446
b. IMF position									- 45	- 23		- 175	40	- 23	84
c. Other official	67	- 106	67	176	168	156	36	- 10	- 55	49	- 47	- 102	- 498	193	30
d. Foreign position of commercial banks	- 14	33	40	25	20	14	26	66	143	47	- 268	40	430	650	- 442
Total	40	- 123	132	83	8	- 80	- 35	- 169	- 721	- 804	- 442	- 577	- 50	1,252	- 774

Sources: OECD, Statistics of Balance of Payments, 1950 - 1961 (Paris, 1964) and Banca d'Italia, Assemblea generale ordinaria dei participanti, Anno 1964 (LXXI) (Rome, 1965).

140

Table 19

Italy: Official International Reserves, 1950-65
(Millions of Dollars)

End of Year	Amount[a]
1950	$ 602
1951	774
1952	696
1953	768
1954	927
1955	1,167
1956	1,236
1957	1,354
1958	2,184
1959	3,056[a]
1960	3,251
1961	3,799
1962	3,818
1963	3,406
1964	3,824
1965	4,414

[a]Italy's creditor position in the European Payments Union is included before 1959.
Source: International Monetary Fund, International Financial Statistics.

Table 20

Value, Quantum, and Unit Value of Total World and Italian
Exports, 1953-65 (Quarterly)
(Millions of Dollars)

Period	Value at Current Prices		Quantum of 1953 Prices		Unit Value, 1953 = 100	
	Total World Exports	Total Italian Exports	Total World Exports[a]	Total Italian Exports	Total World Exports	Total Italian Exports
1953 - 1Q	$ 17,131	$ 342	$ 16,795	$ 329	102	104
2Q	18,008	354	17,830	358	101	99
3Q	18,369	363	18,744	378	98	96
4Q	19,041	432	19,233	424	99	102
1954 - 1Q	17,953	393	18,134	397	99	99
2Q	19,107	390	19,300	398	99	98
3Q	18,109	390	18,292	415	99	94
4Q	19,953	465	20,360	479	98	97
1955 - 1Q	19,623	399	19,821	429	99	93
2Q	19,819	453	20,223	482	98	94
3Q	19,860	495	20,061	532	99	93
4Q	22,265	510	22,265	543	100	94
1956 - 1Q	21,224	501	21,014	545	101	92
2Q	23,170	504	22,941	536	101	94
3Q	22,023	537	21,805	584	101	92
4Q	24,266	615	23,790	699	102	88
1957 - 1Q	24,365	576	23,428	613	104	94
2Q	24,470	624	23,529	664	104	94
3Q	23,601	654	22,693	674	104	97
4Q	24,626	687	24,143	731	102	94

1958 –	1Q	22,724	609	22,327	634	102	96
	2Q	22,758	633	22,758	681	100	93
	3Q	22,284	636	22,284	707	100	90
	4Q	24,602	663	24,602	753	100	88
1959 –	1Q	22,424	627	22,882	721	98	87
	2Q	24,459	651	24,706	757	99	86
	3Q	23,999	777	24,241	925	99	84
	4Q	26,900	858	26,900	1,034	100	83
1960 –	1Q	26,749	882	26,749	991	100	89
	2Q	27,373	921	27,373	1,047	100	88
	3Q	26,190	924	26,190	1,087	100	85
	4Q	28,613	942	28,902	1,121	99	84
1961 –	1Q	27,504	975	27,504	1,161	100	84
	2Q	28,410	993	28,410	1,168	100	85
	3Q	27,792	1,074	27,792	1,279	100	84
	4Q	29,935	1,176	29,935	1,417	100	83
1962 –	1Q	29,016	1,128	29,016	1,359	100	83
	2Q	30,073	1,152	30,073	1,405	100	82
	3Q	28,962	1,164	29,255	1,402	99	83
	4Q	31,395	1,254	31,712	1,511	99	83
1963 –	1Q	29,916	1,185	30,218	1,362	99	87
	2Q	32,760	1,239	32,760	1,441	100	86
	3Q	32,061	1,290	32,061	1,518	100	85
	4Q	35,664	1,362	35,311	1,566	101	87
1964 –	1Q	35,073	1,326	34,385	1,542	102	86
	2Q	36,540	1,461	35,824	1,679	102	87
	3Q	34,920	1,554	34,574	1,766	101	88
	4Q	39,426	1,623	38,653	1,844	102	88
1965 –	1Q	36,081	1,668	35,724	1,940	101	86

aExcluding Italian exports.

Source: Organization for Economic Cooperation and Development (OECD), Statistical Bulletins, Foreign Trade, Series A, Overall Trade by Countries and Main Economic Indicators.

Table 21

Value, Quantum, and Unit Value of World and
Italian Exports of Manufactures, 1960-64 (Quarterly)
(Billions of Dollars)

| Period | Value at Current Prices | | Quantum at 1958 Prices | | Unit Value, 1958 = 100 | |
	World Exports	Italian Exports	World Exports	Italian Exports	World Exports	Italian Exports
1960 - 1Q	$ 12.57	$ .64	$ 12.39	$ .65	101.7	98
2Q	12.98	.68	12.73	.70	101.9	97
3Q	12.20	.68	11.98	.72	101.9	94
4Q	13.58	.70	13.34	.75	102.0	93
1961 - 1Q	12.97	.74	12.66	.84	102.5	88
2Q	13.49	.74	13.09	.78	103.2	95
3Q	12.91	.79	12.46	.85	103.8	93
4Q	14.01	.86	13.56	.95	103.5	91
1962 - 1Q	13.70	.85	13.25	.93	103.6	91
2Q	14.56	.85	14.18	.99	102.9	86
3Q	13.71	.84	13.31	.95	103.2	88
4Q	14.88	.95	14.52	1.06	103.0	90
1963 - 1Q	13.97	.91	13.55	.97	103.6	94
2Q	15.56	.94	15.09	1.00	103.4	94
3Q	14.98	.97	14.56	1.03	103.1	94
4Q	16.87	1.04	16.37	1.09	103.5	95
1964 - 1Q	16.49	1.03	15.84	1.06	104.2	97
2Q	17.50	1.16	16.83	1.20	104.4	97
3Q	16.58	1.20	15.86	1.25	105.3	96
4Q	19.09	1.27	18.21	1.31	106.0	97

Source: United Nations, Monthly Bulletin of Statistics (various issues).

Table 22

Data Utilized in Estimating the Lamfalussy Model

	1951	1952	1953	1954	1955	1956	1957	1958	1959	1960	1961	1962	1963
A. Equation (1)													
1. I/Y	.180	.196	.198	.204	.211	.219	.225	.218	.223	.240	.248	.253	.256
2. y	.071	.019	.070	.048	.070	.042	.063	.042	.080	.073	.086	.066	.048
3. C	1.038	.991	.969	1.000	1.012	1.012	1.017	.964	.997	1.066	1.061	1.064	1.080
4. i	.061	.060	.062	.062	.064	.069	.072	.062	.054	.052	.050	.051	.052
5. $(I/Y)'$	.138	.146	.142	.146	.148	.155	.156	.148	.152	.173	.183	.188	.190
6. y'	.071	.001	.062	.045	.064	.039	.057	.041	.079	.077	.089	.063	.047
B. Equation (2)													
1. S/Y	.171	.168	.171	.184	.197	.205	.225	.228	.244	.237	.248	.245	.219
2. $(S/Y)_{-1}$	.162	.171	.168	.171	.184	.197	.205	.225	.228	.244	.237	.248	.245
3. W/P	.500	.526	.523	.540	.540	.551	.550	.551	.548	.551	.553	.576	.621
C. Equation (3)													
1. y_p	.056	.069	.090	.049	.057	.055	.029	.057	.041	.061	.083	.104	.042
2. y_p''				.083	.069	.047	.052	.036	.083	.082	.059	.061	.040
3. $(I/Y)''$				.109	.111	.118	.118	.110	.113	.131	.142	.147	.151
4. $(I/Y)''_{-1}$				.106	.109	.111	.118	.118	.110	.113	.131	.142	.147
D. Equation (4)													
1. $(X-M)/Y$	-.009	-.028	-.027	-.020	-.014	-.014	.000	.010	.021	-.003	.000	-.008	-.037
2. $(y_p - \gamma)$	.079	.027	.058	.035	.024	.044	.032	.012	.058	.029	.025	-.021	-.074
3. X/Y	.089	.078	.080	.085	.093	.106	.115	.116	.133	.149	.163	.169	.171
4. t_W	.120	-.007	.064	.046	.086	.090	.050	-.019	.069	.114	.036	.050	.079
5. $c_{I,W}$	.079	.027	.058	.035	.024	.044	.032	.012	.058	.029	.025	-.021	-.074
6. $(X/Y)_{-1}$	.083	.089	.078	.080	.085	.093	.106	.115	.116	.133	.149	.163	.169
7. M/Y	.112	.121	.127	.127	.130	.142	.146	.140	.146	.193	.201	.219	.257
8. y''	.065	.038	.070	.041	.062	.043	.050	.032	.069	.099	.083	.076	.077
9. $P_{I,W}$	-.025	-.017	.015	.009	-.011	-.020	-.011	.005	-.012	.001	-.017	.028	.054
10. $(M/Y)_{-1}$	.103	.112	.121	.127	.127	.130	.142	.146	.140	.146	.193	.201	.219

Notes and Sources: Equation (1) - lines 1, 2, 5, and 6 calculated from Tables 2 and 7; lines 3 and 4 from Banca d'Italia calculations.
Equation (2) - lines 1 and 2 from Tables 2 and 7; line 3 from Ministero del bilancio, Relazione generale sulla situazione economica del paese.
Equation (3) - line 1 from Banca d'Italia, Assemblea generale ordinaria dei partecipanti. Equation (4) - lines 1 - 9 calculated from Tables 2, 16, and 17.

Table 23

Data Utilized in Estimating the Beckerman Model

	1951	1952	1953	1954	1955	1956	1957	1958	1959	1960	1961	1962	1963
A. Equation (1)													
1. x	.146	-.100	.046	.130	.177	.186	.141	.039	.263	.202	.188	.127	.044
2. $(1 + P_F - P_I)$	1.005	1.023	1.009	1.000	.997	1.006	1.029	1.019	1.043	1.044	1.070	1.033	.976
3. t_W	.120	-.007	.064	.046	.086	.090	.050	-.019	.069	.114	.033	.048	.080
B. Equation (3)													
1. w_m				.056	.081	.036	.051	.074	.033	.078	.068	.161	.195
2. w'_m				.034	.062	.066	.046	.042	.024	.051	.069	.153	.159
3. w''_m		.050	.024	.035	.062	.064	.045	.048	.027	.049	.068	.151	.186
4. w	.146	.116	.104	.065	.085	.089	.047	.075	.028	.070	.094	.160	.091
5. o				.083	.069	.047	.052	.036	.083	.082	.059	.061	.040
6. o'				.082	.106	.067	.060	.068	.111	.094	.047	.085	.056
7. o''		.033	.088	.063	.087	.068	.056	.064	.099	.069	.055	.080	.053
8. o'''	.056	.069	.090	.049	.057	.055	.029	.057	.041	.061	.083	.104	.042
9. U/L	.101	.100	.097	.093	.087	.082	.076	.075	.056	.042	.035	.031	.025
10. P_I	.077	.032	.018	.015	.024	.034	.010	.026	-.009	.018	.017	.062	.076
11. Pc_I	.093	.043	.020	.030	.029	.047	.018	.044	.000	.025	.033	.056	.083
C. Equation (4)													
1. w_g				.079	.117	.077	.059	.064	.112	.137	.066	.237	.297

Notes and Sources: Equation (1) - lines 1 and 3 calculated from Table 16; line 2 derived from OECD, *General Statistics* and weighted as in Table 16. Equation (3) - lines 1, 2, 4, 5, 6, 8, 10, and 11 from unpublished Banca d'Italia data and from Banca d'Italia, *Assemblea generale ordinaria dei participanti*; lines 3 and 7 from OECD, *General Statistics*. Equation (4) - line 1 from Banca d'Italia, *Assemblea....*

146

Table 24

Italy: Value of Exports by Industry at Current Prices, 1951-63
(Billions of Lire)

Industry	1951	1952	1953	1954	1955	1956	1957	1958	1959	1960	1961	1962	1963
Foodstuffs	82	77	85	88	82	108	135	104	95	106	122	133	135
Beverages	12	13	15	17	18	24	25	27	26	29	31	36	40
Tobacco	4	5	7	7	6	6	7	9	9	10	12	13	10
Textiles	332	171	178	169	176	194	221	200	256	329	380	412	456
Clothing, shoes, and leather	44	40	46	45	55	64	77	87	109	151	184	212	232
Furniture and wood	13	12	10	10	14	15	16	16	17	27	31	34	37
Metallurgy	36	42	41	41	59	98	104	111	118	149	128	126	130
Machinery and metal products	131	141	129	128	161	181	236	267	302	471	559	670	771
Vehicles	55	58	63	73	93	125	172	211	239	258	293	332	341
Stone, clay, and glass products	23	24	20	19	24	28	31	32	37	54	60	69	74
Chemicals and synthetic fibers	63	56	60	74	93	99	108	120	149	189	234	255	278
Petroleum and coal products	29	60	92	113	105	109	117	134	130	134	143	162	174
Rubber	16	9	12	14	18	18	19	17	17	29	36	38	50
Paper	19	7	3	5	6	8	7	6	8	12	12	12	14
Films and printed materials	1	2	2	2	3	3	5	5	7	10	14	19	24
Other manufactures	22	19	21	44	56	51	56	50	50	65	71	81	94
Total	882	736	784	849	969	1,131	1,336	1,396	1,569	2,023	2,310	2,604	2,860

Source: Based upon worksheets kindly supplied by Mario Amendola, who completed the data from the official Italian foreign trade statistics.

147

Table 25

Italy: Value of Imports by Industry at Current Prices, 1951-63
(Billions of Lire)

Industry	1951	1952	1953	1954	1955	1956	1957	1958	1959	1960	1961	1962	1963
Foodstuffs	180	162	157	89	133	180	185	187	201	296	309	321	436
Beverages	2	3	3	4	4	4	4	5	5	7	9	11	14
Tobacco	3	2	8	6	12	8	10	9	6	9	10	30	28
Textiles	281	269	252	241	216	238	292	219	223	313	298	333	376
Clothing, shoes, and leather	23	32	30	30	27	33	41	42	52	72	72	76	90
Furniture and wood	19	28	36	42	50	54	56	56	60	76	84	94	111
Metallurgy	90	113	113	126	133	166	190	156	192	324	386	448	507
Machinery and metal products	106	174	199	206	204	213	238	219	246	358	495	669	856
Vehicles	17	22	24	20	22	29	47	30	32	88	118	174	255
Stone, clay, and glass products	13	19	24	24	27	31	33	31	35	44	70	63	75
Chemicals and synthetic fibers	72	74	74	89	106	135	136	143	162	232	243	270	307
Petroleum and coal derivatives	46	41	40	46	50	56	70	56	53	85	86	82	91
Rubber	2	3	3	4	4	4	4	5	6	9	11	14	18
Paper	30	22	20	26	29	32	39	36	42	58	70	79	100
Films and printed materials	1	1	2	2	2	3	3	3	4	5	6	7	9
Other manufactures	20	21	24	28	33	43	49	39	45	55	57	66	93
Total	905	986	1,009	983	1,052	1,229	1,397	1,236	1,364	2,031	2,324	2,737	3,366

Source: Same as Table 24.

148

Table 26

Italy: Export Price Indexes by Industry, 1951-63

(1953 = 100)

Industry	1951[a]	1952[a]	1953	1954	1955	1956	1957	1958	1959	1960	1961	1962	1963
Foodstuffs, beverages, and tobacco	92.4	90.7	100.0	92.4	87.4	81.2	90.1	88.1	87.6	88.5	84.5	88.6	91.5
Textiles	136.6	112.2	100.0	96.7	91.0	88.5	91.5	87.3	79.8	79.6	74.4	67.3	69.3
Clothing, leather, and shoes	109.8	95.4	100.0	99.4	99.5	98.9	95.5	94.3	91.4	90.2	92.0	88.2	86.6
Furniture and wood	84.5	97.3	100.0	100.2	102.0	104.2	107.0	105.1	104.2	104.1	106.4	108.6	117.2
Metallurgy	109.2	106.5	100.0	80.8	81.5	87.9	90.6	84.4	79.4	89.4	90.2	81.8	87.2
Machinery and metal products	88.4	95.4	100.0	99.7	95.1	93.1	92.9	92.7	95.1	96.5	101.0	100.0	109.9
Vehicles	100.0	95.1	100.0	99.7	91.9	74.4	83.0	79.2	71.1	81.0	70.5	82.7	80.8
Stone, clay, and glass products	109.7	100.0	100.0	100.0	101.4	95.8	99.0	89.1	83.4	81.8	78.9	74.8	78.0
Chemicals	134.3	112.5	100.0	91.3	85.8	86.3	83.1	75.4	65.2	61.1	57.8	50.1	49.2
Petroleum and coal derivatives	109.0	107.1	100.0	94.7	95.1	97.8	108.3	92.0	85.7	80.5	77.2	76.6	72.8
Synthetic fibers	157.0	120.8	100.0	95.0	90.9	86.7	86.0	86.5	86.1	82.0	73.4	76.0	75.8
Paper	142.2	122.3	100.0	94.5	96.4	102.9	105.6	100.1	94.9	94.1	101.4	100.5	104.4
Rubber	130.8	128.9	100.0	94.7	98.1	99.8	107.1	101.2	102.1	102.0	104.6	100.2	97.0
Other manufactures	108.4	109.2	100.0	95.6	99.9	106.2	104.0	103.5	98.8	91.0	87.7	84.7	78.4

[a]Data for 1951 and 1952 were estimated on the basis of the percentage relationships between the new and old series published for 1954.
Source: Istituto Centrale di Statistica, Annuario di statistiche industriali (various issues).

149

Table 27

Italy: Import Price Indexes by Industry, 1951-63
(1953 = 100)

Industry	1951[a]	1952[a]	1953	1954	1955	1956	1957	1958	1959	1960	1961	1962	1963
Foodstuffs, beverages, and tobacco	115.8	105.9	100.0	99.0	98.7	105.6	104.6	100.6	102.7	104.0	96.7	101.2	117.2
Textiles	126.7	98.0	100.0	96.8	89.1	86.2	95.0	82.7	74.6	80.0	79.6	79.0	73.6
Clothing, leather, and shoes	107.9	97.8	100.0	98.9	104.4	99.2	105.9	102.3	103.5	89.2	100.9	87.4	78.9
Furniture and wood	82.9	105.3	100.0	98.8	114.6	117.4	117.9	117.0	111.6	113.9	121.5	123.4	123.9
Metallurgy	98.1	97.4	100.0	89.4	97.6	107.8	102.8	81.4	82.4	86.3	82.8	80.4	76.1
Machinery and metal products	91.5	95.1	100.0	98.7	101.4	103.6	108.4	111.7	107.4	109.4	116.7	121.4	126.1
Vehicles	89.1	92.4	100.0	88.1	97.1	107.5	169.6	115.4	99.5	102.6	96.7	108.3	115.1
Stone, clay, and glass products	112.3	107.5	100.0	92.5	92.6	92.8	96.7	100.3	95.8	98.8	107.1	103.7	88.9
Chemicals	113.0	104.4	100.0	93.0	85.3	75.8	75.3	67.7	60.2	53.7	52.7	50.4	45.9
Petroleum and coal derivatives	108.0	108.1	100.0	88.4	93.5	99.8	97.0	93.8	86.0	91.5	84.7	80.1	77.2
Synthetic fibers	160.2	169.0	100.0	100.2	103.8	103.1	103.1	98.6	92.1	93.0	91.1	85.9	85.9
Paper	206.5	166.9	100.0	110.1	114.5	114.3	114.9	105.3	97.0	101.3	103.0	95.0	92.8
Rubber	143.5	104.4	100.0	104.4	132.2	132.7	114.3	127.4	132.8	128.9	149.5	121.6	109.3
Other manufactures	121.4	116.6	100.0	90.5	92.0	97.1	99.0	93.9	84.5	86.6	84.6	82.4	93.7

[a]Data for 1951 and 1952 were estimated on the basis of the percentage relationships between the new and old series published for 1954.
Source: Istituto Centrale di Statistica, Annuario di statistiche industriali (various issues).

Table 28

Italy: Value of Production by Industry at 1959 Prices, 1951-63
(Billions of Lire)

Industry	1951	1952	1953	1954	1955	1956	1957	1958	1959	1960	1961	1962	1963
Foodstuffs	1,752	1,812	1,878	2,020	2,301	2,276	2,241	2,443	2,729	2,596	2,672	2,759	2,972
Beverages	88	113	91	97	112	110	127	121	152	180	177	203	276
Tobacco	64	67	70	76	77	81	84	86	90	92	96	100	99
Textiles	783	729	783	806	738	783	857	820	903	991	985	1,053	1,093
Clothing, shoes, and leather	610	692	716	734	719	773	875	898	987	1,074	1,149	1,165	1,282
Furniture and wood	311	360	373	377	399	392	408	422	480	515	557	576	585
Metallurgy	398	443	440	522	652	714	803	753	812	1,001	1,091	1,143	1,209
Machinery and metal products	1,292	1,369	1,347	1,365	1,505	1,575	1,742	1,726	1,840	2,208	2,545	2,637	2,892
Vehicles	375	424	522	546	644	760	813	893	985	1,191	1,337	1,571	1,854
Stone, clay, and glass products	260	278	326	350	424	462	498	526	586	682	740	872	924
Chemicals and synthetic fibers	491	444	537	658	728	804	842	950	1,158	1,386	1,602	1,864	2,042
Petroleum and coal derivatives	163	213	271	332	358	398	431	488	524	616	695	822	941
Rubber	110	103	116	136	141	132	138	136	156	201	222	220	266
Paper	145	142	162	169	184	203	222	226	253	283	310	335	355
Films and printed materials	199	206	226	246	271	289	310	322	360	412	453	498	540
Other manufactures	132	136	150	163	180	191	205	213	238	273	300	330	358
Total	7,173	7,531	8,008	8,597	9,433	9,943	10,596	11,023	12,253	13,701	14,931	16,148	17,688

Notes and Sources: The value of production was estimated by multiplying the value of 1959 production defined as "production for sale at factor cost" in the 33 productive sector input-output table for 1959 by the relevant industrial production index with 1959 = 100. The figures for machinery and metal products are the sum of the "seconda fusione" and "industrie meccaniche" sectors; the industrial production indexes for these sectors were estimated for 1951 and 1952 as the weighted average of the indexes for nonelectrical (76.3%) and electrical (23.7%) machinery. The general index for all manufacturing was used for films and printed materials and for other manufactures. The input-output data can be found in Istituto Centrale di Statistica, Primi studi sulle interdipendenze settoriali dell'economia italiana (Tavola economica, 1959), Note and Relazioni, No. 27 (Rome, 1965). The production indexes were taken from Istituto Centrale di Statistica, Annuario statistico italiano (various issues).

Table 29

Italy: Exports as a Percentage of Production by Industry at 1959 Prices, 1951-63

Industry	1951	1952	1953	1954	1955	1956	1957	1958	1959	1960	1961	1962	1963
Foodstuffs	4.4%	4.1%	3.9%	4.1%	3.6%	5.1%	5.9%	4.2%	3.5%	4.0%	4.7%	4.8%	4.4%
Beverages	18.9	16.6	15.6	16.1	16.2	24.1	20.1	17.8	16.9	17.0	17.9	17.3	12.1
Tobacco	6.4	7.7	9.4	9.8	8.2	8.8	8.9	10.6	9.6	10.4	12.8	13.4	9.5
Textiles	24.8	16.7	18.1	17.3	20.9	22.3	22.5	22.3	28.3	33.3	41.4	46.5	48.1
Clothing, shoes, and leather	6.0	5.6	5.9	5.6	7.0	7.7	8.4	9.4	11.0	14.3	15.9	18.8	19.1
Furniture and wood	5.1	3.4	2.8	2.9	3.6	3.9	3.9	3.9	3.5	5.2	5.4	5.7	5.6
Metallurgy	6.5	7.1	7.4	7.8	8.9	12.4	11.3	13.9	14.5	13.2	10.3	10.7	9.8
Machinery and metal products	10.9	10.3	9.1	9.0	10.7	11.7	13.9	15.9	16.4	21.0	20.7	24.1	23.0
Vehicles	10.4	10.2	8.6	9.6	11.2	15.7	18.1	21.2	24.3	19.1	22.1	18.2	16.2
Stone, clay, and glass products	6.7	7.1	5.0	4.6	4.7	5.2	5.2	5.7	6.2	8.1	8.6	8.8	8.6
Chemicals and synthetic fibers	6.3	7.4	7.6	8.2	10.1	9.7	10.3	11.0	12.9	14.5	16.5	17.7	17.8
Petroleum and coal derivatives	14.2	22.6	29.0	30.9	26.3	24.1	21.4	25.6	24.7	23.1	22.8	22.1	21.8
Rubber	11.5	7.1	10.3	10.8	13.1	13.8	13.4	12.4	10.8	14.6	15.8	17.6	19.7
Paper	8.9	3.8	1.9	3.0	3.4	3.4	3.0	2.7	3.2	4.2	3.6	3.5	3.6
Films and printed materials	.7	.7	.8	1.0	1.0	1.1	1.5	1.6	2.0	2.7	3.4	4.4	5.5
Other manufactures	15.1	12.3	13.9	27.6	30.8	24.7	25.7	22.4	21.1	25.9	26.5	28.8	33.1
Total	9.3	8.2	8.3	8.8	9.4	10.7	11.5	12.0	12.8	14.6	15.8	16.8	16.5

Source: Derived from Tables 24, 26, and 28.

Table 30

Italy: Imports as a Percentage of Production by Industry at 1959 Prices, 1951-63

Industry	1951	1952	1953	1954	1955	1956	1957	1958	1959	1960	1961	1962	1963
Foodstuffs	9.1%	8.7%	8.6%	4.6%	6.0%	7.7%	8.1%	7.8%	7.4%	11.3%	12.3%	11.8%	12.8%
Beverages	3.1	3.6	3.6	3.8	4.2	3.6	3.1	3.2	3.6	4.3	5.0	5.3	3.9
Tobacco	5.0	3.9	13.0	9.5	17.5	10.1	12.6	11.7	7.0	9.7	10.9	30.5	25.3
Textiles	21.1	28.1	24.0	23.0	24.5	26.3	26.8	24.1	24.7	29.5	28.3	29.9	34.9
Clothing, shoes, and leather	3.6	4.9	4.3	4.2	3.7	4.4	4.6	4.7	5.3	7.7	6.4	7.7	9.2
Furniture and wood	8.3	8.2	10.7	12.6	12.1	13.0	13.1	12.6	12.6	14.5	13.9	14.8	17.1
Metallurgy	19.0	21.6	21.1	22.2	17.3	17.7	18.9	21.0	23.7	30.9	35.2	40.2	45.4
Machinery and metal products	9.6	14.3	15.9	16.4	14.4	14.0	13.5	12.2	13.4	15.9	17.9	22.5	25.2
Vehicles	4.9	5.6	4.5	4.2	3.4	3.6	3.4	2.9	3.3	7.2	9.0	10.2	11.9
Stone, clay, and glass products	4.2	6.1	6.9	7.2	6.5	6.9	6.5	5.7	5.9	6.2	8.4	6.7	8.8
Chemicals and synthetic fibers	7.9	9.5	8.8	9.2	10.5	13.5	13.1	13.4	14.0	18.5	17.2	17.1	19.5
Petroleum and coal derivatives	22.2	15.4	12.6	13.4	12.8	12.2	14.4	10.5	10.1	13.0	12.6	10.7	10.7
Rubber	1.5	3.7	3.4	3.3	2.6	3.3	3.6	3.6	3.9	4.7	4.6	7.1	8.1
Paper	9.6	9.0	12.3	13.4	13.3	13.4	14.7	14.9	16.8	19.5	21.2	24.0	29.5
Films and printed materials	.4	.4	.6	.6	.7	.8	.7	.8	1.0	1.1	1.2	1.4	1.6
Other manufactures	10.5	11.4	13.7	16.0	17.0	19.4	20.6	16.4	18.8	19.5	19.0	20.6	23.5
Total	9.9	11.6	11.4	10.6	10.3	11.2	11.5	10.7	11.1	14.7	15.4	16.8	18.7

Source: Derived from Tables 25, 27, and 28.

Table 31

Italy: Fixed Investment by ISTAT Sample Industries at Current Prices, 1951-61 [a]

(Billions of Lire)

Industry	1951	1952	1953	1954	1955	1956	1957	1958	1959	1960	1961
301. Foodstuffs and beverages	22.7	24.5	30.1	25.3	32.5	29.4	29.7	26.0	30.9	44.0	46.6
302. Tobacco	3.4	3.6	3.1	3.4	5.3	6.0	4.4	6.3	4.8	5.9	4.7
303. Silk and cotton textiles	16.9	17.3	18.7	16.3	13.7	14.1	17.4	24.9	27.5	31.7	37.3
304. Woolen textiles	6.2	5.9	6.2	7.5	5.2	5.7	7.0	6.8	7.4	9.1	10.8
305. Hard fiber and other textiles	6.3	6.5	4.9	4.6	5.0	5.5	7.0	7.1	7.0	12.1	12.1
306. Clothing and accessories	.6	.7	.5	.5	.8	.8	.9	.8	.9	1.3	3.6
307. Shoes	.4	.4	.5	.5	.4	.6	.5	.5	.5	.6	.9
308. Leather	.7	.7	.7	.8	1.0	1.0	.9	.8	.9	1.8	2.1
309. Furniture	.3	.3	.3	.3	.5	.5	.7	.8	.8	.6	.7
310. Wood	1.2	1.6	1.3	1.8	2.2	2.0	2.1	2.5	3.2	3.9	3.7
311. Metallurgy	56.4	60.8	62.0	39.3	42.2	55.0	79.9	76.3	74.7	73.2	135.2
312. Nonelectrical machinery	14.4	14.7	11.6	11.0	16.7	17.6	21.5	17.6	21.5	31.0	48.2
313. Electrical machinery	6.9	5.9	6.2	6.4	7.9	8.2	10.8	9.8	10.7	13.8	19.9
314. Precision instruments	2.6	2.5	1.9	3.4	4.5	3.9	4.2	4.0	3.1	4.8	17.1
316. Vehicles	26.0	25.3	26.9	35.9	50.4	60.0	75.4	42.6	35.1	62.6	112.9
317. Stone, clay, and glass products	11.2	11.0	14.6	15.3	17.7	22.5	23.0	26.1	30.8	30.7	43.5
318. Chemicals	30.0	42.6	35.2	37.8	39.8	43.1	46.7	55.9	61.2	80.2	115.2
319. Petroleum and coal derivatives	11.9	18.9	21.1	16.3	19.7	18.8	28.2	24.0	16.7	11.4	10.6
320. Rubber	5.8	5.2	4.8	8.6	11.1	9.5	7.9	8.1	7.8	14.5	19.9
321. Synthetic fibers	10.4	9.3	10.0	9.0	6.9	9.4	10.2	8.9	18.3	29.6	35.6
322. Paper	5.7	7.8	8.0	8.0	10.0	8.1	11.0	13.0	12.7	12.0	13.1
323. Graphic arts and printed materials	3.9	3.4	3.7	4.6	4.3	5.2	5.7	6.5	10.4	10.2	11.5
324. Photographs, films, and recordings	.5	.5	.5	.6	.5	1.0	1.2	1.1	1.0	.3	.4
325. Other manufactures	1.7	1.8	1.6	1.9	2.7	2.8	3.1	3.4	3.8	5.3	5.4
Total	246.1	271.2	274.4	259.1	301.0	330.7	399.4	373.8	391.7	490.6	711.0

[a]Industry 315, Machinery repairing, has been excluded from Tables 31-34 because it was not involved in foreign trade.
Source: Derived from ISTAT, Il valore aggiunto delle imprese nel periodo 1951 - 1959, Note e Relazioni, No. 18 (Rome, March, 1962).

154

Table 32

Italy: Sales by ISTAT Sample Industries at Current Prices, 1951-61
(Billions of Lire)

Industry	1951	1952	1953	1954	1955	1956	1957	1958	1959	1960	1961
301. Foodstuffs and beverages	598	655	742	785	850	949	1,037	1,039	1,082	1,127	1,209
302. Tobacco	71	71	77	85	97	106	116	123	133	124	120
303. Silk and cotton textiles	455	394	385	386	368	397	424	410	440	500	521
304. Woolen textiles	170	164	184	178	172	180	201	186	205	226	228
305. Hard fiber and other textiles	118	116	110	117	127	136	150	139	154	174	184
306. Clothing and accessories	25	27	29	30	29	33	36	34	40	45	50
307. Shoes	15	16	18	18	18	20	25	26	28	31	31
308. Leather	26	28	29	29	30	33	35	36	46	48	50
309. Furniture	7	8	9	10	11	12	14	15	16	18	18
310. Wood	32	38	41	46	56	63	68	66	70	76	85
311. Metallurgy	412	481	465	497	629	744	844	763	840	1,052	1,131
312. Nonelectrical machinery	233	254	263	277	312	344	398	399	438	519	594
313. Electrical machinery	144	155	172	192	208	233	257	278	315	362	425
314. Precision instruments	32	35	38	45	64	77	94	95	108	138	176
316. Vehicles	403	513	540	613	672	752	803	840	880	1,015	1,223
317. Stone, clay, and glass products	119	137	152	172	203	221	237	239	262	293	339
318. Chemicals	317	342	376	422	480	550	614	638	659	764	853
319. Petroleum and coal derivatives	266	285	292	324	339	385	473	494	504	439	453
320. Rubber	115	110	111	130	142	148	150	147	168	204	224
321. Synthetic fibers	78	63	79	86	96	104	110	120	158	193	216
322. Paper	102	88	89	99	122	144	158	158	167	193	214
323. Graphic arts and printed materials	71	77	84	91	106	118	138	148	158	181	203
324. Photographs, films, and recordings	5	6	6	7	8	7	7	10	10	11	16
325. Other manufactures	38	39	42	48	54	62	66	67	79	93	104

Source: Same as Table 31.

155

Table 33

Regression Results for Changes in Gross Fixed Investment by Manufacturing Subindustry in Italy, 1953-61

| Industry | Δy_t | Change in Sales | | Lagged Investment i_{t-1} | $\bar{r}^2$ or $\bar{R}^2$ |
		$(.5\,\Delta y_t + .5\,\Delta y_{t-1})$	$(.33\,\Delta y_t + .67\,\Delta y_{t-1})$		
303A. Silk textiles		.05 (.01)			.57
		.04 (.04)		.04 (.10)	.54
303B. Cotton textiles		.11 (.05)			.43
		.13 (.10)		-.02 (.10)	.36
303C. Synthetic fiber textiles			.27 (.08)	-.57 (.22)	.70
305A. Hard fiber textiles			.15 (.09)	-.23 (.13)	.00
305B. Other textiles		.14 (.10)		-.12 (.20)	.36
312A. Foundries	.21 (.05)			-.32 (.12)	.84
312B. Motors			.95 (.25)	-1.62 (.53)	.80
312C. Machine tools	.41 (.19)			-.65 (.36)	.55
312D. Agricultural and industrial machinery and products	.12 (.05)			-.07 (.12)	.67
312F. Other metal products			.12 (.04)	-.18 (.09)	.75

Table 34

Italy: Unit Labor Costs in ISTAT Sample Industries, 1951-61[a]

(1953 = 100)

Industry	1951	1952	1953	1954	1955	1956	1957	1958	1959	1960	1961
301. Foodstuffs and beverages	97.9	94.7	100.0	103.2	98.9	96.8	98.9	102.1	100.0	107.4	115.8
302. Tobacco	93.9	105.6	100.0	96.7	125.8	110.3	118.3	114.1	97.2	118.3	124.4
303. Silk and cotton textiles	108.2	102.1	100.0	101.8	99.3	90.7	93.2	94.6	86.8	85.0	87.1
304. Woolen textiles	120.5	104.2	100.0	104.6	112.1	107.1	104.2	115.5	102.5	113.0	115.9
305. Hard fiber and other textiles	118.6	103.2	100.0	96.5	94.4	87.4	87.7	91.9	80.4	82.1	85.3
306. Clothing and accessories	104.4	98.2	100.0	103.0	111.4	107.4	104.8	107.7	102.6	101.5	109.2
307. Shoes	107.8	100.6	100.0	104.5	107.2	102.4	91.6	94.0	91.6	94.3	90.4
308. Leather	118.1	105.2	100.0	95.2	91.6	84.3	82.3	75.9	77.9	82.3	85.1
309. Furniture	87.8	99.2	100.0	97.2	98.1	95.6	100.0	100.6	100.3	98.1	100.6
310. Wood	92.2	107.8	100.0	97.6	106.3	111.4	108.6	112.2	111.4	102.7	111.0
311. Metallurgy	118.4	125.5	100.0	93.3	83.9	83.9	76.4	80.9	77.5	71.5	74.5
312. Nonelectrical machinery	105.2	104.1	100.0	95.4	90.7	90.2	90.4	96.2	89.9	84.2	85.5
313. Electrical machinery	100.3	103.0	100.0	90.5	93.5	95.0	95.5	93.2	88.7	89.0	91.7
314. Precision instruments	103.2	102.0	100.0	85.6	70.6	73.9	77.3	78.3	74.3	69.0	69.2
316. Vehicles	104.7	102.3	100.0	94.6	83.2	80.2	81.5	88.6	81.5	75.2	77.9
317. Stone, clay, and glass products	96.0	102.3	100.0	97.4	90.3	86.0	86.8	90.0	83.1	82.5	84.8
318. Chemicals	102.7	97.3	100.0	95.5	89.3	89.7	86.2	89.7	84.4	79.5	83.5
319. Petroleum and coal derivatives	104.5	104.5	100.0	106.0	109.0	117.9	107.5	106.0	104.5	117.9	116.4
320. Rubber	92.6	98.9	100.0	97.2	99.3	102.1	97.2	102.5	90.4	78.4	81.2
321. Synthetic fibers	88.4	109.4	100.0	85.0	82.8	71.5	71.9	70.8	67.0	59.2	61.8
322. Paper	114.2	110.6	100.0	93.7	94.9	86.6	86.6	93.7	81.5	77.6	84.3
323. Graphic arts and printed materials	99.2	98.1	100.0	98.1	91.3	94.3	92.7	92.7	87.5	88.0	89.4
324. Photographs, films, and recordings	105.3	118.0	100.0	98.9	131.7	162.4	148.7	134.9	125.4	124.3	97.9
325. Other manufactures	93.8	96.4	100.0	87.6	80.8	79.8	83.4	83.7	75.9	69.1	72.6

[a]Computed by dividing wages per employee by production per employee. Production was estimated by adding the totals given for net sales and the change in inventories.

Source: Same as Table 31.

APPENDIX II

APPENDIX II   METHODOLOGICAL NOTE TO CHAPTER 2

I. The statistical procedure adopted for the analysis of changes in Italy's exports was as follows:

X = Italy's total exports in 1955;

X' = Italy's total exports in 1959 (and later years);

r = increase in world exports to all importing areas other than Italy from 1955 relative to 1959 (and later years);

i = subscripts (1, 2, 3, ... 7) denoting one of the following commodity groups: Food, Beverages, and Tobacco (SITC 0 and 1); Crude Materials, Oils and Fats (SITC 2 and 4); Mineral Fuels and Related Materials (SITC 3); Chemicals (SITC 5); Machinery and Transportation Equipment (SITC 7); Other Manufactured Goods (SITC 6 and 8); All Other Goods (SITC 9);

j = subscripts (1, 2, 3, ... 10) denoting one of the following importing areas: North America; Latin America; EEC (excluding Italy); EFTA; Other Western Europe; Australia, New Zealand, and Union of South Africa; Japan; Other Asia and Africa; Eastern Europe; and All Other Countries.

Thus, for example, X_i represents Italy's exports in 1955 of commodity group i to all markets, and X_{ij}, the exports of commodity group i to market j. r_i and r_{ij} represent the percentage increases from 1955 to 1959 (and later years) in world exports of commodity group i to all markets and to market j, respectively. X'_i and X'_{ij} represent Italy's actual exports in 1959 (and later years) of commodity i to all markets and to market j, respectively.

The effect of the increase in total world trade on Italy's exports is:

$$\sum_{i=1}^{7} r X_i - \sum X_i \tag{1}$$

The effect of the commodity composition of the increase in world trade on Italy's exports is:

$$\sum_{i=1}^{7} r_i X_i - \sum r X_i \tag{2}$$

The effect of the market distribution of the increase in world trade on Italy's exports is:

$$\left(\sum_{j=1}^{10} r_{1j} X_{1j} - r_1 X_1 \right) + \left(\sum_{j=1}^{10} r_{2j} X_{2j} - r_2 X_2 \right) \ldots$$

$$= \sum_{i=1}^{7} \sum_{j=1}^{10} r_{ij} X_{ij} - \sum_{i=1}^{7} r_i X_i \tag{3}$$

The effect of the increased competitiveness of Italy's exports is:

$$\sum_{i=1}^{7} \sum_{j=1}^{10} X'_{ij} - \sum_{i=1}^{7} \sum_{j=1}^{10} r_{ij} X_{ij} \tag{4}$$

Thus, the increase in Italy's exports between 1955 and 1959 (and later years) is due to the combined influence of the four preceding factors:

$$X' - X = \left(\sum_{i=1}^{7} r X_i - \sum X_i \right) + \left(\sum_{i=1}^{7} r_i X_i - \sum r X_i \right)$$
$$+ \left(\sum_{i=1}^{7} \sum_{j=1}^{10} r_{ij} X_{ij} - \sum_{i=1}^{7} r_i X_i \right)$$
$$+ \left(\sum_{j=1}^{7} \sum_{j=1}^{10} X'_{ij} - \sum_{i=1}^{7} \sum_{j=1}^{10} r_{ij} X_{ij} \right) \tag{5}$$

Note that the effects of the increase in total world trade on

Italy's exports could also be measured by $\sum\limits_{j=1}^{10} r\, X_j - X_j$. Similarly, the effect of the market distribution could be measured by $\sum\limits_{j=1}^{10} r_j\, X_j -$ $r\, X_j$, in which case the effect of the commodity composition would be:

$$\sum_{i=1}^{7} \sum_{j=1}^{10} r_{ij}\, X_{ij} - \sum_{j=1}^{10} r_j\, X_j \; .$$

As will be evident from a comparison of Tables 2 and 3, this latter formulation gives somewhat, but not very, different over-all results.

II. The statistical procedure adopted for the analysis of changes in Italy's imports was as follows:

M = Italy's total imports (c.i.f.) in 1955;

M' = Italy's total imports (c.i.f.) in 1959 (and later years);

r = percentage increase in Italy's imports (c.i.f.) from all regions from 1955 to 1959 (and later years);

i = subscripts (1, 2, 3, ... 7) denoting the main commodity groups as used in the analysis of exports;

j = subscripts (1, 2, 3, ... 10) denoting the regions of origin of Italy's imports as used in the analysis of exports.

The effects of the increase in Italy's total imports broken down by commodity class and by region of origin are:

$$\sum_{i=1}^{7} r\, M_i - \sum M_i \text{ and } \sum_{j=1}^{10} r\, M_j - \sum M_j \tag{6}$$

The effects of the increase by commodity class and by region of origin with respect to the increase in total imports are:

$$\sum_{i=1}^{7} \sum_{j=1}^{10} r_{ij}\, M_{ij} - \sum_{i=1}^{7} r\, M_i \text{ and}$$

$$\sum_{i=1}^{7} \sum_{j=1}^{10} r_{ij}\, M_{ij} - \sum_{j=1}^{10} r\, M_j \tag{7}$$

The effects of the changes in competitiveness by region of origin are:

$$\sum_{i=1}^{7} \sum_{j=1}^{10} M'_{ij} - \sum_{i=1}^{7} \sum_{j=1}^{10} r_{ij} M_{ij}$$

Examination of the expressions in (6) will reveal that they should sum to the actual increase in imports for a given year, M', with respect to the initial year, M. Expressions (7) and (8) should, accordingly, sum to zero since they refer to the increases in imports of all commodities from all regions, or, what is the same thing, the imports from all regions of all commodities.

APPENDIX **III**

UNIT LABOR COSTS AND

PRICES IN ISTAT SAMPLE

INDUSTRIES, 1951-63

Figure 1

Unit Labor Costs and Prices for Foodstuffs and
Beverages (301) and Tobacco (302), 1951-63

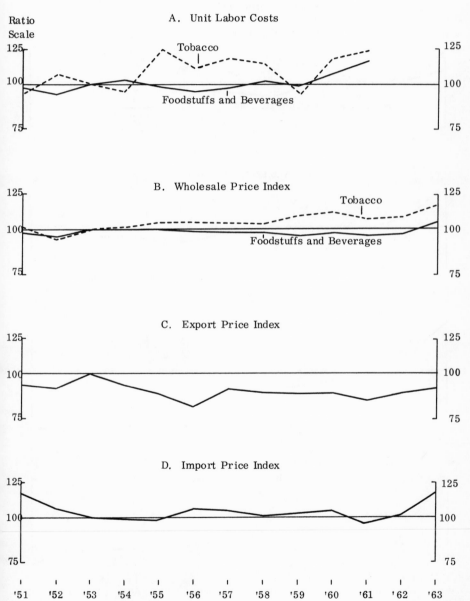

Source: This figure and all those following are based upon data listed in
Appendix I, Tables 10, 26, 27, and 34.

167

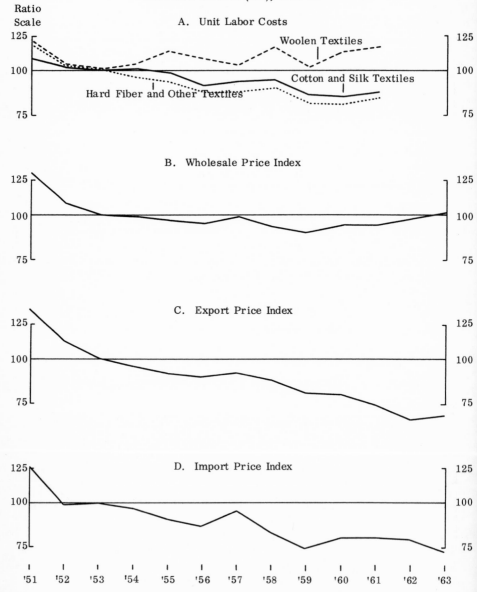

Figure 2

Unit Labor Costs and Prices for Cotton and Silk
Textiles (303), Woolen Textiles (304), and Hard Fiber
and Other Textiles (305), 1951-63

Ratio
Scale

A. Unit Labor Costs

Woolen Textiles

Cotton and Silk Textiles

Hard Fiber and Other Textiles

B. Wholesale Price Index

C. Export Price Index

D. Import Price Index

'51 '52 '53 '54 '55 '56 '57 '58 '59 '60 '61 '62 '63

Figure 3

Unit Labor Costs and Prices of Clothing (306),
Shoes (307), and Leather (308), 1951-63

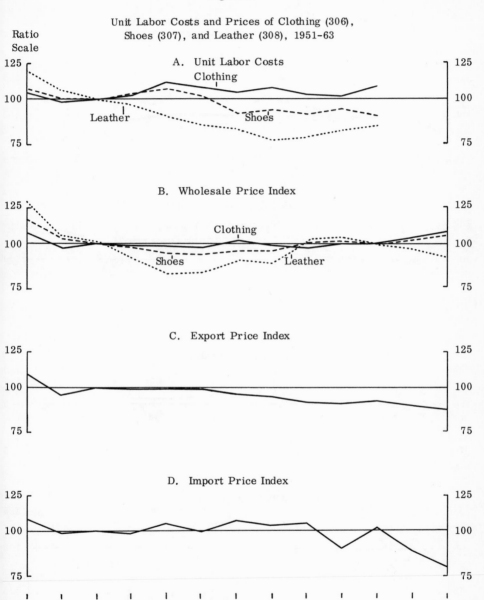

169

Figure 4

Unit Labor Costs and Prices for Furniture (309)
and Wood (310), 1951-63

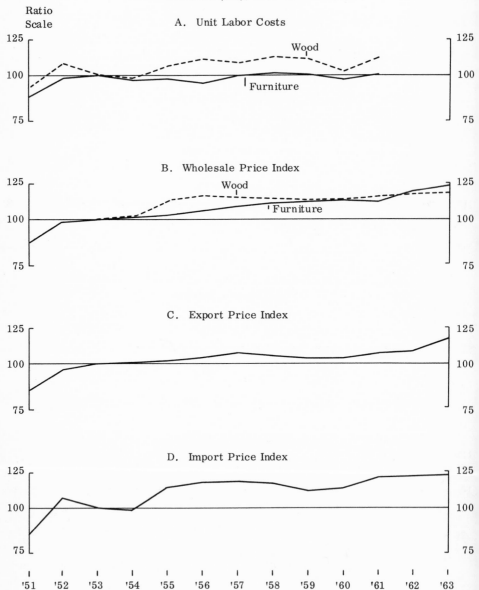

Figure 5

Unit Labor Costs and Prices for Metallurgy (311), 1951-63

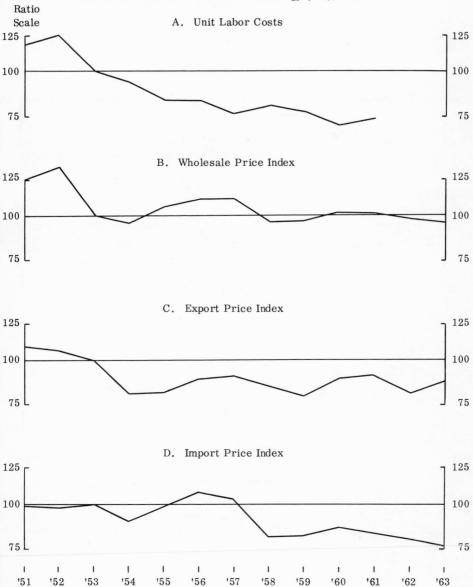

Figure 6

Unit Labor Costs and Prices for Nonelectrical
Machinery (312), Electrical Machinery (313), and
Precision Instruments (314), 1951-63

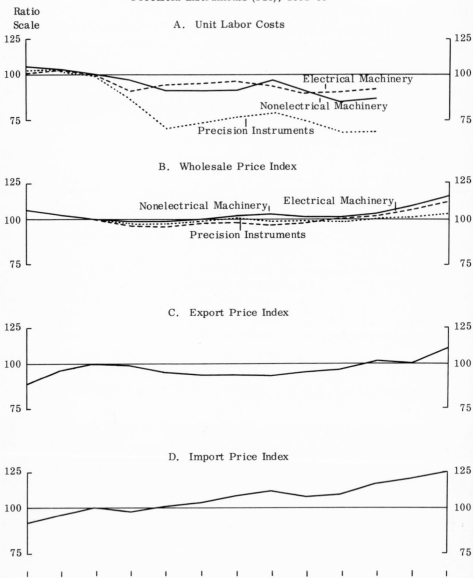

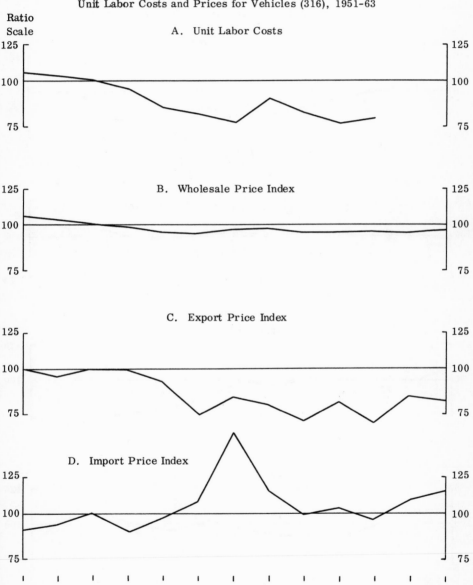

Figure 7

Unit Labor Costs and Prices for Vehicles (316), 1951-63

A. Unit Labor Costs

B. Wholesale Price Index

C. Export Price Index

D. Import Price Index

Figure 8

Unit Labor Costs and Prices for Stone,
Clay, and Glass Products (317), 1951-63

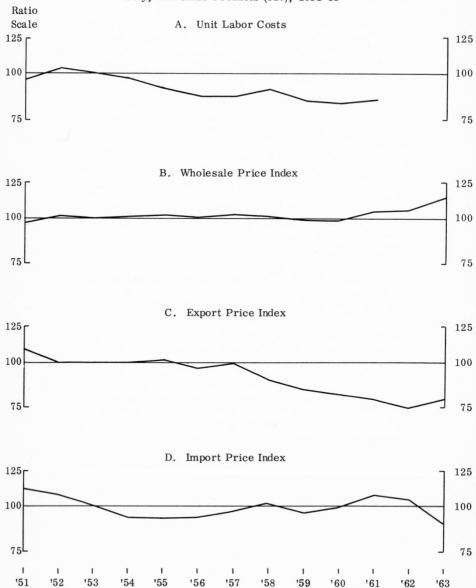

Figure 9

Unit Labor Costs and Prices for Chemicals (318), 1951-63

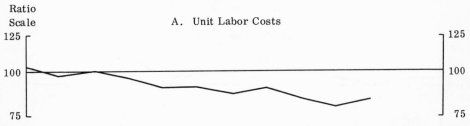

A. Unit Labor Costs

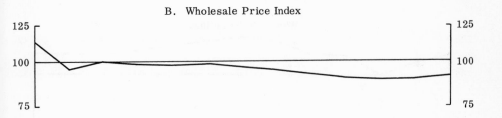

B. Wholesale Price Index

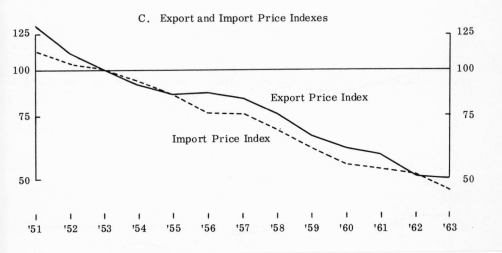

C. Export and Import Price Indexes

Export Price Index

Import Price Index

'51 '52 '53 '54 '55 '56 '57 '58 '59 '60 '61 '62 '63

Figure 10

Unit Labor Costs and Prices for Petroleum
and Coal Derivatives (319), 1951-63

Ratio
Scale

A. Unit Labor Costs

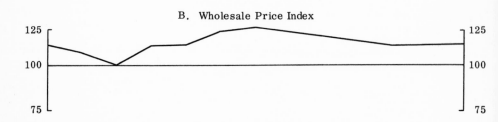

B. Wholesale Price Index

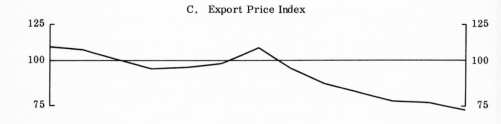

C. Export Price Index

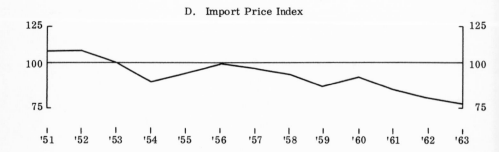

D. Import Price Index

'51   '52   '53   '54   '55   '56   '57   '58   '59   '60   '61   '62   '63

Figure 11

Unit Labor Costs and Prices for Rubber (320), 1951-63

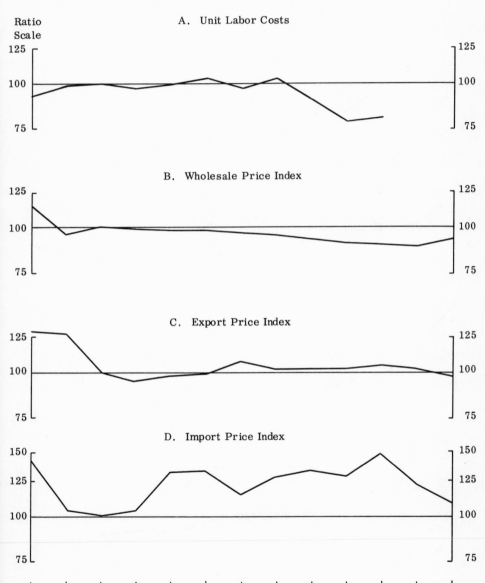

Ratio Scale

A. Unit Labor Costs

B. Wholesale Price Index

C. Export Price Index

D. Import Price Index

Figure 12

Unit Labor Costs and Prices for Synthetic Fibers (321), 1951-63

Figure 13

Unit Labor Costs and Prices for Paper (322), 1951-63

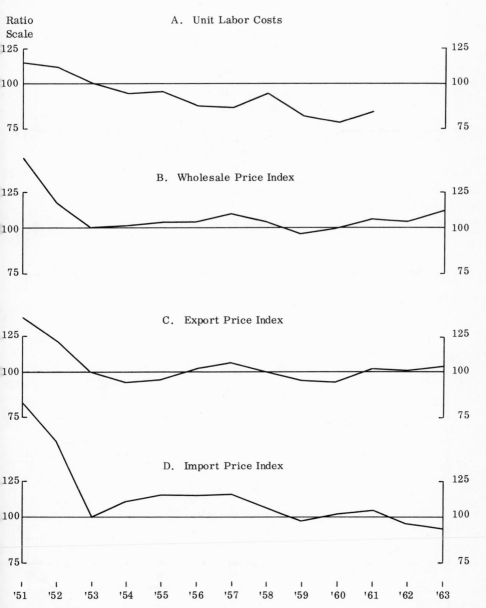

Ratio
Scale

A. Unit Labor Costs

B. Wholesale Price Index

C. Export Price Index

D. Import Price Index

'51 '52 '53 '54 '55 '56 '57 '58 '59 '60 '61 '62 '63

179

Figure 14

Unit Labor Costs and Prices for Graphic Arts and Printed
Materials (323), Photographs, Films, and
Recordings (324), and Other Manufacturing (325), 1951-63

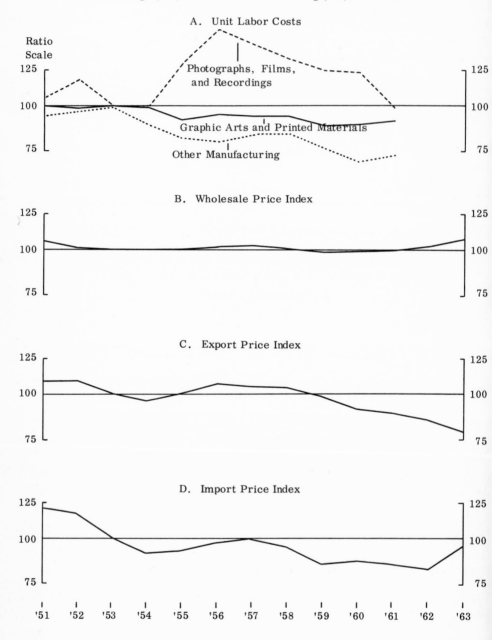

A. Unit Labor Costs

Ratio
Scale

Photographs, Films,
and Recordings

Graphic Arts and Printed Materials

Other Manufacturing

B. Wholesale Price Index

C. Export Price Index

D. Import Price Index

'51 '52 '53 '54 '55 '56 '57 '58 '59 '60 '61 '62 '63

NOTES

NOTES

PREFACE

1.   The averages are based on annual percentage rates of increase
in real GNP computed from data published by the Organization
for Economic Cooperation and Development (OECD), Statistics
of National Accounts, 1951-1961 (Paris, 1964) and General
Statistics. Further details for Italy can be found in Tables 1 and
2 of Appendix I. It should be noted that the official Italian national income data have been revised since the Appendix tables were
prepared. These revisions were unfortunately not available in
time to use in the present study.

2.   This idea of trade serving as an "engine of growth" is of course by
no means a new one. Exports were an important factor in the
early industrial development of Great Britain and in the subsequent development of many other of today's industrialized nations.
While the experience of growth through trade did not figure
centrally in the classical and neoclassical theory of international
trade, its importance was nevertheless clearly recognized in such
influential writings as those of Marshall and in the work of certain
economic historians. It seems fair to say, however, that it has
been only since World War II that trade has become a center of
focus in its contribution to growth. What is interesting in the
postwar period is the difference in views among countries at different levels of development concerning the adequacy of exports
as an inducement to their economic growth. Indeed, this adequacy has come increasingly to be questioned in many newly
developing countries which have accordingly sought a development
path designed in some cases to ignore and in other cases to reduce their dependence upon and vulnerability to changes in the
level and terms of trade. In contrast, the Common Market
countries and Japan in particular have looked to exports to provide an important stimulus to their economic growth. It is the
apparently successful experience with this reliance upon exports
in the specific case of Italy that this study seeks more fully to
understand. Hopefully in the process we will shed some light on
the experience of some of the other industrial countries.

CHAPTER 1

1.   See, for example: George H. Hildebrand, Growth and Structure
      in the Economy of Modern Italy (Cambridge: Harvard University
      Press, 1965), esp. Ch. II-IV and the references cited therein;
      E. Tosco, "Economic Policy in Italy, 1949 to 1961," in E. S.
      Kirschen and others, Economic Policy in Our Time, Vol. III
      (Amsterdam: North-Holland Publishing Company, 1964); P. Baffi,
      "Monetary Stability and Economic Development in Italy, 1946-1960,"
      and "Monetary Developments in Italy from 1961 to 1965," Banca
      Nazionale del Lavoro, Quarterly Review (March, 1961, and March,
      1966). Annual developments can be followed in the Organization
      for Economic Cooperation and Development (OECD), Economic
      Surveys of Italy and in the reports of the Banca d'Italia.

2.   Hildebrand, op. cit., Ch. II, contains an excellent discussion of
      the inflationary forces present during the 1945-49 period and the
      monetary policies implemented to bring these forces under con-
      trol.

3.   According to studies made by the Istituto Nazionale per lo Studio
      della Congiuntura (ISCO), the postwar period can be divided into
      a number of distinct "reference cycles" along the lines suggested
      in work by the National Bureau of Economic Research. Thus,
      "peak" phases in activity were recorded during 1951, 1955, 1957,
      1960, and 1963, while there were "trough" phases in activity
      during 1952, 1956, 1958, 1961, and 1964. It should be noted, of
      course, that these phases really identify changes in the rate of
      growth rather than actual declines. See Tosco, op. cit., pp. 165-
      211, for an extended discussion of the important economic forces
      and policy measures characterizing the different phases up to
      1961.

4.   This reference to 1965 experience and all of the others to be men-
      tioned below are based on preliminary and incomplete data for
      1965 contained in the early 1966 issues of the International Mone-
      tary Fund, International Financial Statistics and the monthly letter
      from the Banca Nazionale del Lavoro, Italian Trends.

5.   The comparative stability of wholesale prices in contrast to the
      more or less continuous upward movement of the GNP deflator,
      consumer prices, and the cost of living has been attributed in
      large measure by Hildebrand, op. cit., esp. pp. 60-61, to dif-
      ferential movements in wages and labor productivity in the manu-

facturing and nonmanufacturing sectors. That is, as will be noted shortly, wage increases in manufacturing were more than offset by increases in productivity. Thus, wholesale (and export) prices remained comparatively stable or fell. In the nonmanufacturing sectors where increases in productivity were more difficult to attain, increased wages were more quickly reflected in higher prices. It may also be noted that some part of the upward movement during the 1950's in the GNP deflator and in the consumer price and cost-of-living indexes was due to the decontrol of such prices as rentals and the raising of public utility charges and the salaries of government workers which had been maintained at somewhat inequitable levels. It is also possible that the consumer price and cost-of-living indexes overstate the increase in prices since they reflect higher prices of consumer goods and services that may in fact be attributable to improvements in quality. There may have been some interaction, finally, between the agricultural price indexes and the consumer price and cost-of-living indexes. That is, harvest shortfalls may have raised agricultural prices temporarily. But because of sliding scale wage arrangements, these temporary price increases possibly resulted in permanent wage increases, which in turn may have caused additional inflationary pressures. On the foregoing points, see Hildebrand, op. cit., esp. pp. 60-61 and Baffi, op. cit., esp. pp. 4-5.

6.   Citing official evidence which differs somewhat from that contained in our Appendix Table 14, Baffi noted: "In the ten years 1951-1960, the supply of labor (employed and jobless) increased by about 2.2 million units, of which 800,000 were absorbed by emigration." Baffi, op. cit., p. 16. For some data on the natural population increase, emigration, and the estimated increase in population of working age for the period 1951-59, see Vera Lutz, Italy: A Study in Economic Development (London: Oxford University Press, 1962), p. 74. Hildebrand, op. cit., Ch. V and VI, has a comprehensive discussion of the major changes in population and the labor force for both the prewar and postwar periods.

7.   The net emigration figures cannot be added to get a total net outflow because of the fact that some emigration was essentially temporary and the possibility that workers may have emigrated and returned more than once during the period.

8.   It should be evident that we are not distinguishing in the employment data the number of workers "underemployed" that may have been substantial in agriculture especially. While some estimates

of underemployment do exist, they were not considered to be sufficiently comprehensive or reliable for our purposes. For a discussion of the question of underemployment in Italy, see Hildebrand, op. cit., esp. pp. 174-81.

9. The data on unemployment noted in Appendix Table 14 are based upon sample survey estimates made by the Istituto Centrale di Statistica (ISTAT). However, according to Hildebrand, op.cit., p. 165, these estimates may be on the low side as compared to those of the Ministry of Labor which are based upon the number of unemployed registered at the local official labor offices. Even though these latter figures may be inflated, Hildebrand argues that the system of local registration gives a more accurate picture because such registration is required by law. But in any event, both the ISTAT and Ministry of Labor series for unemployment show sharp declines, especially after 1958.

10. It will be recalled from Figure 7 that the wholesale price index for manufactured products fell somewhat during this period, while as will be noted below in Figure 10, the export price index declined significantly. It thus appears that the increase in productivity in manufacturing was taken out partly in increased wages, partly in lower wholesale and export prices, and the remainder evidently in higher profits. These profits were important for they permitted a substantial proportion of manufacturing investment to be financed from internally generated funds.

11. Thus, prices increased considerably in these years so that the wage share grew at the expense of profits.

12. It would thus appear that the decline in Italy's export prices had a solid foundation in view of the substantial increases in productivity which were noted in the preceding section.

13. These changes which were taken from the balance-of-payments table do not agree with the changes implied in the table showing the growth of official reserves. The differences prior to 1959 are due to the inclusion in the latter totals of Italy's net position in the European Payments Union and thereafter to differences in the foreign exchange value component of official reserves.

14. Baffi, op.cit., pp. 15-16 et seq. It should be noted that this paragraph and the four that follow rely heavily on Baffi's work.

15. These are preliminary figures for 1965 taken from the sources

cited in footnote 4.

CHAPTER 2

1. For an alternative view of the major developments in Italy's
    foreign trade with reference especially to the annual percentage
    changes in the values of imports and exports, the ratios of trade
    to national income, and the balance of trade in total and by major
    economic categories, see Gastone Micone, "Foreign Trade in the
    Last Ten Years (1954-1963)," Banco di Roma, Review of the
    Economic Conditions in Italy, Vol. XVIII (March, 1964). See
    also, Francesco Masera, "The Balance of Payments," Statist,
    April, 1962, and "L'evoluzione dell'economia italiana ed in
    particolare i recenti sviluppi della bilancia dei pagamenti,"
    Economia Internazionale, XVII (February, 1964), esp. 100-104.
    For some regression analyses of the demand for Italy's exports
    and imports, see Guido M. Rey, "Problemi e prospettive della
    bilancia commerciale italiana," and Guido M. Rey and Sergio
    Sgarbi, "Previsioni del commercio con l'estero," Banca d'Italia,
    Servizio Studi (processed 1963 and 1964). Somewhat more compre-
    hensive results pertaining to Italy's demand for imports in the
    postwar period can be found in E. Volpe di Prignano, Indagini in
    tema di elasticita delle importazioni con referimeno alla recente
    esperienza italiana (Rome: Istituto Nazionale per lo Studio della
    Congiuntura, 1963); this work is summarized in an article by the
    same author, "L'elasticita delle importazioni nell'economia
    italiana," L'Industria, No. 3, 1963.

2. For a discussion of these and related matters, see S. J. Prais,
    "Econometric Research in International Trade: A Review,"
    Kyklos, XV, Fascicle 3, esp. 560-70.

3. According to J. J. Polak, who was one of the first to use this
    formulation in his An International Economic System (Chicago:
    University of Chicago Press, 1953), the volume of world trade is
    actually to be preferred over world income as an explanatory
    variable in this type of relation on two counts (pp. 50-51). The
    first is that the use of world income makes no allowance for inter-
    country differences in the marginal propensity to import, and
    second that the world income variable may be affected by any
    general shift in the relation between income and imports in the
    other trading countries. While Polak's use of the world trade
    variable may thus be defensible on the grounds indicated, it is

by no means the last word especially since we think ordinarily of a country's exports as being a function of changes in income in other countries. This applies particularly to industrial countries, although for less-developed countries changes in foreign exchange availabilities rather than domestic incomes may be the determining factor affecting their imports from other countries. It is for this reason that we eschew the use of the term "income elasticity" in discussing our results in favor of the term "elasticity with respect to total world exports. "

For some recent results using the world trade variable to explain changes in United States exports for the period 1948-61, see Rudolf R. Rhomberg and Lorette Boissoneault, "The Foreign Sector," in J. S. Duesenberry and Others, The Brookings Quarterly Econometric Model of the United States (Chicago: Rand McNally and Company, 1965), esp. pp. 380-89.

4.   The individual equations are thus a linear logarithmic transformation of the more general expression: $X_I = a\, X_W^{\alpha}\, \dfrac{P_{XI}}{P_{XW}}^{\beta}\, e^{u}$,

in which the export and relative price terms correspond to those in the text, a is a constant term, e is an error term, and α, β, and u are coefficients.

5.   The partial correlation coefficients for the world trade and relative price variables were .95 and -.69 for equation (1) and .94 and -.59 for equation (2). Equation (2) was also run with the independent variables lagged one quarter. The results were, however, inferior to those noted in the text.

6.   Actually, as noted in Table 16 of the Appendix, this relationship refers only to the industrial countries since comprehensive data are not available for total world trade in manufactures. But these data limitations are not particularly serious, since the exports of manufactured goods from the nonindustrial countries do not bulk very large in the totals. There may, however, be some question about the exact significance of the calculated price elasticities. As noted in Table 16, the method of weighting the individual country export price indexes followed the procedure employed by the United Nations. Thus, for 1950-58 the weights applied were those for the value of each country's trade in 1953, and for 1959-64 the weights referred to trade in 1959. It would have been preferable to have used different weights each year in order to bring out more clearly the impact of the price substitution effects on each country's export volume. Time and resources

unfortunately precluded trying this procedure.

7.   The partial correlation coefficients for the world trade and rela-
     tive price variables were .75 and -.52 for equation (3) and .94
     and -.71 for equation (4). Lagging the independent variables
     in equation (4) did not improve upon the results noted.

8.   This discussion of exports and the one for imports to be noted
     presently are based in large measure on my article, "Develop-
     ments in the Commodity Composition, Market Distribution, and
     Competitiveness of Italy's Foreign Trade, 1955-1963," Banca
     Nazionale del Lavoro, Quarterly Review, No. 72 (March, 1965).
     An Italian translation of this article was published in Banca
     Nazionale del Lavoro, Moneta e Credito, Vol. XVIII (March,
     1965).

9.   For a more extended discussion of these various factors, see
     J. M. Fleming and S. C. Tsiang, "Changes in Competitive
     Strength and Export Shares of Major Industrial Countries,"
     International Monetary Fund, Staff Papers, V (August, 1956),
     esp. 219-22.

10. This procedure was first suggested in an article by H. Tyszynski,
     "World Trade in Manufactured Commodities, 1899-1950," The
     Manchester School, Vol. XIX (September, 1951). It has since
     been further developed and utilized in a number of other studies,
     among which may be mentioned: I. Svennilson, Growth and Stag-
     nation in the European Economy (Geneva: United Nations, 1954);
     R. E. Baldwin, "The Commodity Composition of Trade: Selected
     Industrial Countries, 1900-1954," Review of Economics and Sta-
     tistics, Vol. XL (February, 1958, Supplement), and "Implication
     of Structural Changes in Commodity Trade," in U. S. Congress,
     Joint Economic Committee, Factors Affecting the United States
     Balance of Payments (Washington: Government Printing Office,
     1962); Stephen Spiegelglas, "World Exports of Manufactures,
     1956 vs. 1937," The Manchester School, Vol. XXVII (May, 1959);
     "Effets de Structure et Effets de Concurrence," Etudes et Conjonc-
     ture (May, 1960); P. R. Narvekar, "The Role of Competitiveness
     in Japan's Export Performance, 1954-58," International Monetary
     Fund, Staff Papers, Vol. VIII (November, 1960); Anne Romanis,
     "Relative Growth of Exports of Manufactures of United States
     and Other Industrial Countries," International Monetary Fund,
     Staff Papers, Vol. VIII (May, 1961); A. Lamfalussy, The United
     Kingdom and the Six (Homewood: Richard D. Irwin, Inc., for the
     Yale University Economic Growth Center, 1963), esp. pp. 47-58

and pp. 137-40; and S. J. Wells, British Export Performance: A Comparative Study (Cambridge: University Press, 1964), esp. pp. 5-9. See also the references cited and results contained in the study by Helen B. Junz and Rudolf R. Rhomberg, "Prices and Export Performance of Industrial Countries, 1953-63," International Monetary Fund, Staff Papers, Vol. XII (July, 1965).

11.   Changes in competitiveness can also be thought of as occurring in response to changes in the domestic level of income and employment insofar as these latter changes affect the availability of goods for export and thus are reflected in the various price and non-price factors mentioned.

12.   As more data points became available, it would perhaps be worth-while to perform some regression analyses of the relations between the calculated residuals of competitiveness and measures of relative export prices by region and for total exports. This is in effect what Fleming and Tsiang, op. cit., attempted to do. There is also the possibility of using a method of analysis in which the commodity composition, market distribution, and world demand influences are approximated by the use of dummy variables. For some preliminary results based upon a procedure of this kind in a different context, see Alan L. Ginsburg and Robert M. Stern, "The Determination of the Factors Affecting American and British Exports in the Interwar and Postwar Periods," Oxford Economic Papers, Vol. 17 (July, 1965).

13.   Less aggregative data comparable to those used in the present study are available in the United Nations (U.N.), Monthly Bulletin of Statistics, for the following seven SITC commodity subgroups: cereals; textile fibers; metalliferous ores and metal scrap; textile yarn and fabric; base metals; other manufactured metal products; and passenger and road vehicles and their parts. A more detailed breakdown according to importing area could be constructed, but only with considerable difficulty, from the U.N., Commodity Trade Statistics.

14.   The year 1955 was chosen as the starting point because world export data for earlier years were arranged in the U.N., Monthly Bulletin of Statistics, according to different and noncomparable regions of destination.

15.   For a recent study of the effects of economic integration which gives substantial weight to the influence of tariff reductions in increasing trade among the EEC countries, see P. J. Verdoorn and

F. J. M. Meyer Zu Schlochtern, "Trade Creation and Trade
Diversion in the Common Market," Integration Europeenne et
Realite Economique (European Integration and Economic Reality),
(Bruges: de Tempel for the College of Europe, 1964). See,
however, George H. Hildebrand, Growth and Structure in the
Economy of Modern Italy (Cambridge: Harvard University Press,
1965), p. 82, for a calculation which purports to show that the increase after 1958 of Italy's exports to the other EEC countries
may have been due in large measure to continuation of a trend
which existed prior to this time.

16.   Although no direct information is available, it might be conjec-
      tured that the 1963 results possibly reflect in part the relatively
      lower prices of export deliveries contracted in earlier years. It
      is perhaps also worth noting that in itself a decline in the propor-
      tion of the increase in exports due to increased competitiveness
      by no means signifies a reduction in competitiveness. If such a
      reduction did occur, the data would disclose an absolute negative
      figure. This was actually the case with Italy's exports to the
      EFTA countries from 1962-63, although it is difficult to say
      whether this was due really to a decline in competitiveness or was
      the reflection of certain special circumstances affecting exports
      for that year.

17.   It may also be noted that there is an index number problem raised
      by the method of calculation because base year export values are
      used throughout. For a discussion of this point and of related
      issues, see Gottfried Haberler, "Introduction," to the Papers and
      Abstracts of Papers at a Universities-National Bureau Committee
      for Economic Research Conference on Problems in International
      Economics, Review of Economics and Statistics, XL (February,
      1958, Supplement), esp. 4-5; R. E. Baldwin, "The Commodity
      Composition of Trade . . .," pp. 56-57; and A. Lamfalussy, op.
      cit., esp. pp. 50-52.

18.   The remarks made earlier in connection with exports about the
      difficulties in estimating and interpreting elasticities apply equally
      to imports.

19.   The untransformed expression for imports is basically similar to
      the one for exports noted above in footnote 7.

20.   In order to test whether the income variables were in fact so pre-
      dominant, one could reestimate the import equations with elastici-
      ties of particular magnitudes preassigned to the price variables.

These elasticities might be taken, if available, from the experiences of other countries that were similar to those of Italy.

21.   The relatively high intercorrelations of the variables in each equation can be seen from the correlation matrices noted below. The symbols noted refer to the variables utilized in each equation:

Equation (1)

	M_T	GNP	P_{M_T}	P_{GNP}
M_T	1.00	.99	-.87	.95
GNP		1.00	-.89	.96
P_{M_T}			1.00	-.78
P_{GNP}				1.00

Equation (2)

	M_C	C	P_{M_C}	P_C
M_C	1.00	.99	-.84	.92
C		1.00	-.80	.95
P_{M_C}			1.00	-.62
P_C				1.00

Equation (3)

	M_I	I	P_{M_I}	P_I
M_I	1.00	.98	-.13	.81
I		1.00	-.10	.74
P_{M_I}			1.00	.13
P_I				1.00

Equation (4)

	M_{AM}	MP	$P_{M_{AM}}$	P_{AM}
M_{AM}	1.00	.997	-.94	-.58
MP		1.00	-.93	-.57
$P_{M_{AM}}$			1.00	.75
P_{AM}				1.00

22.   It is perhaps worth mentioning that all of the import regressions
       were run with price ratios as well as with the price indexes taken
       separately, and also with wholesale prices used instead of the
       GNP deflators. There were no appreciable differences in the
       results obtained in comparison to those noted in the text. For
       this reason and the others also mentioned, further experimenta-
       tion might well be confined to individual commodities or commodity
       groups that are less aggregative and more homogeneous than the
       ones used here.

23.   It would be of interest to determine what part, if any, of the EFTA
       decline in competitiveness evident in Table 5 might be due to the
       differential impact of changes in Italy's commercial policy with
       respect to the EEC. This cannot be assessed, unfortunately,
       without detailed information on tariffs and other changes. How-

ever, the increased competitiveness noted for regions other than the EEC might suggest that changes in commercial policy have not been decisive with respect to altering EFTA's share of Italy's imports. This view is borne out by the results in Verdoorn and Meyer Zu Schloctern, op. cit., that suggest that the decline noted for EFTA may in fact have been attributable to reduced competitiveness rather than to changes in Common Market commercial policies.

CHAPTER 3

1. For some economic history references in which trade has figured importantly, see C. P. Kindleberger, Foreign Trade and the National Economy (New Haven: Yale University Press, 1962), esp. pp. 196-98 and also his Economic Growth in France and Britain, 1851-1950 (Cambridge: Harvard University Press, 1964), esp. pp. 264-77. Among Kindleberger's other writings dealing with trade and growth, see his "Foreign Trade and Economic Growth: Lessons from France and Britain, 1850 to 1913," Economic History Review, Vol. 14 (December, 1961); "Foreign Trade and Growth: Lessons from British Experience Since 1913," Lloyd's Bank Review (July, 1962); "Protected Markets and Economic Growth," in U. S. Congress, Joint Economic Committee, Factors Affecting the United States Balance of Payments (Washington: U. S. Government Printing Office, 1962); and Economic Development (2d ed.; New York: McGraw-Hill, 1965), esp. pp. 304-16.

2. Kindleberger, Economic Growth in France and Britain, 1851-1950, pp. 324-5.

3. Ibid., p. 264.

4. According to Kindleberger, exports may be a balancing sector in the sense of providing an outlet for production in excess of domestic needs and of permitting the importation of goods which are not produced in sufficient quantity domestically. Exports may also lag behind growth because of a deficiency in foreign demand resulting from relatively low income elasticities of demand for many raw materials and foodstuffs, economies of utilization, and technological substitution in the importing countries. For additional details concerning these other two models, see Kindleberger, Foreign Trade and the National Economy, pp. 205-11, and Economic Development, pp. 306-13.

5. Kindleberger, Economic Growth in France and Britain, 1851–1950, p. 265.

6. Kindleberger, Foreign Trade and the National Economy, pp. 199–203.

7. Because his discussion is so highly compressed, Kindleberger does not always distinguish clearly, as in his first submodel, the autonomous from the induced changes in trade. These latter changes are the ones which set into motion the various factors connecting exports and growth.

8. For a verbal statement of the model, see A. Lamfalussy, The United Kingdom and the Six: An Essay on Economic Growth in Western Europe (Homewood: Richard D. Irwin, Inc., for the Economic Growth Center, Yale University, 1963), esp. pp. 110-20; a formal statement of the model is presented in A. Lamfalussy, "Contribution a un theorie de la croissance en economie ouverte," Recherches Economiques de Louvain, Vol. XXIX, No. 8 (1963).

9. In the United Kingdom and the Six, pp. 111-12, Lamfalussy made the assumption that there is no tendency to fall short of full employment either spontaneously or through the inadequacy of government expansionary policies. This assumption was not completely consistent, however, with his subsequent point (pp. 117-18) that the origins of competitive advantage in the Common Market countries, especially Germany, Italy, and the Netherlands, may have been due to undervalued exchange rates and/or a relatively more elastic supply of labor due to unemployment or underemployment. The lack of consistency is mainly with reference to the point involving labor supply conditions since the expansion of exports will encourage more rapid growth based upon the fuller employment of existing resources. I have consequently chosen Lamfalussy's assumption about policy goals from his "Contribution . . .," p. 718, because it posits the promotion of full employment rather than its necessary and continuous realization.

10. Lamfalussy, "Contribution . . .," pp. 719-20.

11. This statement of an accelerator type of investment function differs from the one postulated by Lamfalussy in The United Kingdom and the Six, p. 112, to depend upon increased profits arising from the increase in exports. While it may be the case, as Gardner Ackley has pointed out in his Macroeconomic Theory (New York: Macmillan, 1961), pp. 499-500, that these alterna-

tive functions based upon the accelerator or upon profits may formally be the same, Lamfalussy's discussion in his book had some puzzling aspects. That is, by his assumption of full employment, he ruled out the possibility of expanding production for export to compensate for a decline in domestic demand in order thereby to insure that expanded exports would result in higher profits. However, as mentioned above in footnote 9, there was some inconsistency between his assumption concerning full employment and the origin of competitive advantage due to a relatively greater potential supply of labor.

In my view, Lamfalussy apparently had in mind in his book a situation in which a more rapid rate of increase in foreign demand as compared to home demand made it relatively more profitable to expand production for export. Production could be expanded, however, only if domestic cost conditions permitted and if home demand was restricted by insufficient purchasing power and by relatively high prices for the goods in question. But if costs were bid up with the expansion of output, the export position would be less favorable. The profits position would also deteriorate unless domestic prices were raised to compensate for the higher costs. Lamfalussy seemed, thus, to be dealing with a special case in which foreign demand was booming relative to domestic demand and available factor supplies and existing policies permitted domestic costs and consumption demand to be restrained in favor of profits.

12.   Thus, if $\dfrac{S_t}{Y_t} = \dfrac{Y_t - cY_{t-1}}{Y_t}$ and $Y_t = Y_{t-1}(1 + y)$ and if the second

equation is substituted into the first and both numerator and denominator of the right-hand side are divided by Y_{t-1}, we obtain

$\dfrac{S_t}{Y_t} = \dfrac{(1 + y) - c}{1 + y} = 1 - \dfrac{c}{1 + y}$. If we assume c, the marginal

propensity to consume, to be constant, variations in y will produce variations in the savings ratio.

13.   This is reached by substituting for both sides in equation (5) to obtain: by $+ \beta = ay + \alpha + c(y_p - \gamma)$. Substituting equation (1) into equation (3) for y_p, the foregoing expression becomes: by $+ \beta = ay + \alpha + c(pay + p\alpha + \pi - \gamma)$. By collecting terms and simplifying, this latter expression can be solved for the equilibrium rate of growth, y. Note that in order for negative rates of growth to be avoided, the following condition must hold: $[\alpha + c(p\alpha + \pi - \gamma)]$

$> \beta$ and $b > a(1 + cp)$.

14.   Thus, if $y_p < \gamma$ because of a reduction in the rate of increase in productivity and/or a more rapid rate of increase in domestic money wages relative to foreign unit labor costs, a negative value of c will cause a dimunition in the rate of growth.

15.   Lamfalussy, "Contribution . . .," p. 728.

16.   As Lamfalussy notes in ibid., p. 731, any decline in y may be more than proportional to the decline in employment because the decline in y will have an adverse effect upon productive capacity.

17.   While within the context of the model the considerations mentioned are partly empirical in nature, it may be noted that these considerations were more central in Lamfalussy's The United Kingdom and the Six, where his investment function was formulated to depend upon the increase in profits associated with the increase in exports. What Lamfalussy did not make clear in his book and what is still, in my judgment, left unresolved is how investment was determined in the nonmanufacturing sectors. This was an important omission in his earlier statement of the theory of export-led growth and his attempt to show that Britain was caught in a vicious circle compared to the virtuous circle of growth in the major Common Market countries. A substantial part of his explanation of Britain's difficulties lay in the relatively less efficient investment observed in the nonindustrial sectors of the British economy. But what was left unclear was how and why this situation came about and particularly how it was related to British export performance.

18.   This was also a point of criticism in F. Machlup's well-known article dealing with Alexander's original formulation of the absorption approach. See F. Machlup, "Relative Prices and Aggregate Spending in the Analysis of Devaluation," reprinted from the American Economic Review, Vol. LXV (June, 1955) as Ch. VIII of his International Payments, Debts, and Gold (New York: Charles Scribner's Sons, 1964), pp. 185-86 and 188-90.

19.   The full reference is F. Dewhurst et al., Europe's Needs and Resources (New York: Twentieth Century Fund, 1961). Beckerman's review was entitled "Projecting Europe's Growth," and it appeared in the Economic Journal, Vol. LXXII (December, 1962).

20.   Beckerman, op. cit., p. 914.

21.   Beckerman, op. cit., pp. 918-19. Note that whereas Beckerman
       used α to represent the relative price level of the given country in
       equation (1), I have found it a little clearer to write this as P/P_f.
       Equation (4), it should be pointed out, was not intended by Becker-
       man to be merely an identity. Strictly speaking, then, it should
       be written with a coefficient for (w-o) in order to specify some-
       thing about distributive shares. As it stands now, it assumes that
       distributive shares will remain unchanged.

22.   For the "uncompetitive" country, equation (1) would be x = a - b
       $(1 - P/P_f)$. Note that the sign of bd in equation (6) below will
       thus be changed, and that the "uncompetitive" country will have
       a less than average increase in its rate of productivity.

23.   As Beckerman puts it in op. cit., p. 921, borrowing Kaldor's
       terminology, it is being assumed "that technical dynamism may
       be heavily influenced by export growth and favourable foreign
       balance conditions. . . ."

24.   Beckerman, op. cit., p. 920. Other possibilities for convergence
       that he mentioned (pp. 921-22) were through: (1.) transmission
       of rising prices from the slower-growing to the faster-growing
       country in the form of higher import prices which in turn might
       result in higher wages and prices in the latter country; (2.) im-
       ports induced by the changes in income in the different countries;
       (3.) a fall (rise) in d in equation (2) in the fast (slow) - growing
       country; and (4.) differences in the basic parameters as between
       countries so that, for example, a small, relatively less diversi-
       fied, and trade dependent economy might be more prone to the
       rapid importation of overseas inflation.

25.   Bela Balassa, "Some Observations on Mr. Beckerman's 'Export-
       Propelled' Growth Model," Economic Journal, LXXIII (December,
       1963), 782. The alternative formulations of equation (3) are con-
       tained in Beckerman, op. cit., p. 920.

26.   Balassa, op. cit., p. 782.

27.   According to Balassa, this formulation of equation (3) was to be
       preferred because Beckerman's formulation was not borne out by
       empirical studies of wage determination in the United Kingdom
       and United States. Balassa also argued along lines suggested by

"Phillips curve" analysis that wage changes certainly cannot be considered independently of the state of the labor market.

28.   W. Beckerman, "Some Observations on Mr. Beckerman's Export-Propelled Growth Model: A Reply, "Economic Journal, Vol. LXXIII (December, 1963).

29.   Ibid., p. 786.

30.   As Beckerman stated in ibid., "...this constant...will reflect many factors, such as differences in the wage-negotiation machinery, the bargaining strength of trade unions at given levels of unemployment, the long-run trends in productivity (based largely on experience over the last few years) and the rate of increase in money wages which has become accepted as a customary 'norm' but which will gradually change."

31.   Bela Balassa, "Some Observations on Mr. Beckerman's Export-Propelled Growth Model: A Rejoinder," Economic Journal, Vol. LXXIV (March, 1964).

32.   W. Beckerman, "Professor Balassa's Comments on my 'Export-Propelled' Growth Model: A Rebuttal," Economic Journal, Vol. LXXIV (September, 1964).

33.   Bela Balassa, "Some Observations on Mr. Beckerman's Export-Propelled Growth Model: A Further Note," Economic Journal, Vol. LXXIV (September, 1964).

34.   Beckerman, op. cit., Economic Journal (December, 1963), p. 787.

35.   Balassa, op. cit., Economic Journal (March, 1964), pp. 241-42.

36.   The expansion of the model might be obviated by considering the alternative formulations of the wage equation as suggested by Beckerman in his original article (p. 920). In particular, his equation (3c), $w = m + no + gp$, might well suit those instances in which the rate of increase in wages was related not only to productivity but to the rate of increase in prices as well. As noted above, Beckerman considers this possibility as arising from the importation of inflation from the slower-growing country. But he does not make clear how this outside influence gets transmitted into higher rates of increase in prices and wages within the framework of his model.

CHAPTER 4

1.   Since the meaning of the Durbin-Watson statistic is not clear in a
      distributed lag formulation, it was not computed for those equa-
      tions in which the lagged dependent variable was treated as an
      explanatory variable.

2.   Thus, in formulating the investment equations in his econometric
      model of Italian postwar growth, Gardner Ackley placed great
      emphasis upon the autonomous character of investment in the
      sectors mentioned. See his Un modello econometrico dello svilup-
      po italiano nel dopoguerra, SVIMEZ Monograph Series 7 (Rome:
      Giuffre Editore, 1963), pp. 26-29 and 32-36.

3.   There is perhaps some difficulty in specification here since both
      the investment ratio and the long-term interest rate may be rela-
      tively high in booms and low in recessions.

4.   This was the case also for a number of alternative formulations
      of the productivity equation that were tested but are not reported
      here. These included various lagged formulations of the invest-
      ment ratio and the ratio of investment to changes in employment,
      and measures of the rate of change in Italy's total public and pri-
      vate capital stock per employee and the private capital stock
      per private employee.

5.   Some indication of the importance of input and productivity con-
      siderations for the period 1951-61 has been provided by Augusto
      Graziani in his Sviluppo del mezzogiorno e produttivita delle
      risorse, University of Naples, Cassa Per Il Mezzogiorno, Centro
      di specializzazione e ricerche economico agrarie per il mezzo-
      giorno (Naples: Edizioni Scientifiche Italiane Napoli, 1964). On
      the basis of total productivity indexes constructed for the major
      sectors and for the economy as a whole, Graziani concluded that
      the major portion of the increase in total output as measured by
      value added in 1951-61 was due to the increase in the productivity
      of resources as compared to increased inputs of labor and capi-
      tal. His estimates may be summarized as follows from Table 2.6
      (p. 34) of the aforementioned work:

Percentage Distribution of the Increase in Output by Sector Attributed
to Labor, Capital, and the Increase in Productivity, 1951-61

| Sector | ———Increase in Output Due to——— | | | | Percentage Increase in Output |
	Greater Number of Employees	New Investment	Increase in Productivity	Total	
Agricul- ture	-30.7%	35.0%	95.7%	100.0%	31.0%
Extrac- tive indus- try	- 3.7	24.3	79.4	100.0	⎫
Manufac- turing	19.5	11.2	69.3	100.0	⎬ 134.4
Other in- dustry	8.3	38.6	53.1	100.0	⎭
Transpor- tation and communica- tion	32.7	14.3	53.0	100.0	78.1
Construction	-	110.5	-10.5	100.0	23.1
All sectors	9.5	20.3	70.2	100.0	87.1

Additional information on sectoral productivity which became
available after the completion of the present study can be found
in Giuseppe de Meo, "Productivity and the Distribution of Income to Factors (1951-63)," Banca Nazionale del Lavoro,
Quarterly Review (March, 1966).

6.   The simple correlation between these two measures was -.81.

7.   The basic equations were fit also in terms of levels by multiplying through by Y in order to determine if the poor results
were due to the ratio formulations employed. This failed to
produce any clear improvement in the estimations. Multiplying
through by Y also resulted in the specification of some independent variables whose economic significance was far from ob-

vious.

8.   The choice of the shorter period was indicated by the fact that
Banca d'Italia productivity estimates were not available prior
to 1954.

9.   The estimate of equation (1a) for 1951–63 was as follows:

$$x = -2.28 + 2.32 \ (1 + P_F - P_I) + 1.66 \ t_W \quad \bar{R}^2 = .61 \ D.W. = 1.62.$$
$$\quad\quad\quad (.73) \quad\quad\quad\quad\quad\quad (.42)$$

This equation was also computed using measures of the rate
of change in relative GNP prices, relative export prices, relative wholesale prices, and relative prices of private consumption goods with results generally inferior to those noted.

10.   But there appears to be some inconsistency compared with the
results noted above of equation (4) of the Lamfalussy model in
that the merchandise export ratio was positively correlated
with the rate of change in the ratio of relative GNP prices.
This may be due to the different specifications of these variables computed for purposes of the Lamfalussy model.

11.   It may be worth noting that equation (3) was estimated using a
distributed lag formulation in which the different measures of
w_{t-1} were treated as an explanatory variable. These results
all proved to be inferior to those based upon the hypothesis
that the current levels or rates of change in the variables
specified accounted for most of the current variation in the
rate of change in wages. The introduction in equation (3) of
the rate of change of $\frac{U}{L}$ also proved not to be significant.

12.   An example of the difficulties of data reliability can be illustrated from the following result for 1951–63, in which w''' refers
to the rate of change in the annual remuneration per employee
for the economy as a whole and o''' refers to the rate of change
in the productivity per employee in the economy as a whole
based upon Banca d'Italia data:

$$w''' = -.03 + 1.05 \ o''' + .30 \ \frac{U}{L} + .97 \ p_I \quad \bar{R}^2 = .95 \ D.W. = 2.15$$
$$\quad\quad (.11) \quad\quad (.08) \quad (.09)$$

The trouble with this result is that the coefficient of $\frac{U}{L}$ has a
positive rather than a negative sign. Since the data refer to

the economy as a whole, the wages of part-time workers, who may have been counted as being unemployed, were included in the data for wages per employed worker. Thus, a positive correlation between the errors in w''' and $\frac{U}{L}$ might have accounted for the unexpected positive sign of the coefficient for $\frac{U}{L}$.

13. Equations (3c) and (3d) were also computed using the rate of change in the cost-of-living index as an explanatory variable in view of the fact that the index figured directly in wage determination in some sectors and that it might pick up other general influences on wages. The results of using the index, p_{cI}, which are shown below, were not quite as good as those noted in the text based upon p_I, the rate of change in GNP prices:

$$(3c')\ w' = .02 + .41\ o' - .74\ \frac{U}{L} + 1.62\ p_{cI} \quad \bar{R}^2 = .81 \quad D.W. = 2.48$$
$$\ (.37)\ (.30)\phantom{\frac{U}{L}}\ (.38)$$

$$(3d')\ w'' = .01 + .48\ o'' - .70\ \frac{U}{L} + 1.87\ p_{cI} \quad \bar{R}^2 = .88 \quad D.W. = 2.93$$
$$\ (.34)\ (.21)\phantom{\frac{U}{L}}\ (.31)$$

For some additional regression results relating to the change in wages which bear a close resemblance to the ones presented here, see George H. Hildebrand, Growth and Structure in the Economy of Modern Italy (Cambridge: Harvard University Press, 1965), esp. pp. 242-245.

14. See ibid., p. 222; also note the column for the ratio of money wages to profits, $\frac{W}{P}$, in Table 20 of Appendix I.

15. Equation (4a) was also computed for 1951-63 using the rates of change in wages and productivity for the economy as a whole as defined in footnote 13, with the following result:

$$p_I = .002 + .89\ w''' - .85\ o''' \quad \bar{R}^2 = .80 \quad D.W. = .94$$
$$\ (.13)\ (.22)$$

16. The endogenous variables were x, o, w, p_I, and P_I, while the exogenous variables were p_F, t_W, $\frac{U}{L}$, and w_g. P_I was defined for computational purposes as $p_I \cdot P_{I_{t-1}}$. These endogenous and exogenous variables, it may be noted, were sufficient so that the individual equations could be identified in the statistical sense.

CHAPTER 5

1.   For example, 31.6 per cent of total imports of foodstuffs in
        1959 were used as inputs in the foodstuffs industry, 15.0 per
        cent (probably animal hides mainly) in clothing, shoes, and
        leather, and 7.5 per cent in chemicals. Some 4.9 per cent of
        beverages imports went into the foodstuffs industry and 19.5
        per cent into the beverages industry itself. The clothing,
        shoes, and leather industry absorbed 46.8 per cent of imports
        of this sector's imports.

2.   The textiles industry used 46.8 per cent of textiles imports;
        the furniture and wood industries accounted for 91.0 per cent
        of furniture and wood imports; 48.0 per cent of metallurgy im-
        ports went into the metallurgy industry itself, 33.3 per cent
        into machinery and metal products, and 7.5 per cent into
        vehicles; the chemical and synthetic fibers industry absorbed
        57.7 per cent of its imports; 10.7 per cent of rubber imports
        were used in the machinery and metal products industry and
        27.0 per cent in vehicles; and the paper and paper products
        industry absorbed 50.0 per cent of its imports. It perhaps
        should also be mentioned that a substantial proportion of im-
        ports of stone, clay, and glass products was taken by the con-
        struction industry, while the transportation industry took a
        large share of the imports of petroleum and coal derivatives
        and of rubber.

3.   The 29.8 per cent shown for imports of vehicles probably con-
        sisted mainly of parts used by the vehicle industry itself,
        while the 19.2 per cent shown for other productive sectors
        went chiefly to the transportation industry.

4.   Ackley presented the rationale for this formulation on pp. 20-
        21 of the original English language mimeographed version of
        his Un modello econometrico dello sviluppo italiano nel dopo-
        guerra (see corresponding p. 22) as follows:

                Thus, if the technically-required or the eco-
                nomically-optimum capital to output ratio is
                represented as C, investment should occur in
                the amount necessary to bring the capital stock
                to Cy, where y is the rate of output. This in-
                vestment should occur in the amount (Cy - K)
                where K is the existing stock of capital. How-

ever, this investment (or disinvestment, if K
exceeds Cy) may not occur at once, either
because of limitations on the output of new
capital goods (or on the rate of wearing out of
existing ones), or because entrepreneurs deli-
berately spread the required investment over
a period of time, or are forced to do so for financial reasons. Thus the extent of investment in any given period may be proportional
to (by a factor β) but not equal to the gap between the optimum capital stock (Cy) and the
existing stock (K_{t-1}). . . .

We can therefore write $i_t = \beta(Cy_t - K_{t-1}) = \beta Cy_t - \beta K_{t-1}$ or
$i_t = \beta(Cy_{t-1} - K_{t-1}) = \beta Cy_{t-1} - \beta K_{t-1}$. This latter expression
can be simplified to $i_t = \alpha y_{t-1} - \beta K_{t-1}$, which is the equation
noted in the text above. If this is rewritten as $i_t = \beta(\frac{\alpha}{\beta} y_{t-1} - K_{t-1})$, it is evident that $\frac{\alpha}{\beta}$ may be taken as an approximation
of C. It may be noted, as Ackley pointed out, that the equation
in the text is identical to the simplest version of James Duesenberry's investment theory in which investment is assumed to
depend on profits, which in turn are assumed to depend on
sales and the existing capital stock.

5.   This might be considered acceptable, as Ackley, op.cit.,
        p. 24, mentioned, on the grounds that depreciation should be
        relatively stable or at least subject to some trend movement,
        whereas $\triangle i_t$ and $\triangle y_t$ would be expected to vary considerably.

6.   For these and other details, consult ISTAT, Il valore aggiunto
        delle imprese nel periodo 1951-1959, Note e Relazioni, No. 18
        (Rome, March, 1962), esp. pp. 5-16. Data for 1960-61 were
        kindly provided in part by ISTAT from unpublished worksheets
        which underlay the tables published in their Annuario Statistico
        Italiano in the section entitled "Bilanci Delle Imprese."

7.   The new sample data were published for the first time in the
        1964 volumes of ISTAT, Annuario Statistico Italiano and Com-
        pendio Annuario Statistico. The plans are apparently to have
        the new sample cover the period of 1961-71. Hopefully, ar-
        rangements will be made to provide for backward and forward
        continuity in these new series in order to make them more use-
        ful and relevant for research purposes. It may also be noted
        that some investment figures by industry are available in the

publications of the Confederazione Generale dell'Industria
Italiana, Le prospettive dell'industria italiana nel triennio....
These figures date only from recent years, however, and may
not be comparable to the ones published by ISTAT.

8.   In order to test some alternative specifications of the model,
the regressions were run also with the inclusion of a profits
variable separately and in addition to sales, and with an index of capacity utilization in individual industries jointly with
sales and lagged investment. Profits were defined for this
purpose from the ISTAT data as value added minus wages.
But since this was a measure of gross profits inclusive of depreciation, it produced some apparently spurious results.
This was because the dependent variable measuring gross investment included depreciation as a matter of definition. It
was decided consequently that use of the sales variable was
more defensible. The index of capacity utilization proved not
to be significant in practically every case. This was in contrast to the results of equation (1e) of the Lamfalussy model
noted in the preceding chapter in which the index of capacity
utilization for industry as a whole was an important determinant of the aggregate investment ratio. The most likely explanation of this phenomenon is that the sales and lagged investment variables used in the disaggregated relationships must
have reflected in great part the variations in capacity utilization for the individual industries.

9.   It should be mentioned that the R^2's in Table 13 were computed
according to the following formula applicable to a homogeneous
regression (i.e., one without a constant term) which Robert H.
Rasche kindly supplied to me:

$$R^2 = \frac{n \sum Y \hat{Y} - \sum Y \sum \hat{Y}}{\sqrt{[n \sum Y^2 - (\sum Y)^2][n \sum \hat{Y}^2 - (\sum \hat{Y})^2]}}$$

where n = the number of observations, Y = the actual value of
the dependent variable, and $\hat{Y}$ = the estimated value of the dependent variable computed from the regression results. The
corrected R^2's were calculated according to the usual formula.

10.   The results for the subcategories of the textiles industries are
given in Table 33 of Appendix I. The simple regression coefficients for sales were significant for silk (303A) and synthetic
fiber textiles (303C) and nearly so for cotton textiles (303B).
Lagged investment showed up in synthetic fiber textiles, but
not in the others. The results for hard fiber textiles (305A)

looked plausible but the $\bar{R}^2$ turned out to be zero. The results
for other textiles (305B) had the expected signs, but the standard errors were sizable and the $\bar{R}^2$ low.

11.   The results for the subcategories of the nonelectrical machinery
        and metal products industry which are given in Table 33 of
        Appendix I corroborate in general those for the industry as a
        whole in Table 13.

12.   It may be noted that in the paper industry (322) while unit labor
        costs declined during the period, the prices indexes fluctuated
        more or less around the base level after 1953. Unit labor costs
        also fell in the graphic arts and printed materials (323) and
        in the other manufacturing industries (325). Both export and
        import prices in these industries fell considerably after 1956-
        57.

BIBLIOGRAPHY

BIBLIOGRAPHY

PUBLIC DOCUMENTS

Banca d'Italia. Assemblea generale ordinaria dei participanti.

International Monetary Fund. International Financial Statistics.

Italy, Associazione per lo sviluppo dell'industria nel Mezzogiorno (SVIMEZ). L'aumento dell'occupazione in Italia dal 1950 al 1957. Rome, 1959.

Italy, Istituto Centrale di Statistica (ISTAT). Annuario di statistiche industriali.

_____. Annuario statistico italiano.

_____. Compendio annuario statistico.

_____. Il valore aggiunto delle imprese nel periodo 1951-1959. Note e Relazioni, No. 18. Rome, March, 1962.

_____. Primi studi sulle interdependenze settoriali dell'economia italiana (Tavola economica, 1959). Note e Relazioni, No. 27. Rome, January, 1965.

Italy, Istituto per lo Studio della Congiuntura (ISCO), Quadri della contabilita nazionale italiana per il periodo 1950-1964. Rome, 1965.

Italy, Ministero del Bilancio. Relazione generalle sulla situazione economica del paese.

Organization for Economic Cooperation and Development (OECD). Economic Surveys: Italy.

_____. General Statistics.

_____. Main Economic Indicators.

_____. Statistical Bulletins. Foreign Trade, Series A, Overall Trade by Countries.

_____. Statistical Bulletins. Foreign Trade, Series B, Analytical Abstracts.

_____. Statistical Bulletins. Foreign Trade, Series C, Trade by Commodities.

_____. Statistics of Balance of Payments, 1950-1961. Paris, 1964.

_____. Statistics of National Accounts, 1951-1961. Paris, 1964.

Organization for European Economic Cooperation (OEEC). Statistical Bulletins. Foreign Trade, Series IV, Italy, Foreign Trade by Commodity and Area of Origin and Destination.

United Nations. Commodity Trade Statistics.

_____. Monthly Bulletin of Statistics.

_____. Yearbook of International Trade Statistics.

BOOKS

Ackley, G. Macroeconomic Theory. New York: Macmillan, 1961.

_____. Un modello econometrico dello sviluppo italiano nel dopoguerra. SVIMEZ Monograph Series 7. Rome: Giuffre Editore, 1963.

Dewhurst, F., and Others. Europe's Needs and Resources. New York: Twentieth Century Fund, 1961.

Graziani, A. Sviluppo del mezzogiorno e produttivita delle risorse. University of Naples, Cassa per il Mezzogiorno, Centro di specializzazione e ricerche economico agrarie per il mezzogiorno. Naples: Edizioni Scientifiche Italiane Napoli, 1964.

Hildebrand, G. H. Growth and Structure in the Economy of Modern Italy. Cambridge: Harvard University Press, 1965.

Kindleberger, C. P. Economic Development. 2d ed. revised. New York: McGraw-Hill, 1965.

_____. Economic Growth in France and Britain, 1851-1950. Cambridge: Harvard University Press, 1964.

_____. Foreign Trade and the National Economy. New Haven: Yale University Press, 1962.

Lamfalussy, A. The United Kingdom and the Six: An Essay on Economic Growth in Western Europe. Homewood: Richard D. Irwin, Inc., for the Yale University Economic Growth Center, 1963.

Lutz, V. Italy: A Study in Economic Development. London: Oxford University Press, 1962.

Polak, J. J. An International Economic System. Chicago: University of Chicago Press, 1953.

Svennilson, I. Growth and Stagnation in the European Economy. Geneva: United Nations, 1954.

Volpe di Prignano, E. Indagini in tema di elasticita delle importazioni con referimento alla recente esperienza italiana. Rome: Istituto Nazionale per lo Studio della Congiuntura, 1963.

Wells, S. J. British Export Performance: A Comparative Study. Cambridge, England: Cambridge University Press, 1964.

ARTICLES AND PERIODICALS

Baffi, P. "Monetary Developments in Italy from 1961 to 1965," Banca Nazionale del Lavoro, Quarterly Review (March, 1966).

_____. "Monetary Stability and Economic Development in Italy, 1946-1960," Banca Nazionale del Lavoro, Quarterly Review (March, 1961).

Balassa, B. "Some Observations on Mr. Beckerman's Export-Propelled Growth Model," Economic Journal, Vol. LXXIII (December, 1963).

_____. "Some Observations on Mr. Beckerman's Export-Propelled Growth Model: A Further Note," Economic Journal, Vol. LXXIV (September, 1964).

_____. "Some Observations on Mr. Beckerman's Export-Propelled Growth Model: A Rejoinder," Economic Journal. Vol. LXXIV (March, 1964).

Baldwin, R. E. "The Commodity Composition of Trade: Selected Industrial Countries, 1900-1954," Review of Economics and Statistics, Vol. XL (February, 1958, Supplement).

_____. "Implication of Structural Changes in Commodity Trade," in U. S. Congress, Joint Economic Committee, Factors Affecting the United States Balance of Payments. Washington, D. C.: Government Printing Office, 1962.

Banca Nazionale del Lavoro. Italian Trends (1964-66).

Beckerman, W. "Professor Balassa's Comments on my 'Export-Propelled' Growth Model: A Rebuttal," Economic Journal, Vol. LXXIV (September, 1964).

_____. "Projecting Europe's Growth," Economic Journal, Vol. LXXII (December, 1962).

_____. "Some Observations on Mr. Beckerman's Export-Propelled Growth Model: A Reply," Economic Journal, Vol. LXXIII (December, 1963).

De Meo, G. "Productivity and the Distribution of Income to Factors (1951-63)," Banca Nazionale del Lavoro, Quarterly Review (March, 1966).

"Effets de Structure et Effets de Concurrence," Etudes et Conjoncture (May, 1960).

Fleming, J. M., and Tsiang, S. C. "Changes in Competitive Strength and Export Shares of Major Industrial Countries," International Monetary Fund, Staff Papers, Vol. V (August, 1956).

Ginsburg, A. L., and Stern, R. M. "The Determination of the Factors Affecting American and British Exports in the Interwar and Post-war Periods," Oxford Economic Papers, Vol. 17 (July, 1965).

Haberler, G. "Introduction," to the Papers and Abstracts of Papers at a Universities - National Bureau Committee for Economic Research Conference on Problems in International Economics, Review of Economics and Statistics, Vol. XL (February, 1958, Supplement).

Junz, H. B., and Rhomberg, R. R. "Prices and Export Performance of
    Industrial Countries, 1953-63," International Monetary Fund,
    Staff Papers, Vol. XII (July, 1965).

Kindleberger, C. P. "Foreign Trade and Economic Growth: Lessons
    from France and Britain, 1850 to 1913," Economic History Re-
    view, Vol. 14 (December, 1961).

_____. "Foreign Trade and Growth: Lessons from British Experience
    Since 1913," Lloyd's Bank Review (July, 1962).

_____. "Protected Markets and Economic Growth," in U. S. Con-
    gress, Joint Economic Committee, Factors Affecting the United
    States Balance of Payments. Washington, D. C.: Government
    Printing Office, 1962.

Lamfalussy, A. "Contribution à un theorie de la croissance en economie
    ouverte," Recherches Economiques de Louvain, Vol. XXIX (1963,
    No. 8).

Machlup, F. "Relative Prices and Aggregate Spending in the Analysis
    of Devaluation," American Economic Review, Vol. LXV (June,
    1955); reprinted in International Payments, Debts, and Gold.
    New York: Charles Scribner's Sons, 1964.

Masera, F. "The Balance of Payments," Statist (April, 1962).

_____. "L'evoluzione dell'economia italiana ed in particolare i
    recenti sviluppi della bilancia dei pagamenti," Economia Inter-
    nazionale, Vol. XVII (February, 1964).

Micone, G. "Foreign Trade in the Last Ten Years (1954-1963),"
    Banco di Roma, Review of the Economic Conditions in Italy, Vol.
    XVIII (March, 1964).

Narvekar, P. R. "The Role of Competitiveness in Japan's Export Per-
    formance," International Monetary Fund, Staff Papers, Vol.
    VIII (November, 1960).

Prais, S. J. "Econometric Research in International Trade: A Review,"
    Kyklos, Vol. XV (1962).

Rey, G. "Problemi e prospettive della bilancia commerciale italiana," Banca d'Italia, internal report, 1963.

Rey, G., and Sgarbi, S. "Previsioni del commercio con l'estero," Banca d'Italia, internal report, 1964.

Rhomberg, R. R., and Boissonneault, L. "The Foreign Sector," in The Brookings Quarterly Econometric Model by J. S. Duesenberry and Others. Chicago: Rand McNally and Company, 1965.

Romanis, A. "Relative Growth of Manufactures of United States and Other Industrial Countries," International Monetary Fund, Staff Papers, Vol. VIII (May, 1961).

Spiegelglas, S. "World Exports of Manufactures, 1956 vs. 1937," The Manchester School, Vol. XXVII (May, 1959).

Stern, R. M. "Developments in the Commodity Composition, Market Distribution, and Competitiveness of Italy's Foreign Trade, 1955-1963," Banca Nazionale del Lavoro, Quarterly Review, No. 72 (March, 1965). The same article in Italian, Banca Nazionale del Lavoro, Moneta e Credito, Vol. XVIII (March, 1965).

Tosco, A. "Economic Policy in Italy, 1949 to 1961," in Economic Policy in Our Time, Vol. III by E. S. Kirschen and Others. Amsterdam: North-Holland Publishing Company, 1964.

Tyszynski, H. "World Trade in Manufactured Commodities," The Manchester School, Vol. XIX (September, 1951).

Verdoorn, P. J., and Meyer Zu Schlochtern, F. J. M. "Trade Creation and Trade Diversion in the Common Market," in Integration Europeenne et Realite Economique (European Integration and Economic Reality). Bruges: de Tempel for the College of Europe, 1964.

Volpe di Prignano, E. "L'elasticita delle importazioni nell'economia italiana," L'Industria, No. 3 (1963).

ABOUT THE AUTHOR

Robert M. Stern is a Professor of Economics at the University of Michigan in Ann Arbor, where he also heads the graduate seminar in international economics and has served as Director of Graduate Studies in Economics. Before joining the Michigan faculty in 1961, he was Assistant Professor of Economics at Columbia University.

Most of the research for this book was done in 1964-65 while Professor Stern was in residence at the Banca d'Italia as a Ford Foundation Faculty Research Fellow. After receiving his Ph.D. in economics from Columbia University, Professor Stern studied in the Netherlands in 1958-59 under a Fulbright fellowship.

Professor Stern has written extensively on international economics. His published works include studies of changes in the commodity structure of world trade, factors influencing the production of export commodities in less-developed countries, the determinants of comparative advantage and international trade in manufactured goods, and questions of international economic theory and policy applicable to both advanced and less-developed countries.

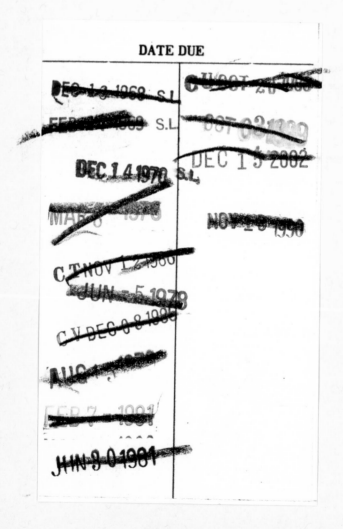

DATE DUE